DAVID LIVINGSTONE
FAMILY LETTERS
1841–1856
★

Volume One
1841–1848

DAVID LIVINGSTONE
Family Letters 1841–1856

*

VOLUME ONE
1841–1848

*Edited with
an Introduction by*
I. SCHAPERA

1959
CHATTO & WINDUS
LONDON

PUBLISHED BY
CHATTO AND WINDUS LTD
42 WILLIAM IV STREET
LONDON WC2

★

CLARKE, IRWIN AND CO LTD
TORONTO

PRINTED IN GREAT BRITAIN BY
BUTLER AND TANNER LTD
FROME AND LONDON

CONTENTS

Introduction

On 8 December 1840 David Livingstone, at the age of twenty-seven, sailed from London in order to start work as a missionary among the Native peoples of Bechuanaland. On 9 December 1856, sixteen years later almost to the very day, he arrived back in London, to be greeted triumphantly and with much public honour as the greatest of African explorers. The first eight and a half of those years he had spent on missionary teaching and travel in southern Bechuanaland and adjoining regions. Two and a half more were devoted largely to seeking a suitable site for a new mission station in the distant North-West. Then, after going to Cape Town to send his wife and children to England, and subsequently being detained for several months at Kuruman by fear of the Boers, he made the magnificent journeys of more than three years' duration that took him to Luanda on the West coast and back again right across Africa to Quelimane in the East. From there he sailed to England, via Mauritius, Ceylon, and the Red Sea, never to return to Bechuanaland.

The story of this first period, the longest of the three that Livingstone spent in Africa, has been told very often: by himself in his book *Missionary Travels and Researches in South Africa* (1857), and by many biographers, historians, and others. But as hitherto told it is neither complete nor scrupulously accurate. Nearly four-fifths of Livingstone's own account deals with the journeys of 1853–6. The preceding phases he describes much more sketchily, and, as shown by his letters of that time, he is not always trustworthy in his recollections and also omits a good deal. His biographers, whether uncritical hero-worshippers or not, have without exception made mistakes of various kinds: sometimes through slavishly following if not embellishing what he says in his book, sometimes through blatant carelessness, sometimes through faulty chronology, and most often perhaps through failure to consult other relevant sources of information. Even such recent and generally painstaking writers as Debenham, Simmons, Seaver, and Gelfand, are not wholly reliable on matters of fact, however much they may have added in other respects to our knowledge and understanding of Livingstone.[1]

The present work should help to ensure that future accounts are more comprehensive and authentic. Based primarily upon collections held by two of his descendants, Dr Hubert Frank Wilson and Miss Diana Livingstone Bruce, it comprises all that could be traced of the many letters he wrote to his own relatives or his wife's during the period of his first residence in Africa. A few have already been published, though not in full, by Blaikie or Chamberlin,[2] and extracts from others are given by Blaikie or later biographers, but the great majority, especially of those to Robert Moffat, have not previously been available in print.

These letters do not and cannot be expected to reflect the whole range of Livingstone's interests and activities. He was a prolific and voluminous correspondent, and despite frequent repetition what he wrote necessarily varied with the person whom he was addressing. Moffat, for example, had come to Bechuanaland in 1820, and was thoroughly familiar with the country and its inhabitants; he and Livingstone also met from time to time, occasionally for lengthy periods, between December 1843 and December 1852. Consequently much that Livingstone communicated to people in Britain or elsewhere was already known to Moffat or could have been told to him orally. Similarly, Livingstone's letters to kinsmen in Scotland or America inevitably often dealt with their domestic concerns, discussion of which left him relatively little time and space for dilating upon other topics. His missionary work and opinions are in fact described most fully to officers and supporters of the London Missionary Society, his scientific discoveries to professional men such as Bennett and Maclear, and his personal activities and prob-

---

[1] Some examples of their mistakes are given in the annotations to the letters.

[2] W. G. Blaikie, *The Personal Life of David Livingstone*, 1880; D. Chamberlin (ed.), *Some Letters from Livingstone*, 1940.

lems to such intimate friends as Watt, Moore, MacLehose, and Mrs Sewell.

The present collection, nevertheless, contains much new and important material. Livingstone's letters to his own kin, for example, tell us far more about him as son and brother than has hitherto appeared in any of his biographies. His writing as if he never expected to see his parents again, and his occasional likening of himself to the biblical Joseph, "separate from his brethren", show that he felt his isolation from them keenly. He was constantly mindful of his obligations. Although his own means were so scanty that he was sometimes troubled by debt, he sent money to Scotland and to his brother Charles in America; he wanted his parents and sisters to emigrate so that they could live in greater comfort; and his concern about their ill health finds expression in frequent medical advice, though he must have known it could seldom reach them sooner than four or five months after being written. And if now and then he is obviously impatient of their vacillating attitude to emigration, their religious views, and their homoeopathic tendencies, it is because of affectionate dismay, not intolerant superiority; or if he seems to apologize too much for not writing more often, it is because he himself so evidently missed hearing frequently from home. To Charles, similarly, he displays an elder brother's pride and partiality that help one to understand the unfortunate inclusion of that young man in the Zambesi expedition of 1858–63.

In contrast, Livingstone's letters to his wife may seem to some modern readers deficient in emotional quality. Certainly the way he wrote while they were engaged rarely suggests the ardent lover, memorable though a few phrases are, and the letters she received in England, when they had long been apart, are relatively brief, prosaic, and undemonstrative. He never, so far as we know, wrote to her as extensively and easily as he did to some of his personal friends, nor as intimately and sympathetically as for example Moffat did to Mrs Moffat. Again, that he had much pleasure and delight in his young children is apparent from what he says about them to his parents and others; but one wonders if the children themselves would have derived that impression from the lectures on religion and education that form the main and sometimes sole content of his letters to them. None of Livingstone's biographers, with the possible exception of Seaver, has dealt at length with him as husband and father; the letters published here suggest that this aspect of his family life needs more careful study if we are ever to know his character fully.

The letters to Moffat do not have to be judged similarly in terms of the behaviour conventionally expected towards next of kin. The marked cordiality they display may perhaps have been due partly to the affinal connection, but it is evident also that Livingstone found his father-in-law personally and intellectually very congenial. To no one else did he reveal himself so fully.

Because Moffat lived within comparatively easy reach and knew Bechuanaland so well, Livingstone could write to him both often and about many local affairs of little interest to people abroad. The Moffat letters are consequently an unrivalled source of historical information about the interior of Southern Africa at that time. They record in great detail the movements and raids of the local Native tribes, their relations with the Boer Voortrekkers of the Transvaal, and the changes produced in their way of life by missionaries and by visiting hunters, traders, and other European or Native travellers. There is also matter of incidental interest in what Livingstone says about the activities and conduct of Gordon Cumming and several less-known adventurers.

Again, because Moffat was not only a fellow-missionary but also a sympathetic relative, Livingstone could discuss missionary politics and personalities with him more freely than with officers of the London Missionary Society and other colleagues. Missionary work itself inevitably receives a good deal of attention; and the story of Sechele's conversion and fall illustrates one of the problems that had to be overcome, just as the occasional linguistic notes reflect another. Moffat's experience and technical skill also made him a useful mentor in regard to the practical difficulties confronting the pioneer settler; and the many requests Livingstone sent him for tools and other supplies, and for advice about gardening, building, smithing, etc., indicate the extent to which early missionaries often had to subordinate their vocational activities to the necessity of erecting a home and getting their daily food.

In the light of all these letters, and others written during the same period, two aspects of Livingstone's career in Bechuanaland require special comment. One is his relations with his fellow-missionaries. He is understandably silent about this in his book, and his biographers usually mention only the quarrel with Edwards, whose resentment at being treated as "a mere appendix" they regard as the cause of Livingstone's departure from Mabotsa. Livingstone's letters show clearly that he despised several of his colleagues. But they show also that except in regard to Ross, whom he disliked from the start, that was a later reaction. Of Edwards, in particular, he at first wrote with respect and admiration, and his scornful contempt of Inglis from 1844 onwards contrasts strangely with the eager desire previously expressed for his companionship in the field. He may have had good reason for turning against Edwards, though not himself wholly blameless for the disagreement he so minutely records; but his condemnation of his old student friend Inglis before they had even met again in Africa was due almost certainly to Moffat's influence. The factionalism to which Moffat was a party proved contagious, and before long the man who had once noted with disgust the evils of missionary gossip was himself regaling his father-in-law with spiteful comments on colleagues, often merely repeating hearsay. That Livingstone was deeply religious is certain, but, like Moffat, he did not always practise tolerance and charity towards his fellow-workers. And if he could write in 1850 that "there is no more Christian affection between most if not all the brethren and me than between my riding-ox and his grandmother",[1] his own statements show that the obvious defects of those "brethren" were reinforced, in producing mutual antipathy, by his personal resentment of criticism and by the starkness of his judgements. How far this state of bitter feeling was one of the factors inducing him to abandon Bechuanaland has not received the attention it seems to deserve.

[1] See below, vol. ii, p. 81.

The traditional version of Livingstone's relations with the Boers also needs some correction. Unquestionably he was completely justified in many of the allegations he made about their treatment of Native peoples. But, despite his assertions to the contrary, there is also no doubt that the BaKwena, relying upon possession of firearms, were at times unduly provocative; and his own letters to Moffat show too that the BaKwena were much better armed than he implies in his book. He himself, as is well known, was accused by the Boers of having helped to furnish those arms. That charge he emphatically denied. In 1853, for example, a Cape Town newspaper published a statement (written the year before) in the course of which he said: "My reply to both Missionaries and Boers was, and is, if you can prove that I either *lent* or *sold*, or *gave* a gun . . . to Secheli, I shall willingly leave the country." [1] Although faithfully echoed by almost all his biographers, the denial was literally untrue: Livingstone's letters to Moffat show that he did in fact occasionally supply arms and ammunition to Sechele and other Natives.

However, the same letters also prove convincingly that he supplied relatively little, and that sometimes he simply acted as Moffat's agent. His attitude was that the Natives needed fire-arms both for hunting and for protection against the Boers. But although willing to help them (and at least once he refused the BaKwena gunpowder which he thought they wished to use in attacking another tribe), he was normally satisfied to let them deal with traders and others, who were unquestionably their main source of supply. What he gave was primarily in exchange for food and similar commodities, not for financial gain; indeed, as shown by letters to his parents, he was strongly opposed to any form of commercial trading by missionaries.

One other fact may be noted briefly. Whatever Livingstone wrote, in his book and elsewhere, about the damage the Boers did to his mission station at Kolobeng, was based

---

[1] *Cape Town Mail,* 26 April 1853; italics in original. The statement was sent to the Editor by W. Thompson, the LMS agent at Cape Town, who introduced it by saying: "The substance of the following paper was communicated to me orally by the Rev. Dr Livingstone, about twelve months ago, and at my request was afterwards furnished to me in writing."

entirely on hearsay. As shown especially by his letter to his wife in January 1853 (No. 94 of the present collection), he himself never again saw Kolobeng after passing through it at the end of 1851 when on his way to the Cape.

(ii)

I have referred particularly to certain omissions and in-accuracies in Livingstone's own publications, because of their perpetuation by his biographers. The letters in this book provide the corrective. They also help us to under-stand more fully why he gave up his missionary work in Bechuanaland. Writing from Kuruman on 2 November 1852 to Dr A. Tidman, Foreign Secretary of the London Missionary Society, he himself described that work as a "failure".[1] During the whole of his residence in Bechuana-land his only convert was Sechele, chief of the BaKwena; but within six months of baptism Sechele had broken his vows and been suspended from holy communion. When Living-stone finally abandoned the BaKwena in April 1851, it was with the knowledge that, as he put it, the people had "wilfully rejected the gospel".[2]

We are so accustomed to thinking of him, in view of his later career, as "one of the greatest and most influential missionaries in the history of mankind",[3] that his lack of success in Bechuanaland has tended to be minimized. By and large, he followed essentially the same methods as his fellow-missionaries, and the difficulties he met were neither unique nor insuperable. He himself says that the BaKwena could not, or rather would not, listen to him because they were "pinched by hunger and badgered by the Boers". But the Boers were some distance away, and did not attack the BaKwena until more than a year after he had left; and short-age of food owing to failure of the crops often also occurred elsewhere in Bechuanaland. Moffat and the other pioneers at Kuruman had had even greater obstacles to overcome

---

[1] Cf. Chamberlin, *op. cit.*, p. 186.

[2] Letter to Tidman 2.xi.1852; the passage in which the phrase occurs is omitted by Chamberlin.

[3] K. S. Latourette, *A History of the Expansion of Christianity*, vol. 5 (1943), p. 345.

before they began to make converts. And, unlike Moffat, Livingstone was well received by the tribes with whom he settled, soon mastered the language, inspired confidence and respect because of his medical profession, and came to be sympathetic in his approach to the people and their customs. He was in fact better placed to succeed in his mission than were any of his predecessors in the country.

But, again unlike Moffat, he was too impatient. Although well aware that he should not expect rapid conversions, he was not prepared to remain indefinitely and work steadily with any one group of people. He started his mission among the BaKwena in August 1845, yet by March 1847 he was writing to Tidman: "I tell my Bakwains that if spared ten years I shall move on to the regions beyond them. Now is their opportunity and if they do not learn, the guilt will rest on their own heads." [1] In fact he remained with them for less than six years, during which he was often away; and, as shown by the experience of missionaries in other parts of Bechuanaland, he was hardly justified in hoping to do more in that time than he did.

His objection to prolonged residence with a single tribe was due to a conception of missionary policy differing markedly from what was then fashionable in Southern Africa. He believed that mission stations should not be maintained indefinitely by financial aid and human replacements from the mother country. Once a local church had been established, it should become self-sufficient and support its own minister; and those missionaries who preferred evangelical to pastoral work should then advance to a still heathen country. Even the formation of a church was not an essential prerequisite. "It would perhaps conduce to the efficiency of missions," he wrote to Freeman of the London Missionary Society in January 1850, "if it were known that except in special instances a tribe would not be favoured with a European missionary beyond a certain number of years." And to his friend Watt he expressed his basic doctrine still more simply (September 1851): "We ought to give all if possible a chance, and not spend an age on one tribe or people." [2]

[1] Chamberlin, *op. cit.*, p. 109.
[2] LMS archives. Neither letter is published by Chamberlin.

Consequently, when his discovery of Lake Ngami revealed the existence of a population much larger than in the southern parts of Bechuanaland, a population moreover still completely ignorant of the gospel, he had little hesitation in deciding what to do. The BaKwena had heard and rejected his message; he left them to their fate, and proceeded to carry "the good tidings" elsewhere.

The reason why he went to Lake Ngami at all he stated most precisely in a letter he wrote to Tidman on 24 May 1849, shortly before his departure. The relevant passage may be quoted in full, since it also emphasizes his views on missionary policy. After referring to a recent journey Eastward, which had brought him into unpleasant contact with the Boers, he continues:

"No other missionaries having ever visited the numerous tribes in that direction, the commandant repeatedly asked why I did not remain with the Bakwains till they were all converted. I suppose they concluded if they could procure the recal of this one they would be permitted to follow their future policy towards the Natives undisturbed. But I hope other missionaries will be induced to pity the condition of these perishing thousands, and if not of our Society of some other. There are no elements in the Bechuana character calculated to encourage the belief that conversions will occur precipitously. They are truly *slow* of heart to believe. It is therefore imperatively necessary to endeavour to extend the *gospel to all* the surrounding tribes. This although it involves a great many weary journies is the only way which permits the rational hope that when the people do turn to the Lord it will be by groups. When Native teachers can be furnished, that is of course still better than occasional visits, and now that the way to the East seems in a measure closed for the latter mode of working, we have turned our thoughts Northward. When I had made every preparation for a journey thither, a party of seven men who had never before seen a white man came from the Lake in order to invite us to come. I am on the point of starting." [1]

[1] This letter also is not published by Chamberlin.

15

It has sometimes been suggested, because of his subsequent activities, that Livingstone was really more interested in geographical discovery than in the conversion of the heathen. But he himself always denied such an explanation of his movements; and certainly his letters show that, during the period with which we are here concerned, every one of his journeys into the interior was dictated primarily by his conception of missionary work, and only incidentally if at all by thoughts of exploration or discovery. In fact, we learn more about the route of his first journey from his companion Edwards than himself; and we need only compare what he wrote during and immediately after his two journeys to Shoshong in 1842–3 with similar accounts by, say, Bain and Moffat, to realize that if his career had ended then his scientific reputation would not have been higher than theirs. Even his initial reports about the discovery of Lake Ngami are inferior to Oswell's, which gives more information both about the route followed and about the Lake itself.

It was partly owing to the fame he achieved by that discovery, and the encouragement he received from the Royal Geographical Society and others, that Livingstone now for the first time began to pay special attention to making and recording the observations that are so outstandingly valuable a feature of his later writings. Almost certainly he was influenced also by an official letter from Tidman, dated 14 April 1852,[1] the postscript of which reads:

> "We have sent extracts from your correspondence to the Geographical Society, and shall be happy to furnish that Society with such information as it comes to hand; but in order to give additional attraction to your reports, we would suggest that you keep a regular journal recording any remarkable events, notices of the manners and customs of the different tribes, the natural history of the country, and other topics which as the result of observation at the time are more likely to prove of permanent interest and value than the more vague and general impressions conveyed in a hastily written letter."

Livingstone had in fact already started to keep a journal,

[1] Copy in LMS archives.

but the entries preceding the latter half of 1852 are decidedly more sketchy and unsystematic than what comes afterwards.

It was thus not scientific curiosity that made Livingstone go to Lake Ngami and beyond. Nor was it desire for personal renown. On the eve of setting out for the Lake in 1849, he wrote to his brother Charles that he was awaiting Oswell, and added: "The honour of discovery will probably be given to him, but I shall have the privilege of first preaching Jesus and the resurrection on its shores"; and in July 1850 he wrote to Moffat that he was "regardless of the fame of discovery".[1] There is no reason to suspect either statement of concealing his true thoughts.

But Livingstone did have personal motives, though of another kind: he was unwilling to carry on work started or shared in by others, and sought always to go where no one had preceded him. Not only does he often refer complacently in his letters to having been farther inland than any other missionary before him, but in January 1845, at least two months before his return to Mabotsa and the quarrel with Edwards, he wrote to a friend from Kuruman, where he had gone to be married:[2]

"At Mabotsa matters go on pretty well. But I don't expect to remain there long. The sphere is too small for two missionaries. As I am the younger I purpose to go on to the Bakwains of either Bubi or Sechele. If I remained at Mabotsa the utmost I could hope for would be the part of introduction of the gospel to a tribe, while by going to another it would be an introduction of the gospel wholly by my instrumentality."

And in January 1850, after his first journey to Lake Ngami, he wrote to Freeman:

"I cannot help earnestly coveting the privilege of introducing the gospel into a new land and people. When I heard the new language and saw a few portions of the people, I felt that if I could be permitted to reduce their

[1] See below, vol. ii, pp. 50, 85.
[2] Letter to B. Pyne of Ongar, 28.i.1845 (Scottish National Library, Edinburgh, Acc. 1064).

language to writing and perhaps translate the Scriptures into it, I might be able to say that I had not lived in vain. I have had a strong desire ever since to be the first in the great undertaking. Perhaps it arises from ambition, but it is not of an ignoble sort."

His conviction that the message of Christ should be carried to all who had not yet heard of it, and his personal aspiration to be foremost in that work, were perhaps the two dominant forces shaping Livingstone's career in Southern Africa. In the very first letter of the present collection, written to his sisters soon after his arrival at Cape Town, he defined aptly the abiding impulse that drove him ever farther into the depths of darkest Africa and on to glorious achievement: "I would never build on another man's foundation. I shall preach the gospel beyond every other man's line of things." To that high resolve he was consistent in his endeavours.

(iii)

With but a few exceptions, every one of the 115 letters in this book is published in full. The exceptions are of three kinds. (1) The original texts of five letters, if they have been preserved at all, could not be traced. I have therefore copied those letters as they appear in Blaikie's *Life*. (2) In ten letters to members of the Livingston family in Hamilton, occasional and on the whole brief passages were heavily obliterated, presumably after receipt and because they contained matter deemed unsuitable for others to read. Those passages I have not tried to decipher. (3) In deference to the wishes of the owner (Dr H. F. Wilson), I have myself omitted a few short passages in five of the same series of letters; such omissions are specifically indicated wherever they occur, and a slight indication of their nature is given. Occasionally I have had to add a word or portion of a word to make good either a tear in the paper, usually at the seal, or an inadvertent omission by Livingstone himself when starting a new page; such additions are all enclosed within brackets.

The address is included only when it forms part of the

letter as preserved. Wherever possible I have indicated the approximate or actual date of receipt, as shown in the postmark or by other endorsement. I have indicated also which letters have previously been published (whether substantially or through quotation of extracts), and in the footnotes have cited renderings in those publications that do not conform to the manuscript. Insignificant deviations have not as a rule been so noted, as it would have been tiresome if not pedantic to list them all; they occur in virtually every instance.

To facilitate reading, I have broken up into more convenient size the often very lengthy paragraphs of the original, and have also tried to apply modern canons of punctuation. Spelling has been a difficult problem. Livingstone consistently used or favoured such forms as "Wedensday", "recieved", "agreable", "bretheren", "untill", "ajacent", etc.; sometimes he varied, alternating for example between "despair" and "dispair"; and in writing Native names and other words he used the orthography then in vogue, the main feature of which is that "c" represents the modern "ts" or "tš" and "oe" the modern "we". With some hesitation I have decided against trying to correct the spelling or substitute the modern Tswana orthography. The knowledge that one is reading Livingstone as he actually wrote will, I trust, be some compensation for the occasional shock of finding that his spelling was not faultless. But although his spelling of the family surname has accordingly also been retained everywhere just as it occurs in the manuscript, in my own headings I have used "Livingstone" for himself, his wife, and his children, and the older form "Livingston" for his parents and others; the main reason has been the necessity of distinguishing between his sister Agnes and his daughter of the same name.

(iv)

The publication of this book would have been impossible without the great generosity of Dr Hubert Wilson and Miss Diana Bruce, both of whom readily agreed to the inclusion in it of all their Livingstone letters for the period it embraces. For their kindness in lending me the originals, their help with information about family history, and their friendly interest and encouragement, I am most grateful. To Dr Wilson I am further indebted for securing me access to the letters owned by his sister Mrs R. MacDonald and her daughters Mrs G. R. Morgan and Mrs M. M. Chesson, who graciously placed them at my disposal; Dr Wilson also made possible my use of the letters to Charles Livingston now preserved in the Livingstone Memorial, Blantyre, of whose Board of Trustees he is Chairman.

To Miss Irene Fletcher, Librarian of the London Missionary Society, I am deeply obliged for the loan of many letters and books, and for cheerful readiness at all times to respond to inquiries about the Society's work in Bechuanaland. The National Library of Scotland (Edinburgh), Wellcome Historical Medical Library (London), Central African Archives (Salisbury, S. Rhodesia), Rhodes-Livingstone Museum (Livingstone, N. Rhodesia), and Rhodes House (Oxford), kindly supplied me with photostat or typed copies of letters in their respective collections. Mr D. H. Varley, Librarian of the South African Library, Cape Town, procured for me extracts from old South African newspapers not available in London, and helped in many other ways; Mr D. C. Cameron, Warden of the Livingstone Memorial, made local inquiries on my behalf about some of the places in and around Blantyre mentioned by Livingstone; and the Librarians of the Royal Anthropological Institute and of the London School of Economics sought out for me useful works of reference. To all of them, as to Mr E. Kedourie, Mr D. G. MacRae, and other colleagues who helped in various ways, I wish to express my gratitude.

List of Letters

VOLUME I

1841

21

1845

No.	Date	Addressee	Written from	Page
19.	April 1	Robert Moffat	Mabotsa	110
20.	May 12	Robert Moffat	Mabotsa	111
21.	May 14	Mrs Livingston	Mabotsa	120
22.	June 6	Robert Moffat	Mabotsa	123
23.	July 18	Robert Moffat	Mabotsa	136
24.	August 13	Robert Moffat	Mabotsa	137
25.	September 5	Robert Moffat	Mabotsa	143
26.	September 22	Robert Moffat	Mabotsa	148
27.	October 1	Mr & Mrs Livingston	Mabotsa	150
28.	November 1 (?)	Robert Moffat	[Chonwane]	154
29.	November 11	Agnes Livingston	Chonwane	155

1846

No.	Date	Addressee	Written from	Page
30.	January 17	Mr Livingston	Chonwane	159
31.	February 11	Robert Moffat	Chonwane	163
32.	March 11	Robert Moffat	Chonwane	170
33.	July 1	Robert Moffat	Chonwane	174
34.	September 8	Robert Moffat	Chonwane	178
35.	October 5	Robert Moffat	Chonwane	181
36.	October 27	Robert Moffat	Chonwane	183

1847

No.	Date	Addressee	Written from	Page
37.	March 15	Mr & Mrs Livingston	Kuruman	186
38.	March 16	Charles Livingston	Kuruman	189
39.	May 4	Mrs Livingston	Kuruman	195
40.	July	Robert Moffat	"Banks of Ñotoane"	200
41.	August 13	R. Moffat, jr.	Kolobeng	202
42.	September 29	Robert Moffat	Kolobeng	211
43.	November 7	Janet Livingston	Kolobeng	226
44.	November (?)	Robert Moffat	Kolobeng	231

1848

No.	Date	Addressee	Written from	Page
45.	March (?)	Robert Moffat	Kolobeng	234
46.	July 5	Mr & Mrs Livingston	Kolobeng	243

1855

1856

Abbreviations, etc., used in Footnotes.

Biographers of Livingstone, and compilers of dictionaries, are generally cited by name only, e.g. Blaikie, Brown, Campbell; the titles of their works are given in the "List of References", Vol. II, p. 297.

Letters written by Livingstone are cited simply by date and name of addressee, e.g. 14.xii.1848 Tidman means "letter from Livingstone to Tidman, 14 December 1848".

Cross-references to footnotes are given by number of Letter and footnote, e.g. 40.12 means "note 12 to Letter 40".

Other abbreviations commonly used include the following:

D. L.   David Livingstone
D.N.B.   *Concise Dictionary of National Biography, I.*
            To 1900
Journal   Livingstone's manuscript journals
LMS   London Missionary Society
Oswell   *William Cotton Oswell,* by W. E. Oswell
Register London Missionary Society: *A Register of*
            Missionaries, Deputations, etc., from 1796
            to 1923. Fourth ed., 1923.
Travels   *Missionary Travels and Researches in South*
            Africa, by D. Livingstone

1841

1: To JANET AND AGNES LIVINGSTON
30 March 1841

Address: Miss Janet Livingston, Almada St., Hamilton, N.B.
Postmark: Hamilton, JUN 2, 1841. [Wilson Collection.]

Cape Town
30th March 1841[1]

My dear Sisters J. & Agnes,

Here I am sitting in Dr Phillip's house. . . .[2] Are you purling? . . .[3] I suppose you have got the garden again in trim, while here winter is just commencing, and those who have been long here say they feel it cold; to us it is as warm & pleasant as ever we felt it in England. It is very delightful weather indeed, and then this is just the end of the grape season. The oranges are just coming in, and the second crop of figs may be had in abundance. The pomegranate I always thought from reading the Bible to be a most delicious fruit, but though very beautiful to look at, and very much like a large apple ☖ of beautiful colour, yet it is filled with seeds around each of which is a very thin film filled with wine-coloured juice of an astringent taste. The seeds are not eaten. The outer rind has an abominable taste. Take it as a whole, a bunch of roans[4] are as good if not better than a pomegranate. They grow very abundantly on hedges round

[1] D. L. had arrived at Cape Town on 15 March, having sailed from London on 8 December 1840.

[2] John Philip (1775–1851), born in Scotland; superintendent since 1820 of LMS missions in S. Africa, author of *Researches in South Africa* (1828), vigorous and outspoken champion of the Coloured and Native peoples; lived at 5 Church Square, Cape Town.

[3] The dots represent passages of about three and seven words respectively that have been cut out of the MS.

[4] Rowans (berries of the mountain ash).

some gardens here, but are a useless sort of fruit. The figs
are not very fine, but the grapes are excellent & very cheap.
I wish I could send you a bunch or two, but I daresay you
don't thank me for tempting you with discriptions of fruits
which you can never taste in Hamilton.[5]

I wish I could transport you all to America, where if you
did not get these fine fruits you would at least get a good
supply of the more substantial necessaries of life. I have
spoken about my money affairs to the Dr, & find I can draw
as freely on my present salary as I choose,[6] but I have a
great many things to purchase before I leave. We have as it
were to lay in a stock for some years to come. I therefore
won't be able to send £30 or £40 of it as I intended. Nor
can I do more than give you a lift of about £15. I shall try &
make it £20. This will be £10 for Mr Moore[7] & £10 for
yourselves. I am very sorry for this, but if I did more now I
should not then be able in the following year . . . take you
all . . . extricate you a little from your . . . perhaps place
you in a better position for [the follow]ing spring.[8] I do not
enclose it in this, but will in my next. Perhaps I may send it
to Mr Moore, perhaps to you. I am not decided yet.

I shall take no tea or coffee, & live as cheaply as possible,
that you may not be in any way disappointed in the following
year. You might not have been able to have got out this year
although I had sent all I intended, as it would have been late
in the season before you could have made the necessary
arrangements. Much as I should like to send it all just now,
it will not be prudent. Large draughts at the very commencement somehow become known amongst the missionaries, &
conjectures arise, for we are a great deal like other men. I
should not however care a straw for gossip if I could have
done it with a good grace in relation to other matters. You
may depend upon me, I won't fail, if God will, to do all I

[5] A town about 11 miles south-east of Glasgow. The Livingston family had
moved there in 1840 from Blantyre (3 miles north-west).

[6] D. L.'s salary as a bachelor was £75 per annum; married men were paid £100.

[7] Possibly Joseph Moore (1816–93), D. L.'s fellow-lodger and intimate friend in
London and Ongar; missionary in Tahiti 1843–4, subsequently a pastor in Cheshire
(Blaikie, pp. 25 ff.; Register, p. 55).

[8] Portions of MS. cut away (approximately four, three, and three words respectively).

intended as soon as I possibly can. I have not changed my mind in the least. I hope it is from a motive to the promotion of the glory of God that we desire to change our country. I hope it is so with all of us. Let us look at our motives & see that they are such as God approves.

I have preached 4 times since I came here, & am now wishing to get away from this place, that we may get to the acquisition of the language of the country in which I am to spend my life. Dr Phillip's church is all in confusion, divided against itself. I dare say they would take any one as a pastor instead of him. He has given in his resignation to them, but they can stir neither hand nor foot. They have nobody to choose as his successor. The chapel belongs to the Society. It is a sad sight. He never visits them, can't from want of time. They want one who will do so & take some interest in them, but can't find one. He resigned his charge that night we came here.[9] I daresay they would take Mr Ross[10] even, if by that means they could get quit of the Dr. Much is said against & much for him & Mrs P., but I believe we must deduct a large percentage off the statements of both parties to arrive at the truth. Both have been exceedingly kind to me: not the least appearance of domineering, but the very opposite. They seem to have the good of the Mission at heart, & if they have done some things wrong I have no doubt it was done from the best motives. He stated to me that he did not consider himself anything more than a money agent of the Society. My fears with respect to him are all dissappointed. I am thankful they are so.

Our ship has not yet come round from Simon's Bay.[11] We expect her daily. It will be at least 6 weeks from this date before we reach Algoa Bay. The Dr would fain have either

[9] Philip was also minister of Union Chapel, Cape Town, some members of which complained that he devoted more attention to missionary affairs than to his pastoral duties (13.v.1841 Cecil). But he remained in office until a successor arrived from England in August 1844 (*Register*, pp. 20, 33).

[10] William Ross (1802–63); born in Scotland, worked as ploughman and apprentice carpenter, then studied at St Andrews, London, and Edinburgh; joined the LMS 1840; ordained together with D. L. and sailed with him to S. Africa for Bechuanaland (*Register*, p. 51; Mackenzie, *Ten Years North of the Orange River*, 1871, p. 85).

[11] Simonstown, on the False Bay coast; 23 miles south of Cape Town. D. L.'s ship had anchored there on arrival from England.

Mr Ross or myself to remain in his place while he goes up the country, but I think it would be a great pity if either of us remained & soothed up the difference between him & his people. I hope they may act for themselves & never give in untill they get a pastor to look after them. I would not for a moment think of remaining. I shall go immediately when I can get the opportunity. I would never build on another man's foundation. I shall preach the gospel beyond every other man's line of things.

The mail closes in half an hour. I shall write you perhaps by every mail that leaves for England. You see I am hurried for time in this letter. I ought to have begun sooner. I wrote Charles[12] telling him not to stop the Evangelists.[13] The Dr, Mrs P. & son had an argument one evening on the subject of Perfection. I told him that I had been examining these views on my passage, & like them so far as I understood them. He proposed to appoint a time when we should fully discuss the subject; I suppose it will be soon, as I agreed & told him I should be glad to be convinced if wrong.

I write this letter to Janet & Agnes that they may write in answer to me. I have not individualised as I intended when I began. I hope Mother is well. I should like now to hear from you, but I suppose your letter or letters are lying at Port Elizabeth waiting my arrival. Dr P's son & daughter-in-law have not yet heard from Scotland, although they have been out for a considerable time now.[14] I don't know well what to say to Mother & the sisterhood. If I had a letter from them I could answer it & stick to the text, but now it is rather difficult to recollect the particular things which would please them. There are so many things here which claim attention that poor old Scotland is frequently forgotten. If I look out of the window, there I see lofty Table Mountain with its beautiful table cloth of fleecy clouds, the

[12] D. L.'s younger brother (1821–73); then studying at Oberlin College, Ohio, U.S.A., to which he had gone in 1839.

[13] The English journal of that name had ceased publication in 1839. The reference may possibly be to either *The Evangelist* (Cincinnati, Ohio, 1832 onwards) or *The Evangelist and Religious Review* (New York, 1830 onwards).

[14] William Philip (1814–45); born in Scotland, studied at Glasgow, married there in April 1840 and came to Cape Town with his wife in October (*Scottish Congregational Mag.*, n.s. vol. 6 (1846), p. 8, and information from Mr P. H. Philip).

Lion's head back & rump,[15] the ships at anchor in the Bay, &c &c. So many things new & strange that if you were here I am sure you would say, even Mother would say, "I canna be fash't aye write writing", so if my letters are not all they ought to be, be thankful that they are anything at all.

D. L.

I got Mr J. Allen's[16] brother after searching over all Cape Town, & told him to give his brother a better address than Cape Town. There are 24,000 inhabitants here. He complained that his brother had never answered a letter of his, although he had written frequently from the Cape. I promised to go & visit him at his house, but have not had time yet. Tell Mrs Pyne[17] that I got the boxes from the Colonial Secretary, Colonel Bell.[18] My kind regards to J. Wheelan.[19] I have a letter written for him. Also Mr Drummond,[20] &c &c. My love to John [and] Sarah.[21] I would have written Agnes,[22] but her letter is mislaid.

2: To MR AND MRS N. LIVINGSTON

19 May 1841

Address: Mr Livingston, Almada St., Hamilton, N.B. *Postmark:* Hamilton, AUG 7, 1841. [Wilson Collection; extracts published in Blaikie, *Personal Life*, pp. 40 f.]

[15] Lion's Head (2,175 ft.), a prominent peak adjoining Table Mountain, is on the other side connected by a low ridge (D. L.'s "back") with "Lion's Rump", nowadays known as Signal Hill (1,100 ft.).

[16] Not identified.

[17] Mrs Benjamin Pyne, of "Wildingtree", Ongar, Essex, with whose family D. L. had become very friendly while studying there under Rev. Richard Cecil in 1838–9.

[18] John Bell (1782–1876), Chief Secretary of the Cape of Good Hope Government 1828–41. The boxes had been sent out by Dr Richard Owen, Royal College of Surgeons, for whom D. L. had undertaken to collect biological specimens.

[19] Not identified.

[20] Henry Drummond, of Campbell Street, Hamilton, was a lace manufacturer (for whom Charles L. had worked), and (like D. L.'s father) a deacon of the local Independent church; he subsequently (c. 1844) moved to Glasgow (30.xii.1847 Tidman; Pigot, p. 628). Supplied clothing to D. L. while in S. Africa.

[21] D. L.'s elder brother (born 1811) and his wife Sarah (*née* Mackenzie); then living in Glasgow; migrated soon afterwards to Canada.

[22] Not identified; the beginning of the letter shows that D. L. is not referring to his sister.

Port Elizabeth,
19th May 1841[1]

My dear Parents,

With much pleasure I begin a short epistle to you. I have one somewhere which I wrote some time ago, & not finding an opportunity of transmitting it to the Cape it has somehow become invisible. I am just ready to begin my career of land navigation. My oxen are ready at hand, waggon is loaded, & tomorrow morning I shall weigh anchor & set sail for Bethelsdorp.[2] From thence to Uitenhage,[3] & then I am beyond the inconvenience of living in towns for some time to come.

I like travelling in this country very much. It has so much freedom connected with it. Stop when one chooses, light a fire, for there are abundance of bushes, & cook a meal; no one ever accusing another of tresspassing on his ground. And then besides, if we like, we can enjoy the Nabalish felicity of looking about & saying, *my* 12 oxen, *my* waggon, *my* people, &c. A little of it, a poor fellow like your humble servant must feel as he perhaps whistles "I am the monarch of all I survey".

I may however get wrecked before long, for we [have] roads here such as you can form no conception of. Charles spoke of a jolting he got, but here we have shakings worth speaking about. The huge vehicle is dragged by physical force over every obstacle, down hills so steep that looking down you feel sure that it must be dashed to peices at the bottom after having rushed over & killed all the oxen. And then in going up, no matter how much inclined to the perpendicular the hill may be, up they go, although the cattle may be forced to ascend on their knees.

I have been thinking, & I don't know any place I have seen in Scotland near you which resembles the country over which I travelled to Hankey.[4] The scenery was very fine.

---

[1] D. L. had remained at Cape Town for a month before sailing for Port Elizabeth, which he reached about 19 April (7.vii.1841 Watt, 13.v.1841 Cecil). The visit to Hankey, described below, was made while his wagon was being prepared for the long journey of over 500 miles to Kuruman.

[2] An LMS station about 9 miles north-west of Port Elizabeth. Its inhabitants were mostly Hottentots.

[3] A village about 20 miles north-west of Port Elizabeth.

[4] An LMS station, also inhabited mainly by Hottentots, about 50 miles west-north-west of Port Elizabeth.

The white sand in some places near the beach drifted up in large wreaths exactly like snow. One might imagine himself in Scotland were there not a hot sun overhead. The woods present an aspect of strangeness, for everywhere the eye meets the foreign looking tree from which the bitter aloes is extracted popping up its head over[5] the mimosa bushes & stunted acacias. Beautiful humming birds fly about in great quantities[6] sucking the nectar from the flowers, which are in great abundance & very beautiful. Many of them, such as geraniums &c, you find in English greenhouses. Baboons also frequently take a look at us as we pass & salute us in their own way.

I was much pleased with my visit to Hankey, the station of Rev. E. Williams, a Welshman.[7] I went in Rev. W. Phillip's waggon, who has for wife Mr Fullarton's step-daughter (Alice Bell).[8] You may remember her. We were happy to meet each other as old acquaintances, although our knowledge of each other was confined formerly to face knowledge. Of course we had a long talk about Hamilton, Linnhouse,[9] &c. She desired remembrance to David & Fergus[10] when I wrote. By the way, I ought to write Fergus, & also Mr Drummond, Kirk,[11] &c, but I have so much to think of just now when laying in stores to last for a long time to come & looking after everything about my journey, that

---

[5] "among" (Blaikie). [6] "number" (Blaikie).

[7] Edward Williams (1814–44); LMS missionary; born in Flintshire, stationed at Hankey 1837, returned to England owing to ill health 1843 (*Register*, pp. 38 f.).

[8] Alison Blair Bell (b. 1822), familiarly known as "Alice"; after her father's death (1825), her mother had married Archibald Fullarton, a widower, of Bath Street, Glasgow, who died *c.* 1836 (information from Mr P. H. Philip, great-grandson of W. Philip). She was accompanying her husband, who had been appointed to the mission staff at Hankey.

[9] An estate, with mansion, about one mile south of Cathcart (Glasgow), adjoining the White Cart Water.

[10] Sons of Fergus Ferguson, of Rosebank Cottage, Burnbank, Hamilton, a well-to-do member and deacon of the local Independent church, where he taught a Bible class that D. L. had attended. He and Drummond (1.20) financed D. L.'s journey to London in 1838 to be interviewed by the Directors of the LMS (Campbell, *Livingstone*, 1929, p. 55). The younger Fergus (1824–97) subsequently became a prominent Congregational minister in Glasgow (W. Adamson, *Life of Fergus Ferguson*, 1900).

[11] Rev. John Kirk, ordained 1839, pastor of the Independent Church at Hamilton 1839–45, then moved to Edinburgh (J. Ross, *A History of Congregational Independency in Scotland*, 1900, pp. 231, 248, 251, 258).

my mind is quite unfit for that exercise. I shall however do my duty as soon as I can.

I can give you no idea of Hankey as far as describing the scenery is concerned. But the state [of the] people presents so many features of interest that anyone may talk about it & convey some idea of what the gospel has done. The full extent of benefit received can however be understood only by those who witness it, in contrast with other places which have not been so highly favoured. My expectations have been far exceeded. Everything I witnessed surpassed my hopes, and if this one station is a fair sample of the whole, the statements of the missionaries with regard to their success is far within the truth. They have not been guilty of vain boasting. The Hottentots of Hankey appear to be in a state somewhat similar to what our forefathers were in the days immediately succeeding to the times of the Covenanters.[12] They have a prayer meeting every morning at 4 o'clock *& well attended.* They began it during a visitation of measles amongst them, & liked it so well that they still continue it. The missionary can attend only occasionally, & the good folks having no clocks or watches are sometimes egregiously out of their reckoning. The first one who awakens goes & rings the bell. There are always some wakeful enough, & not unfrequently the whole village is assembled at 11, perhaps 12, 1 or 2.

They expected us, along with their pastor, who had been to the Cape on account of an affection of the throat. Two of them on horseback met us at some miles distance from the village. The children had often come to meet him but were disappointed, so taking the horses Mr W. & I, proceeding before the waggon, had an opportunity of coming on them at unawares. As soon as we were perceived at the first houses, a discharge of musketry announced to the villagers our approach, & to[ld] us that their keen eyes had recognized the strangers. This was responded to by some guns from the opposite side of the village, & immediately from all quarters could be seen running at the top of their speed men women & children, young & old, to welcome us, & then such a

[12] ". . . in a state similar to that of our forefathers in the days immediately preceding the times of the Covenanters" (Blaikie).

shaking of hands, &c &c. Mr W. had lost a little boy by death since he last saw them. To shew their sympathy each had a black hankerchief or a bit of crape around the head. I was much struck by the conduct of a woman who had been his nurse. Approaching with her bosom heaving with emotion, she hastily saluted him & bursting into tears turned aside to weep.

They (the people) gave us an entertainment as soon as the women could bake a sufficient number of "cookies". It consisted of coffee in the morning & tea in the afternoon. Speeches were made & much joy at our arrival expressed in them. I ought to have mentioned that after salutation the women struck up a hymn & conducted us so into the Mission House. Approaching the village the beautifully clear & full Hottentot voices resounded through the whole village.

I returned in one of the people's waggons. Family worship struck me much as resembling the Covenanters. Sitting round a fire in the bush, they made the rocks re-echo to their beautiful singing. They knew all the hymns by "heart", & the prayers seemed earnest. Contrast this with the conduct of a Dutch farmer who came out to us rest[ing on][13] Sunday, & invited me as a medical man to come to his [house] at a little distance. I gave his child some medicine. With [this] attention he seemed much pleased. After coffee, supper of the best he had was prepared, but during the time of preparation his wife & two grown-up daughters were dancing before the house, a black fiddling. He enquired if I should like to see them exhibit themselves in the room in which we were sitting. I just knew enough of Dutch to let him know I disapproved of it. He muttered something (as an excuse) about their being children. He & they were very kind, but pure heathens, knew nothing. They gave me some provisions next morning for the rest of the way, among which were a live fowl, biscuit, &c. I hope this is not a fair specimen of the Dutch Boors.

I am just ready to set off. Part of this I wrote last night, but was too fatigued to finish it. This accounts for its broken sort of narration. I send to Mr Pyne a bill for £20, & he

[13] MS. slightly torn at seal.

will draw it. . . .[14] out of the country. Write to Cheshunt College near London, care of Dr Harris. . . .[15] Pray for me that I may be more spiritually minded & confirmed to the will of Christ. . . .

I have received no letters except one from my good friend Mrs Sewell.[16] My love to Mother, Janet & Agnes. Nobody must see my letters.

Yours ever,
D. L.

I have not written John or Charles. Write frequently. The beads I got from the warehouse girls[17] will, I understand, be valuable as small money. I shall get my belly filled by them sometimes.

Address me always to the care of Dr Phillip, Cape Town. It is much cheaper, & he is not as he is represented to be in England. He has no tyranny, great humility, & no dictatorial spirit. Tell Mr McLehose[18] to address me so, & not to Mr Robson.[19] Also Charles & John. The Dr usually pays our letters. He is a devoted Christian, & very clever, but old age creeps upon him.

3: To MR AND MRS N. LIVINGSTON AND DAUGHTERS

29 September 1841

Address: (Care of Revd. Dr Phillip, Church Square, Cape Town) Mr Livingston, Almada St., Hamilton, N.B. *Postmark:* Hamilton, JAN 15, 1842. [Wilson Collection.]

[14] The dots represent passages (of four, three and a half, and three and a half lines respectively) that have been heavily obliterated in the MS.

[15] John Harris (1802–56), President of Cheshunt College, Cheshunt, Herts. (*D.N.B.*). The obliterated lines probably refer to Joseph Moore (1.7), who studied there after leaving Ongar and before going to Tahiti (*Register*, p. 55).

[16] Keeper of a boarding-house with LMS connections at 57 Aldersgate Street, London, where D. L. had stayed in 1838 and again in 1840. He wrote to her several times from S. Africa.

[17] Presumably the fellow-workers of D. L.'s sisters.

[18] James MacLehose, bookseller and publisher, of 83 Buchanan Street, Glasgow; D. L.'s fellow-lodger at Mrs Sewell's in 1838, and another of his early correspondents while in S. Africa.

[19] Adam Robson (1794–1870), LMS missionary; formerly at Bethelsdorp; since 1832 minister of Union Chapel, Port Elizabeth (*Register*, p. 24).

Kuruman
29th September 1841[1]

My dear Parents & Sisters,

In case I have no other opportunity of writing you previous to setting off towards the North,[2] I now begin. I am sorry I had not one ready yesterday, when a Griqua[3] passed this way. I sent several to friends, & I hope this won't be long behind any of which you may hear.

I am busy learning the language, which is not remarkably difficult. The only impediment is a want of proper aids such as Dict[ionarie]s, Grammars, &c. I hope however soon to conquer it, & then preach Christ & him crucified to the perishing Bechuanas. I have a great deal of work in the way of helping the infirm, & many of them seem attached to me on account of little attentions shewn to themselves or children, of whom they are remarkably fond. Mothers are mothers I see all over the world, if only a little of poor humanity remains uncorrupted by the customs of sin. How is my mother? I hope comfortable. May God bless her and give her an inheritance with the blessed in Heaven by sanctifying her to himself.

I have got no letters as yet from you, & have now written you 5.[4] It is no easy matter to have all the correspondence to oneself, but I hope they are on the way. Well, what shall I tell you about? I suppose Janet & Agnes would like a lion story, or something of that sort. That I can't however give, for I have not dared to look one in the face. A terrible fellow was shot a short distance from this, & the sight of his dead body so (shall I say) frightened me I have no wish to have

---

[1] D. L., with Mr and Mrs Ross, had left Port Elizabeth on 20 May and reached Kuruman on 31 July. They travelled through Uitenhage, Graaff Reinet, Colesberg, Philippolis, Campbell, and Griquatown (where they stayed "9 or 10 days", 5.viii.1841 Mrs Philip).

[2] "I propose accompanying Br[other] Edwards in his journey to the Interior, as I am informed by the bretheren who are best able to judge it will be advantageous for me in many respects" (23.ix.1841 Freeman).

[3] A people of hybrid stock, predominantly Hottentots but with much European admixture. They occupied the regions now known as Griqualand West and the western Orange Free State, their main settlement being at Griquatown (110 miles south of Kuruman), where the LMS had established a mission in 1802.

[4] This suggests that several of D. L.'s letters to his family either did not reach them or have not been preserved. The former is more likely, since letters to other people (e.g., MacLehose and Mrs Sewell) also went astray.

intercourse with his majesty again. I would rather meet with some members of the royal families among men than of beasts, for the former, in this country at least, are an insignificant race of beings, distinguished for nothing but superior impudence in begging, & generally worse looking than any of their attendants.

I have been in company with Waterboer, the Griqua chief.[5] He is rather an exception in point of intellect, although in bodily appearance he is a little Bushman. Old Moteebe, our chief,[6] was here a few weeks ago for the purpose of being baptized & admitted into the church, a feeble decrepit old man, tottering into the grave. After he had carelessly heard the offers of mercy for about 25 years, we trust he has now turned to the Lord. His baptism has caused great excitement through the whole country, particularly amongst the violent opponents of the gospel. I hope it will lead others to think of their state & look for mercy before it is too late.

The Bechuanas are great beggars. Indeed they seem to make it a matter of conscience to neglect no opportunity of asking, & a refusal does not by any means put them out if it is done in a jocular way. It is only occasionally they think it worth while to tell you what their opinion of you is, & really it is ludicrous enough to hear their epithets. Instead of getting vexed by them, they always powerfully excite my risible faculties. Only think of an old grey-headed man or woman coming forward & saluting me with the epithet, "Father, king, gentleman, &c &c", and then after a little conversation requesting as a great favour a knife, handkerchief, or only a little bit of my shirt to bind their heads; & when I give them the hint that though I much wish to gratify my children it is quite out of my power, my father or mother adopts quite a different style & tells me, "Verily thou art a dog, tiger, &c, and whoever marries you will marry a wolf." These paternal addresses have one good

[5] Andries Waterboer, a convert who had taught for some years in the local mission school, was chief of the Griquatown community 1820–52. He was partly of Bushman descent, and, as D. L. also indicates, an extremely able man.

[6] Mothibi, chief of the BaTlhaping 1812–45. He had moved away from Kuruman with part of the tribe in 1825, and later settled at Dikgatlhong, about 100 miles to the east. His baptism is briefly described (by R. Edwards, 24.ix.1841) in the *LMS Chronicle*, vol. 6 (1842), p. 41.

effect, they usually bring something to my mind which sets them off in good humour.

When Moteebe was with us, during the whole fortnight he never begged any, & for this he formerly was notorious. The sisterhood will be amused to know I was physician to his majesty, but I nearly got into disgrace by shouting out to him, as he lay asleep in the middle of the path at midday with his karross[7] over his head, "Hallo, my lad, this is not night." He awakened with a start. When I beheld who it was, I stooped down &, examining his eyes, told him I should give him some ointment for them in the afternoon. He seemed quite well pleased, & thanked me for my care of him.

When talking to him of his past life, he always commenced crying like a child. This is remarkable for a Bechuana, & particularly for a king. They never weep untill the Spirit works upon their hearts, & then they weep like children. Sometimes in the chapel they hide their heads in their karosses & creep under the forms to avoid the eyes of the preacher. This however won't do. They then scream out, & occasionally rush out of chapel fleeing with all their might. It has often made me wonder, for in performing most severe surgical operations they sit, both men & women, as if they had no feeling. In one case of fungous 4 inches in length & nearly 2 in breadth, nearly $\frac{1}{2}$ in height, I employed a severe but quick mode of getting rid of it. During the operation I expected him to get up & dance from the pain. But no, he sat immoveable & talked with as composed a countenance as if he felt nothing. "A man like me never cries", said he with the greatest composure, "It's only children who cry." The spirit of God alone can affect their hearts. Without His aid all our efforts must be ineffectual.

There are many believers scattered up & down the country, even far from this, & where all is opposition (apparently) the missionaries are pleased to know that there is piety even in the centre of the opposition. Pious women particularly are often found where none are expected, and often it is impossible to hold intercourse with them, as it

[7] A South African term, of Hottentot origin, for a cloak made of wild animal skins sewn together.

would subject them to great annoyance from their heathen husbands. Only a word or two can be said where much is needed. We hope however the Lord will uphold his own work in their hearts & enable them to persevere unto the end.

The women have hard work to perform amongst the Bechuanas. They cultivate the ground and build the houses, while the "Lords of the Creation" sew karosses, milk the cattle, & hunt or sleep. They make very neat builders indeed. It would puzzle the men to do half so well, and if the latter are spoken to about it they reply, "O, it is good for them", "it makes them strong", &c. It is only a very few of the younger people who can be induced to do a little of women's work, & I dare say their own opinion that hard work makes their wives look soon old has more influence over them than any of our arguments. When sitting round a fire by our waggon I have sometimes tried to let the women have a share of it, by requesting the men to give way, but that was out of the question. "We are the kings" was quite a sufficient reason for the women being compelled to sit behind in the cold. How would Agnes like this system of things?

The old spectacles mother put into my bag were a most acceptable present to an old woman who made great efforts to learn to read, but her nose not being of proper shape for the antique things to adhere in their own natural way she must hold them always with the hand. The beads are invaluable, money being of very little use & rather a losing concern, as they will take nothing but silver, & they always prefer a few beads or a hankerchief to it.

Mr Hamilton[8] has just returned from an itinerating journey of a month or nearly 200 miles towards E. by North. He met great opposition in some places & encouragement in others. He is quite well in health, & so, I am thankful to say, we all are.

Is Fergus & David still within reach of you? I should

[8] Robert Hamilton (1776–1851), born in Scotland, entered the service of the LMS in 1815 as an artisan; helped to found the mission at Kuruman (1816), where he was stationed for the rest of his life (Register, p. 11). For his own account of the journey mentioned, cf. LMS Chronicle, vol. 6 (1842), pp. 171 f.

have written them, but feared they might be removed ere my letter arrived. I hope to write Mr Naismith soon, as also S[amue]l & J[oh]n.[9] Remember me kindly to them. Could they not write me? My letter will cross theirs on the way if they do. How is Duncan?[10] I suppose gone to America; & J. Wheelan? D[itt]o. The sun shines down our chimneys here.

Yours affectly,
D. L.

I can write no more to Charles. He is a shabby fellow for a correspondent. Tell him I say so. I think frequently of you all, but this language engages many thoughts. I am never pleased with the progress I make, the Natives do jumble their words so together, & then they are so stupid at understanding if there is any blunder in my sentences; but I hope soon to overcome. I shall after returning live entirely amongst them & speak not a word of English. I must conquer. Yesterday a man came to carry medicine for his wife, whom I had just been to see. I gave him instructions to let her have it immediately. Before I could say stop, the fellow had it whisked into his own stomach. Although not very agreable (castor oil, a large quantity), he yiel[d]ed prompt obedience to what he thought I wished, & the reason was I did not use the phrase most commonly employed.

The people here are very much like what the patriarchs must have been. They are all nomadic if they can possibly find a few cattle. Some are mighty hunters, not your red-coated gentry after a fox. I know men here who have attacked lions & killed them with no other weapons than an asagai in one hand & the kaross wound round the other arm to thrust into his mouth. The mill is more original still than that of the two women which I have seen in use in the Colony,[11] a flat stone (broad) with a little roundish one to rub with a sort of shoving motion, as women in Scotland do

[9] John Naismith, tanner and currier; deacon of the Independent Church in Hamilton. Samuel and John were his sons; the latter was then Treasurer of the church (LMS Annual Reports).

[10] Not identified.

[11] The Cape Colony, whose nearest boundary was then about 200 miles to the south of Kuruman.

with their clothes at the bottom of the tub. I can understand why Rachel felt so much at being barren.[12] Nothing is
so great a curse to a B[echuana] wife as want of children;
they are really miserable if without, & children are so
valuable.

The heat is beginning. North winds sweeping over the
long tract of country in that direction become so heated,
when they come here they are like the blast of a furnace;
sometimes crumble the grass into powder.

4: To JANET LIVINGSTON

8 December 1841

Address: (Care of Revd. Dr Phillip, Church Square, Cape Town)
Miss Janet Livingston, Almada St., Hamilton, N.B. *Postmark:* Hamil-
ton, MY 18, 1842. [Wilson Collection; extracts published in Blaikie,
Personal Life, pp. 44 f.]

Kuruman
8th Dec. 1841

My dear Sisters,
The day before yesterday I received my first communication (dated March & May) from home since sailing from
England, & I was made both glad & sorry by the news it
contained. Another letter has been sent, but it has not come
to hand. As it was, I was thankful to hear a little of you all.
It has made me think a little more of home or rather Hamilton, for it is not my home, than I had done for some time
previously. Poor Duncan is gone, and Agnes was nearly off
too. Let us work with all our might in the service of our
Saviour now, for it will soon be said of us all, they have
passed away. I suppose this is the beginning of what I must
expect—a letter every now & then telling me some of my
friends are dead. The voice is explicit. May we not neglect
its warning voice. Long before this reaches you the vividness of the impressions may have worn away. Instead of
saying much in my letter I shall pray that what you have both
seen, & one of you experienced, may be sanctified to you,

[12] Genesis 30: 1–8, 22–4.

43

and thus the object of what I might otherwise have said will be accomplished by a much shorter route than via Cape of Good Hope, viz. up to Heaven & down to Hamilton.

I am sorry your anticipations of crossing the Atlantic are disappointed in the mean time. It is however not for want of will on my part that it was not accomplished. I dare say you find it no joke in this case to take the will for the deed. But I could not do more than I have done. This year, commencing April next, I cannot send anything to anyone. But the year after that I hope to be able, if John can't do the needful in the interval. By what I sent I was afraid I should be run ashore before the year expired, but I have met with an excellent friend in Mr Edwards[1] of this station, who with Mrs E. does all that is needful. Living is much dearer here than in some countries, India for instance. We have everything to buy. But I need not make a poor mouth to poorer sisters than I am, & Father need not if he pleases fill his next letter after receipt of this with how much he was grieved to take anything from me, &c. You must all just take what you can get, & no more about it.

And you Janet, in particular, you are a heineous offender. No more of your poetry if you please, nay I command it; and if you again venture to fill up a letter with such everlasting nonsense, blethers strung up in rhyme, instead of what ought to be in it, you may expect a bull fulminated against your person equal perhaps to the famous one sent after the "alum secret stealing man", or worse still a Campleton one conjured up in your dreams by some of the black art which I am imagined to be possessed of by some of the more ignorant people here.[2] It's very well for you to sit on the bridge & sing these effusions, but what on earth makes you think I care for the Lady or her brother? No more, I assure

[1] Rogers Edwards (1795–1876), born in Lancashire, joined the LMS in 1823 as an artisan, and after serving at two stations in the Cape Colony went to Kuruman in 1831. In 1843 he and D. L. founded the mission at Mabotsa, from which he was expelled by the Boers in 1852. He subsequently worked again in the Cape Colony, chiefly at Port Elizabeth, where he died. (*Register*, p. 24). D. L. boarded with him on first reaching Kuruman, and described him as "a fellow-labourer whom I much esteem & admire" (14.vii.1842 Mrs Sewell).

[2] Writing to Mrs Sewell (7.iv.1842), D. L. remarks that because of his medical practice he had acquired the reputation of being "a great wizard, . . . a doctor who can cure all disease & *raise the dead*".

you, than I do for "Roy's wife of Aldivalloch" & Mars
Niven's brother Bob.[3] I don't know what mother was about
when she allowed it.

But enough of this nonsense. I know it was done with the
best intentions, & perhaps I shall lose my biliousness over
it when I read it some of these days. However, for your
guidance in future I may say poetry must be precious good
stuff indeed before it merits the place where news of home
ought to be. Only think, I have been away on a journey
700 miles long,[4] & killed as the Natives say by an angry
angry sun, & longing to hear from home; a letter comes, &
about ⅓ of it is the effusion (not of my own sisters but) of
some pair of poetastresses who I suppose would have been
much more usefully employed darning their Grannies'
stockings than clinking words together, cruelly murdering
the English language in the attempt.

You must either have a large sheet of foolscap or two full
sheets of the other shorter paper. Postage does not go by
weight in the Colony. Hence of *scraps* beware. If more
sheets than one, mention it on the outside.

We have got newspapers up to May & June, so I am a
little acquainted with the state of the country, corn law
agitation, &c, up to that date. You need not say much respecting general affairs or the state of the country generally;
local & family news is more acceptable.

In our journey, which was undertaken to ascertain the
actual condition of some tribes concerning whom we had
often heard favourable accounts, we had to endure a great
deal of heat & fatigue. You don't know in Scotland what is
meant by heat during the middle of the day. The sun's rays
are so strong, one feels quite afraid of going into them from
under the shade in which you may be stewing. The sand is
burning hot, & the stones too if you sit down on one, even
long after the heat of the day is gone, you feel as if you had

[3] "Roy's Wife of Aldivalloch" is a poem by Mrs Grant of Carron, 1745–1814
(*Edinburgh Book of Scottish Verse*, 1910, p. 432). The other allusions I cannot
explain.
[4] D. L. and Edwards had left Kuruman for the Interior on 18 October, and
returned six weeks later. Among the tribes they visited were the BaKgatla-
baMmanaana near Mabotsa, BaKwena at Shokwane and Dithubaruba, BaNgwaketse
at Setlagole, and BaRolong at Lotlhakane (Edwards to Tidman, 8.xii.1841).

LIVINGSTONE'S FAMILY LETTERS 1841

sat down by mistake on the "girdle".[5] We travelled over hundreds of miles of dreary wilderness, not a soul appearing in sight. Now & then a herd of wild horses, giraffes, ostriches, or different kinds of antelopes served as a relief to the eye, wearied with the monotony of the perpetually recurring thorn bushes & camel thorn trees. It is no wonder that Hagar lifted up her voice in the wilderness & wept when the water was spent in the bottle.[6] We had some Natives with us from the Interior tribes, who came about 300 miles on foot for the purpose of selling a few skins & an elephant's tooth they had got, and at the same time seeing Sunday, a name some of them give Kuruman. They carried water in ostrich eggshells, and when we got beyond the region they knew, nothing would induce them to drink their water (although suffering severely from thirst) untill they saw the next we should come to. Wisdom, taught them by experience, induced them to preserve it carefully in case they should be brought to extremity. We travelled on one occasion between 50 & 60 miles without a drop for the oxen for more than 2 days, this with the sun so hot in the middle of the day that centipedes coming out of their holes are roasted alive. I never saw them so nearly done up.

There is a tribe called the Bakalihari,[7] who live in the desert & have scarcely any water, but Providence supplies the want in a great measure, for through the whole country there abounds a species of bitter melon, which they pierce & collect the juice. The seeds of it serve when roasted as food for them. Amongst this tribe the Bechuanas find their doctors. One day far from any dwelling we came to a tree in the midst of a plain, and 3 little children sitting under it, this in a country where wild animals abound. They shewed that their mothers were up at some mountains in the distance collecting a kind of wild fruit. I gave them some

[5] "Circular iron plate hung over fire for toasting cakes" (*Concise Oxford Dictionary*).
[6] Genesis 21: 14 ff.
[7] BaKgalagadi, the earliest people of Tswana stock to settle in Bechuanaland. They were divided into many separate groups, most of which were either conquered and reduced to servitude, or driven into the Kalahari Desert (whence their name), by later Tswana invaders. "They have scarcely any fountains, no cattle, & subsist by snaring wild animals and eating roots" (8.xii.1841 MacLehose; cf. *Travels*, pp. 49 ff.).

46

buttons which were put into my bag by mother, & a lump
of rhinoceros' flesh, which made them quite happy. Their
mothers returned after some time, but were afraid to come
near, but seeing the children playing about us they at last
ventured. I gave one of them the remains of our dinner. She
afterwards filled the pot with her wild fruit & presented
it to me. Janet, I suppose, will feel anxious to know what the
dinner was; I remember she once asked what my suppers
were in London. Well, we boiled a peice of the flesh of a
rhinosuross, which is toughness itself. The night previous,
the meat was our supper, & porridge made of Indian corn
meal & the gravy of the meat made a very good dinner next
day.[8]

When about 150 miles from home, we came to a large
village. The chief had sore eyes. I doctored his eyes, & he
fed us pretty well with milk & beans & sent a fine buck
after me as a present. When we had got about 10 or 12 miles
on the way, we unyoked for breakfast. Presently a little girl
11 or 12 years of age came up & sat down under my
waggon, having run away for the purpose of coming with us
to Kuruman. She had lived with a sister whom she had lately
lost by death. Another family took possession of her, for the
purpose of selling her as soon as she was old enough for a
wife. But not liking this she determined to run away from
them & come to some friends near K. With this intention
she came, & thought of walking all the way behind my
waggon. I was pleased with the determination of the little
creature, & gave her some food. But before we had remained
long there, I heard her sobbing violently as if her heart
would break. On looking round, I observed the cause. A
man with a gun had been sent after her to bring her back, &
he had just arrived. I did not know well what to do now. But
I was not in perplexity long, for Paumer,[9] a Native convert
who accompanied us, started up & defended her cause. He
being the son of a chief, & possessed of some authority,
managed the business nicely. She was loaded with beads

[8] "We boiled a piece of the flesh of a rhinoceros which was toughness itself, the
night before. The meat was our supper, and porridge made of Indian corn-meal
and gravy of the meat made a very good dinner next day" (Blaikie).
[9] Pôômore, "the son of a chief near Kuruman" (7.iv.1842 Mrs Sewell); I cannot
identify him more precisely.

to render her more attractive & fetch a higher price. These he stript off & gave to the man & desired him to go away. I afterwards took measures for hiding her, & though 50 had come for [her] they would not have got her.

The reason I mention this is that [you] may value your priveleges more. In this country the women are in abject slavery, & have to build the houses, plant the corn, &c &c, and when mere children are bartered for; their consent is never asked, and the men don't care how many wives they have, the more wives the more corn &c he gets into his possession by their means. And the hard work they have to do soon making them look old, they are then thrown off. Forced to subsist on different kinds of wild roots, they are frequently, when ill especially, unable to return home at night, & are devoured by the wolves,[10] or they perish from hunger in the endeavour to get food. Do you ever pray for your sisters who perish by wolves. If you once heard the dismal horrid growl of one you would never forget it.

Pray for this little girl that it may not be to her condemnation that she has seen the light but turned from it. She is now at school. When she was first in my waggon, a law of the country after a kind of national ceremony prevented her speaking to any but those of her own sex.[11] She commenced plaiting grass into necklaces to supply the place of the beads she had lost. I took out a string of black beads (I believe those J. Jack[12] took off her neck in our house), & asked if she would speak to me for these. Her love to the beads overcame all regard for the law of her nation, for she instantly answered, "O yes, I shall speak if you give me them, I love them".

You may mention some of these things to your fellow workers, but not about eating rhinoceros flesh; it would look as if I meant it to be understood I endured great sufferings, while the fact is my appetite was keen, & I relished the

[10] Hyenas (Afrikaans *wolf*). There are no true wolves in S. Africa.
[11] The "ceremony" was probably the *bojale*, by which girls at about the age of puberty were collectively initiated into the social status of womanhood.
[12] Not identified.

flesh of a wild horse as much as I ever did of a cow; it is excellent, but the other has too much the flavour of train oil. In fact it is like a huge pig, & its flesh whale's blubber.

The great livery buttons were very valuable, for they serve as earings—the eye is put through a hole in the ear, and a peice of stick put through that on the inside keeps it fast in its place. Some of them are now in the ears of chiefs & great men, and the bracelets are fastened on the forehead. I think they look better with beads than without. They certainly are finer with them than with animals' bones, paws, claws of tigers, serpents' skins, or their bones of divination. Perhaps my opinion is influenced by the draughts of milk wh[ich] these things are capable of purchasing. It is exceedingly refreshing to get a little milk after a long journey over burning sand.

When at one tribe, we found our way up to the palace, & entering we found some of the chief's wives eating porridge. Being hungry & wishing to gain their confidence, I squatted down beside them & put my hand into the dish too. They were highly amused and, the porridge being too warm, at my complaint one of them spread it up the side of the dish with her hand. I think you say, how nasty. No, it was very good. They had never seen a white man before, and my hair seemed very strange in their eyes, for when I took off my cap[13] & held down my head they ran back, putting their mouths into that expressive form some people do when they see in one's head a great number of lice or an ugly scab. On turning up my shirt, the horrid whiteness of my skin made them stand aghast; & the queen, after she had become a little better acquainted, ventured to put up her hand to my nose, to feel if it were really so far elevated from the level of my face & not like her own little flat thing.

I have got no letter from John or Charles. A few newspapers from the former. How is mother? You must not think of me as dead by lions, &c. Do you still conjure up so many images yet about our possible condition? You must not, for I am sure you cannot form a true idea of my condition, no more than if I were in the moon. I hope Agnes is quite

³ "A common midshipman's cap covers my head" (16.xii.1843 N. Livingston).

recovered now. I enjoy excellent health & spirits. I am entirely separate from ———[14] & am very happy. I shall read an address in Sicuana[15] first time next Sunday.

Yours affectionately,
D. L.

[14] Dash in MS.   [15] SeTswana, the language of the Tswana tribes.

1842

4 April 1842

Address: (Care of Revd. Dr Phillip, Cape Town) Miss A. Livingston, Almada St., Hamilton, N.B. *Postmark:* Hamilton, SP 25, 1842. [Wilson Collection.]

Bakuain Country,
4th April 1842[1]

My dear Agnes,

I ought to have written you long ago, but I need not fill any space with apologies, as they are in my humble opinion about as valuable as Janet's poetry was. I proceed right on to other matters, & first I suppose you wish to know where I am & what I am doing. Well, I am at present on the top of a hill which forms part of a ridge somewhat like Campsie range.[2] It is the residence of Bubi & his people, who are a part of the Bakuain tribe.[3] This hill is surrounded on all sides by precipitous approaches. A path which winds round a part of it is the only way by which a waggon can come up, but after one is up it is very pleasant, for it is much cooler than the plains below & you can see to a great distance a country covered thickly with trees & beautifully green. We

[1] D. L. had left Kuruman on 10 February, on his second journey into the Interior. His main object was to perfect his knowledge of the language "by exclusive intercourse with the Natives", but he also took with him the Native teacher Pôômore (4.9), whom he intended to station with a group of BaKwena that he and Edwards had visited the year before (3.vii.1842 Freeman).

[2] Campsie Fells, a range of hills (in Stirlingshire) about 15–20 miles north-north-west of Hamilton.

[3] The BaKwena, one of the oldest Tswana tribes, had broken apart after the assassination (*c.* 1822) of Motswasele II, father of Sechele. One section, of which Motswasele's agnatic cousin Bubi became chief in 1828 (?), ultimately settled at Dithubaruba, in the Dithejwane Hills, about 30 miles north-west of Kolobeng. D. L. was writing from there.

see another range of mountains in the distance, about as far off as when you look from Hamilton to Benleddi,[4] but it is here a plain between, & instead of Glasgow with its smoke & dirt you would meet with the rhinoceros, cameleopard, buffalo, zebra, and numerous herds of different kinds of antelopes, some of whom are as large as horses. Down there my driver goes every few days and brings back an ox load of butcher's meat. On the East I can see nothing but a continuation of this range of mountains. It is just as if you stood on Campsie & looked away to the Highlands, only the hills are covered all over with trees & plenty of baboons.

It is much more pleasant here than near Kuruman, which is a bleak parched-looking desert, having nothing but stunted thorn bushes which if they seize you must stand & patiently extricate yourself. Most of the thorns are bent backwards like fish hooks, but there are likewise a goodly array of straight ones pointing in every direction ready to do mischief both ways and all villainously sharp & strong. If one gets into a reverie & walks on with uplifted eye & gaping mouth, he will quickly be reminded by that nasty Acacia tortuosa that this is not the land for waking dreams, or perchance a fly will buzz down his throat, for you must know the flies are very impudent here. I suppose their numbers makes them so. At home they are really modest well-bred flies, if I may use the expression, but here nothing is secure from their voracious appetites. They light right into the eyes, & when we knock them off from the face in dozens the villains crawl up the legs of the trowsers, sleeves of jacket, front of shirt, determined to worry you anyhow. They light on the spoon when ascending to your mouth, & have not the sense to get out of the way of certain destruction without almost a box on the ear, besides committing suicide by scores in your coffee if it is warm enough for the purpose. I at first covered milk up with a cloth, thinking that was sufficient, but unless a weight is applied besides you find the surface of the milk black instead of white, these marauders having perished in the spoil.

[4] Ben Ledi (2875 ft.), 4 miles north-west of Callander in Perthshire, and about 35 miles north of Hamilton.

A stream rather larger than Calder at the Prior Bridge[5] winds round part of this hill, and passes through a deep defile which separates this hill from the range on one side. It is a kind of fissure & resembles the Cartlan crags[6] very much, only it is larger & deeper. The rocks are of red sandstone, full of pebbles like those you see on the sea[7] shore, & in some places the ripple or mark of the waves which you have seen very beautifully left on the sand at the bottom of a river is quite apparent in the stone. The strata answer to each other on each side.

Here in this defile I am at work, or rather directing others to work. I am engaged in leading out the water to irrigate a garden for Pomore, a Native teacher. For this purpose we have been obliged to raise a huge dam of earth & stones & dig a canal. The Natives do it all themselves. I am only an overseer, for the first day I got my legs & arms so burnt by the sun, although in the water almost the whole time, I was unable to stimulate them by my example. You don't know what sunburnt means in Scotland. You think, Well, what about it, although his legs were browned, bah. The sun burns red & blisters here, & you don't perhaps know it till you feel a little pricking pain in the part, but it is painfull enough afterwards. The Natives were quite delighted with the idea that I could make rain so (the doctor & rain maker is one & the same), & by this means I hope they will see the folly of trusting any more to their rain doctor.[8] The chief sends 16 men dailly to work under my directions, among whom are his principal under-chiefs & his doctor. These are as many as he can spare at present, for the crops are just now being taken in. A tornado came down two nights ago and swept away a great portion of the dam when we were within two days of its completion. After looking at the work of destruction a little with rueful countenances,

[5] The Rotten Calder, which runs northwards to join the Clyde below Uddingston, is about 80 feet wide in the vicinity of the old priory, Blantyre.

[6] Cartland Crags, 2 miles north-west of Lanark; a vast chasm in the sandstone rocks forming the bed of the Mouse Water.

[7] MS. has "see".

[8] "I proposed to the chief to lead out a river which winds round the bottom of this hill, explaining that by this means I could make rain much more certainly than any of his rainmakers. He was quite delighted with the idea" (7.iv.1842 Mrs Sewell).

we commenced again & hope soon to finish the whole. All the digging has been performed by means of sticks sharpened to a point, & the earth is lifted out in "gowpenfuls"[9] or in a large tortoise shell, sometimes by wooden platters from which they take their food. Their karosses or skin cloaks are the wheelbarrows. O, I should mention we have one spade, viz. mine, but it is without a handle.

The place where the dam is is overshadowed by a perpendicular rock twice as high as the one on which the old Priory stands,[10] & behind it the hill rises to 6 or 7 times that height. Under it I sit & give my orders from sunrise untill the heat becomes intolerable, & then we wend our way up the mountain to our home. You would be amused if you saw us at work & heard the curious expressions of the Natives relating to the work, "Namane a tuna e kholu tiro e,[11] a great great great work is this", of the foreigner. The other day the[y] lightened their labour by songs of which I was the subject, but you will not think the words very complimentary, although to them they caused abundant merriment. "We are killed by Monarri"[12] (Mr), æ æ æ as chorus. "He is making us oxen now &c, we shall see our wives no more &c."

I am thankful that I have so much influence with them as to induce them to engage in a public work of this kind. It is the first instance known of Bechuanas working without pay. The older missionaries had to do all themselves, & if they at any time got the Natives to work they had to pay them handsomely, & not unfrequently they were unable to get them to work even with that. Those here are not contaminated yet by intercourse with Europeans or Natives farther to the South. It was this consideration that induced

[9] Gowpen, "the two hands held together so as to form a bowl" (A. Warrack, *Chambers's Scots Dictionary*, p. 224).

[10] The ruins of Blantyre Priory, three-quarters of a mile north-west of Low Blantyre, are on the summit of a rock about 150 ft. above the bed of the Clyde.

[11] In the modern orthography, *Namane e tona e kgolo tiró e*. Literally, *namane e tona* means "large calf", but the phrase is used idiomatically "to denote anything exceedingly big" (Brown, *Secwana Dictionary*, p. 226). D. L.'s translation is accurate enough.

[12] *Monare*, from Afrikaans *meneer* (Dutch *mynheer*), "a term of respect often employed in South Africa when a minister of the Gospel is addressed or spoken of" (C. Pettman, *Africanderisms*, 1913, p. 331).

me to think of beginning here, & thanks be to our Heavenly Father I have not been out in my reckoning.

Had I not made this effort for these people, I might have been able to have sent you £20 instead of devoting it to this cause. Pomore will remain here.[13] I shall visit him sometimes, & O, may He without whose aid nothing can be done bless our very feeble labours to his own glory. This explanation will I am sure meet your approbation. I thought I saw that good might be done by a vigorous effort, & the only question was whether shall I devote this to the cause of Christ or to my parents. I felt sure you all would say to the former. I hope some friend in England will assist me in this work. I wrote Mr Naismith to see if he would do anything.[14] I shall write him again soon on the same subject.

That the Lord has thus opened up my way I feel thankful. But O, much must still be done. You can form no idea of the state of these people. Nothing but Almighty grace can change them from what they are. The chief is very friendly, sends me milk regularly, & does everything I wish. But only imagine, if you can, the earthly minds of the people, who can think of nothing but what they see around them. Sometimes it would be amusing were it not at the same time seriously distressing. While Pomore is preaching with great fervour, some one burst[s] into a loud laugh, in which most of the congregation join although ignorant of the cause. When he has quelled this & they have sat quiet for 10 minutes, another sees one passing at a distance with sweet reed,[15] & as his thoughts are on some other subject than the sermon he instantly bawls out at the top of his voice, "Hey, man, why don't you bring us some of your sweet reed?"; & then suddenly recollecting himself looks round to me with an expression of fear which would make me smile were I not engaged in so important a work. And again when they sprawl down on their bellies or backs to hear Pomore tell them to sit on their "doups".[16] But I hope this will soon be changed for another state of things. Several families of Christians will

---

[13] However, having fallen ill of malaria he accompanied D. L. back to Kuruman.

[14] D. L. had written to him on 2.xii.1841, asking for financial help to secure a Native catechist "as your representative in the Interior".

[15] *Sorghum dochna* (Forsk.) Snowden.   [16] Buttocks.

come with Pomore,[17] & I hope [and] pray the leaven will spread untill it leavens the whole lump. Remember us in your prayers.

This place is situated on or near the Tropic of Capricorn.[18] The vegetation is quite tropical here & as different from the South as possible. The birds are beautiful. The fig trees grow in abundance on the hills, but I don't know scarcely any of the others. I am told there are many tribes before me, but they are far distant.

I was at this interrupted by one of Bubi's wives bringing me some beans & a draught of [a] curious sort of beer, if indeed it deserves that name. I gave her a string of amber beads & two rings, I believe given me by your companions. In giving them I called her "sister", which pleased her so very much she is determined to act the part of one. Every evening since she sends me a huge bowl of sour porridge or beans or some sweet reeds with the message, "Sister sends you this, as she ought to take good care of her brother." I have not met with any in the Bechuana nation who shewed continued kindness equal to hers. Our people are [so][19] well fed by the people that there is no occasion to draw on [our] own meal sack at all. In return ours share the venison [with] them while I furnish the powder & shot.

Mother will be anxious to hear how I fare. I remember in the only letter I have got from you since I left Eng[lan]d some allusion is made to this. Please tell her, I "aye get a wamefu",[20] and this more than I deserve. "I have been aye provided for, & sae will I yet." Some of the bretheren would kill me with kindness if I lived long with them, they are so grateful for any little medical assistance I render them.

Next month I expect to receive letters from home. What are you all doing? is a question that I sometimes ask myself, but no answer but the still deathlike quietness which you can almost hear in this wide wide wilderness land. Here in the evenings I hear the bleating of sheep & goats, the lowing

---

[17] "The ground we have irrigated will induce a considerable number of the Christians to come hither from Kuruman" (14.iv.1842 Watt).
[18] The latitude (of Dithubaruba) is approximately 24° 30′ S.
[19] Paper slightly torn at seal.   [20] Bellyful.

of oxen & the jabber of the Natives mingling with the yell of the jackall & howling of the wolf. Occasionally the Natives dance & screech their own wild unearthly music the greater portion of the night, but not very often.

Here you cannot fear colds, for a cough is seldom ever heard even among the Natives, who go almost naked. The sun goes down about 7 o'clock, & very soon indeed after it sets it is quite dark. We have scarcely any twilight, & one can sit out in the evenings without dread of rheumatisms or sore throats. The nights are really delightful, but the days we long for clouds as much as you do for an umbrella in a shower. Even after the sun has set the stones are disagreably warm and you can't sit on them with pleasure, but during the day to sit on them would be trying Jock Riddle's cure for the toothache.[21]

I forgot to say in reference to Janet's vomiting, she ought to have her bowels opened freely a day or two previous to the return of the attack, by a pill composed of Compound Rhubarb pill, Blue Pill, and a small quantity of Quinine. If you purchase 4 drachms ($\frac{1}{2}$ ounce) C. Rhub. Pil., 1 Dr[a]chm Blue Pil., mix them well with flour & as much Quinine as will stand on the point of a penknife for each pill you make, it will assist her, I think. Blue Pill contains a mild preparation of mercury, but it will do her no harm. If you fear it, work it all off with common Epsom salts next morning having a few drops of vitriol in the solution. During the interval let her have 10 drops of oil of turpentine morning & evening in a little water. The druggists sell what is called Rectified Spirit of T., it does not taste so nauseously as Com. Turp. Divide the med. specified above into 60 pills. A scruple of Quinine or half a drachm will be sufficient.

The little black spot you speak of is a nervous defect, or as I ought to express it a deficiency of nervous influence, & arises from the same cause as the impaired vision, viz. debility. Take Quinine or some other bitter, keep the bowels open. Gentian with soda is excellent, or Bark with Soda. An ounce to a drachm of Soda (carbonate) & a mutchkin[22] of

21 I cannot explain the allusion.
22 "A liquid measure equal to an English pint" (Warrack).

water, wine glass night & morning. The black spot is called muscae volitantes. The eye being a little out of the axis of vision may be part of the cause, as it often causes it, the light striking directly on a part of the optic nerve which ought not to receive it so powerfully.

No doubt the story of the cockroach pleased you vastly, but unfortunately although "the giant cockroach is a noted reveller in the West Indies" he is not so in the country where the ladies slept (Wales).[23] If the drummer is not in existence in Wales, of course his drumming was not heard.

All my handkerchiefs are gone except 3 or 4, but you need not send any. A few beads would be as valuable as a few Pounds. All sort of trinkets are excellent, & money is of no value at all except in purchasing these things from traders.

This is the largest sheet of paper I have with me on this journey,[24] but it contains more than you[r] "head & thraws"[25] one, so you must be content. It will be long ere you see it, for it is a weary way to the Colony from this. I am about 250 miles Lat. & Long. from Kuruman.[26]

Farewell, yours affectionately,

D. L.

Kind love to Mother. I have written very often to you, but if I don't get letters from you I suppose I shall get tired by & by. I have got no letter from John since I came here. Charles Dᵒ. Dᵒ. Love to all I know.

17th June. Arrived at Kuruman in excellent health.[27] Got one letter from Father dated 15 Jany. /41.

[23] I cannot explain the allusion.

[24] It measures 8·9 by 7·2 inches.

[25] Heads-and-thraws, "with the heads and feet, or heads and points, lying in opposite directions" (*Jamieson's Dictionary of the Scottish Language*, abridged ed., p. 264).

[26] "I am about 250 miles North East of Lattakoo" [Kuruman] (7.iv.1842 Mrs Sewell).

[27] After staying with Bubi for about a month, D. L. had proceeded farther north and visited the BaNgwato and other tribes in the Shoshong Hills before returning to Kuruman.

6: To MR AND MRS N. LIVINGSTON

13 July 1842

Address: (Care of Revd. Dr Phillip, Cape Town) Mr Livingston, Almada St., Hamilton, N.B. *Postmark:* Hamilton, NO 27, 1842. [Wilson Collection.]

Kuruman
July 13th 1842

My dear Parents,
    I received your welcome letter about a month ago. It bears date 4th Nov. '/41. I received in December /41 another, dated March I believe, and these two constitute the sum total of your correspondence with me since I left. I am glad you got the little I sent; I was a little anxious to hear. I have got no letter from either John or Charles since leaving England; I got, however, a few newspapers from John, which shews the grand-juryman is not dead yet, I suppose. I am very sorry to hear Charles has not got my parcels. Janet's dreams & fancies are the only intimation . . .[1] rhymes made something better than "Weep no more". The colloquy might have been thus: O Jock, is that you? Aye, mither, but I'm deed noo. Cam awa, man, ye're in fun. Na, mither, I canna wun.[2] If ye're deed, what brings ye here? I am a puir ghost, ye need na speir, share's death I am like to swarf;[3] gie the cobbler his tools and I'll be aff, &c &c. But this is nonsense I am writing.
    Mrs Ross[4] is near me at this time, but I was never put to any sort [of] trouble by being near her in the way you think of. I live in the house of Mr Edward[s]. Both he & Mrs E. are kind to a fault. Of course when I am away in the Interior I am not dependant on any one for attentions. My people cook, wash, &c for me. I am very much indebted to Mr E. Had he not acted the part of a brother, I should have

---

[1] Four lines heavily obliterated in MS.
[2] A variant of "win", meaning *inter alia* "to go, to come, to have power or liberty to go" (Warrack, pp. 678, 688).
[3] "I am a poor ghost, you need not ask, [as] sure as death I am about to swoon".
[4] The wife of William Ross (1.10). She and her husband had travelled together with D. L. from England.

been in difficulties by sending you what I did, but the Lord provided.

Mrs R. had a child. I was the means of saving its life as clearly as anyone could be, & had I been 4 or 5 minutes later it must have died. She is a regular old maid, Miss Grant stereotyped.[5] In order to get over all sense of obligations to me, she has told several of our sisters that I did nothing! But unfortunately for her fame, Mrs Edwards was present at the confinement, saw the entire inability of the midwife & what was done by me, and lets the sisterhood know what a genius they have got among them. She is, however, a very good sort of woman in the main. She is very anxious to make the bretheren believe that her husband is something extraordinary, but her efforts, together with his strange sort of conduct,[6] make them very suspicious of him. I am however quite apart from them & very comfortable.

I wrote Agnes in the Interior & sent it when I returned. Also one to Mr J. Naismith, Junior. It was a strictly private letter. I told him so, & hope it will not be read in public. I wrote you also previous to going into the Interior, & now I am writing you again before I leave. The country is quite different from this. It abounds with trees. It is much warmer, and far in there are many more people. There are people too who speak another language than the Sicuana.[7] In this last I can now speak with considerable fluency. I preach occasionally without reading what I say. I preached my first sermon beyond Latitude 22° North, I mean without reading it. It was to a people who live on the top of very high rocks.

[5] Writing to Rev. R. Cecil of Ongar on 13.v.1841, D. L. described Mrs Ross as "an old maid when married, seems likely to continue so to the end of the chapter", and as a "blooming bride of 34 or 35". Miss Grant I have been unable to identify.

[6] During the voyage from England, Ross had made a very unfavourable impression upon D. L., who described him as "a foolish weak-minded companion" (7.iv.1842 Mrs Sewell). "He & I are not on good terms, because I speak out & pay no more regard to his opinions on the ground of his 9 years' education (his wife's boast) than if he were my Hottentot boy & could not read. . . . [He] is mule-headed beyond calculation" (7.vii.1841 Watt).

[7] This refers to the MaKalaka, whom D. L. had found in the Shoshong Hills on his recent journey, and of whom he wrote that they "speak a language differing very decidedly from the Sitchuana. None of the Bechuanas I had with me could understand it. But from some of the words which I caught, I am inclined to think it belongs to the same root with their tongue" (3.vii.1842 Freeman). It is, in fact, a dialect of the Shona group of Bantu languages, spoken mainly in S. Rhodesia.

They are called Bakaa,[8] & never saw a missionary before.
They saw a trader a few years ago, & poisoned both him &
his people.[9] Now Mother must be sure & dream that I am
killed & murdered too by them. I did not notice that you
mentioned how she was, but perhaps you did in your last; it
was so mutilated by being tied outside of some packet &
apparently wetted by sea water that I could not read it all.
The people in the Interior have a great dread of white people
in consequence of what they have heard of the guns of the
Boors. When I approached the town of the Bakaa they were
terrified & thought I had come to kill them, so Mother need
not be afraid on my account. The thought is better still,
the Lord is my keeper night & day. My times are in his
hand.

We have no corn laws here, but sometimes it is as bad in
the Interior; but that is nothing, for when we have not corn
we have flesh. I don't know how you would like to sit down
to a meal composed of flesh. It is very good if one is hungry,
& if we are not we should not eat at all. The fat kitchens[10]
the lean, & down it goes like curds & cream. I was without
bread for a month when in, & when I came to a place called
Mosika,[11] perhaps a 150 miles North of this, a Griqua
woman who lives there made me a loaf composed of Native
& Indian corn meal mixed, & it seemed the best bread I
had ever tasted, and this although I was not tired of the
meat regimen.

The work of God goes on here notwithstanding all our
infirmities. Souls are gathered in continually, and sometimes
from among those we could scarcely have expected to see
turning to the Lord. 24 were last month added to the

[8] A people of Tswana stock, the BaKaa were an early offshoot from the BaRolong,
and after migrating northward had by the middle of the eighteenth century settled
in the Shoshong Hills. Cf. Schapera, "Notes on the History of the Kaa", *African
Studies*, vol. 4 (1945), pp. 110 f.

[9] But in *Travels*, p. 10, D. L. writes: "The Bakaa mountains had been visited
before by a trader, who, with his people, all perished from fever." This corresponds
with information given to the explorer Andrew Smith in 1835, within a year of the
event; cf. Schapera, *op. cit.*, pp. 113 f. The trader's name was Gibson.

[10] Seasons, gives a relish to food.

[11] Despite the conclusion suggested by the spelling, D. L. is probably referring,
not to Mosega (see below, 11.20), but to Mosita (26° 9′ S., 24° 45′ E., marked
"Mosito" on modern maps), about 80 miles by road west-south-west of Mafeking.

church, and there are several inquirers. At Moteeto,[12] too, a French station about 35 miles North by East of this, there has been an awakening, & I hope much good will result. May the cause go on & prosper. I have good news too from Rio De Janeiro. The Bibles that have been distributed are beginning to cause a stir. A priest had, during the week my friend there wrote, inserted a furious letter against all Protestants in general & him in particular. The writer of the letter is an archbishop, & says he is surprised to see with what avidity the people, whose ignorance is notorious, & the priests, who are if possible still more ignorant, receive the Bible. My friend remarks the priests won't thank him for the compliment.[13]

I wish I could promise to do something more for you than I have done, but I fear I must wait a little yet. I can't at present do anything for Charles. If you had a few beads or hankercheifs they would be valuable, but you must not purchase anything for me. I received a letter from A. Brownlee[14] & will answer it as soon as possible. I think of writing Mr Moir[15] & Fergus, but I don't know where to address the latter. Give my kind regards to J[ame]s Wheelan. I thought he would have been in America, or perhaps I should have written him. But my time is very scarce, & it is very difficult to get a sufficient length of it free from interruptions for a letter. I hope he will try himself next time, and if he gets

[12] Motito, now known as Bothithong (27° 4′ S., 23° 49′ E.). The Paris Evangelical Missionary Society had established a station there in 1832. Its Native inhabitants were chiefly BaRolong.

[13] On the voyage from England, D. L.'s ship had put in at Rio for repairs. While there he lived with "an American Episcopal methodist missionary" named Justin Spaulding, "a good sort of fellow, once a chaplain in the American Navy, & devoid of the characteristic cant of English Wesleyans" (7.vii.1841 Watt). For further details about him, cf. 5.iii.1841 Prentice (in Chamberlin, *Some Letters from Livingstone*, p. 18).

[14] Alexander Brownlee, a physician living at 22 Orr Street, Mile End, Glasgow. A letter to him from D. L., dated 17.vii.1843 and beginning "Your kind and excellent letter reached me some months ago", was published in the *Glasgow Medical Journal*, vol. 128 (1937), pp. 161 ff.

[15] Rev. John Moir, ordained 1835, pastor of the Independent (Congregational) Church, Hamilton, 1835–9; afterwards joined the Free Church of Scotland and became Presbyterian minister in Wellington, New Zealand (Ross, *Congregational Independency in Scotland*, pp. 251, 257; Blaikie, p. 19 n.). In August 1837 he had written to the Directors of the LMS strongly recommending D. L. as a prospective missionary (Campbell, *Livingstone*, p. 55 n.).

over & goes as far into the country as where John is, there is no probability he will wish to come back. Remember me to Mr Taylor.[16] I expect a letter from him when I return from the Interior five or 6 months hence. My love to Mother & the sisterhood. So you thought I was married, did you? I am not afflicted in that way yet. I cannot write any more at present.

Yours affectionately,
D. Livingston

I am now certain I have only got two letters from you.

P.S. I have just noticed that there is a bit of one letter written by Janet. I suppose this is then the third I have got, you will perhaps remember better, or was this the one which contained Janet's poetry? What she has said is a peice of blarney about "nice brothers". Bah! Good luck to them.

7: To MR AND MRS N. LIVINGSTON

26 September 1842

Address: (Care of the Revd. Dr Phillip, Cape Town) Mr Livingston, Almada St., Hamilton, Lanarkshire, N.B. *Postmark:* Hamilton, FE 1, [1843]. [Wilson Collection (Mrs. R. MacDonald, Edinburgh).]

Kuruman
26th Septr 1842

My dear Parents,

I am still in this quarter, although when I last wrote I expected to have been in the Interior. I had everything prepared and all in the waggon, when I was completely non-plussed for want of a leader to my four-footed subjects. I suppose you know we need a man to go before & lead the two oxen in front while another propels them with a huge fishing rod of a whip from behind. Well, there I was at a dead stand, & I am so still, for nobody will trust his precious

---

[16] Probably Joseph van Someren Taylor (1820–81), later a missionary in India, who had been with D. L. at Ongar and then studied at Glasgow Theological Academy 1841–5 (*Register*, p. 60; Ross, *op. cit.*, p. 259; Campbell, pp. 68 f.; Blaikie, p. 27).

black body where there is the least probability of it being scathed.

The country is a dreadful scene of confusion. They have been fighting or rather stealing from each other in every direction, and there is no possibility of saying when it will stop. Mahura[1] commenced it by falling upon the defenceless Sebegwe[2] and murdering 36 of his people. Sechele, the chief of the Bakwain,[3] next fell upon him, but was repulsed with the loss of about 20 men. While he was away from his town Pillanie, another Bakwain chief,[4] came to fight him, and finding nobody in his town but old men, women and children, of course Pillanie like a valiant Bechwana murders the most of these, burns the town, & seizes all the cattle. Sechele was met in the field by a fugitive woman from his own town, who told him what had happened & gave him an opportunity of escaping. Had he fallen into the hands of Pillanie after his recent defeat by Sebegue, it is probable he with his people would have been cut off. Thus he who left for the purpose of destroying Sebegwe met destruction himself from another quarter than he dreamed of. Pillanie not having an opportunity of fighting, or rather inflated by having acted so valiantly against the helpless women & children,—I do not speak in irony, the murder of a child is in the eyes of a Motchuana a very brave deed, and they are not ashamed to boast of it afterwards,—fell upon Sebegue

[1] Chief (1825-69) of one section of the BaTlhaping, then living at Taung (about 90 miles east of Kuruman). He and his people had seceded from the rule of his half-brother Mothibi (3.6).

[2] Chief (1825-44) of one section of the BaNgwaketse. In 1830 or soon after, he and his people had been forced by repeated attacks from the MaTebele to retreat across the Kalahari Desert to the vicinity of Lake Ngami. On hearing that the MaTebele had withdrawn northwards (1837), he returned towards his former home, despite a warning sent him by D. L. that other enemies were awaiting him. The outcome was the disaster mentioned. Cf. Schapera, "A Short History of the BaNgwaketse", *African Studies*, vol. 1 (1942), pp. 6 ff.

[3] Sechele, after living abroad in privation for several years following the assassination of his father (*c.* 1822), had become chief of the main section of BaKwena in 1831, and ruled until his death in 1892. D. L. settled with him as a missionary in 1845, and refers to him repeatedly in correspondence; cf. also *Travels*, pp. 14 ff. and *passim*, and A. Sillery, *Sechele: The Story of an African Chief* (1954).

[4] Pilane was actually chief, 1825(?)-48, of the BaKgatla-bagaKgafêla (not to be confused with the BaKgatla-baMmanaana, with whom D. L. worked in 1843-5). As D. L. subsequently noted (Letter 8), the attack referred to was in fact made not by him, but by the MaTebele of Moselekatse.

after he had just experienced a reverse in an engagement with Bubi, & succeeded in killing a great number of women & children & carrying off a great number of cattle.

A marauding expedition was also sent against poor Sebegue by two tribes in this direction, and they without killing any of his people succeeded in carrying off a number of cattle. So poor S. is now, from being the richest in cattle in the whole country, reduced to wander up & down the wilderness with only a handful of people, scarcely any women or children, & only his shield to sleep on at night. Another expedition went out from a town 14 miles from this, and attacked the chief actor against Sebegwe and drove off a number of his cattle. It was for these, which may be called the gods of the Bechuanas, that he in conjunction with Mahura attacked Sebegwe, & now he in turn will feel some of the misery Sebegwe felt. All will be at him directly. No fewer than three large parties are away with the intention of plundering him.[5] Very likely Bubi will fall into their hands. If so, woe be to him.

The Lord is punishing the people of this land & making them scourges to one another. We don't know when it will end. At present all their minds are on the stretch & no good can be done. The news of war & plunder, and the thousand false reports dailly spread, fill the mind to the exclusion of anything that would make them think on the truth which so much concerns their immortal souls. War never appeared so thoroughly disgusting as now, when close upon the seat of it & knowing many of its victims. May the time soon come when war shall cease. But that never will, unless the gospel is carried to them who are now delighting in blood.

The population in this country is very thin indeed, & they are making it still thinner. I don't know what the new missionaries will think of it when they come.[6] My opinion is they would have been more usefully employed somewhere

[5] The reference is to Sebego's senior half-brother Segotshane, then living with a fugitive section of BaNgwaketse at Dikhukhung on the Molopo River. After the attack mentioned by D. L., which was made by a group of BaTlharo from near Kuruman, he and his people moved to the South and settled with Mahura at Taung. Cf. Schapera, *op. cit.*, p. 10.

[6] These were the recruits (Ashton and Inglis) accompanying Moffat on his return to Bechuanaland from England.

else. There are no fewer than 12 missionaries to about 40,000 Bechuanas, while in India one missionary may have five or six hundred thousand. I have been at pains counting the Bechuanas, & no one else has been so far into the Interior, yet however Mr Moffat[7] may speak I am fully convinced to send more missionaries here, while the wants of India, China &c, are so great, is nothing less than missplaced benevolence. Tell Charles so. He must not come to Africa. I would tell him myself, but I don't know whether he ever received a letter from me. I have never heard from either him or John since I left home.

I suspect Mr M.'s book will be a . . .[8] Not to say the Bechuanas here are not improved when compared with what they were & what the Interior tribes now are. The change is very great indeed. But yet after all if you saw them & knew the deeds of believers, your independant princi[ples][9] would prompt you to dissolve the church. Only think of church members receiving presents of cattle from Mahura immediately after they had seen him shedding human blood in order to procure them, and mightily offended because the missionary remonstrated with them for doing so. But a good deal of this can be traced to the ungodly talk of a wicked trader here,[10] who has been telling them that the missionaries are too hard upon them. "Stand up for your rights", says he, "the teachers should do a great deal more for you than they do, they are paid for it." The believers would not behave so badly as they sometimes do were it not for this wicked man. I fear he will take many of the people here down to the bottomless pit along with himself. The people at this station, I believe, are the least advanced of any. Yet

[7] Robert Moffat (1795–1883), the senior missionary at Kuruman, where he had been stationed since 1821, after working in Namaqualand (1817–19). He went to England on official business in 1839, and while there did much preaching and lecturing on missionary work in Bechuanaland.

[8] Three words (presumably derogatory) heavily obliterated. Moffat's *Missionary Labours and Scenes in Southern Africa* was published in the spring of 1842 by John Snow, London.

[9] Small tear in paper.

[10] Presumably David Hume (1796–1863), who after making several trading expeditions into the Interior (including one as far north as the BaNgwato in 1833) had established a permanent trading-store at Kuruman in 1838 (cf. Moffat, *op. cit.*, p. 605). His life and travels are briefly described in S. le Roux, *Pioneers and Sportsmen of South Africa*, 1939, pp. 29–31.

when I look at the Interior, the people here seem quite civilized in comparison. May the Lord carry on the work which I trust he has begun in many of their souls, and may the whole world soon be filled with the glory of the Lord.

If mother could send me a few seeds I should be glad, the seeds of rhubarb, not old musty stuff that will not grow, of henbane, hemlock, the real sort has spotted stems, dandelion or pissabed, the crocus, colchicum, or any other medicinal plant, you will oblige me. You must not buy them, for you can seldom get them worth anything from dealers. If you knew any gardener, he would be the best hand for it. A small cannister or box a few inches in diameter, made of tin & soldered down, would preserve them. The seeds of the honeysuckle, dog-rose or fir taken out of the cone might at some future period be useful in ornamenting a station, but if you would be put to trouble or expense by it you must not mind them.

I have received no letter from you of late, but I write in order to let you know I am not yet gone to the Interior & don't know when I shall go. May the Lord make plain my path & direct [me] in the way which shall be most for his glory.

Have not yet heard from Mr Drummond or Kirk, or indeed from anybody else in Scotland. My love to Mother, Janet & Agnes. All the bretheren here are well. Mr Hamilton remembers Betty Finletter (Mrs J. Naismith)[11] better now. He was talking to me about her last night.

The grace of the Lord Jesus be with your spirits is the prayer of

D. L.

I preached twice yesterday & usually take my turn in the services here, but the state of the country is such I fear but little good is done by any of us. It is a season of darkness. May it soon be dispelled.

Please tell John his promise to write me once a month seems to me to have nothing else than a bottle of thin air. A few newspapers on one occasion are the only things I got to apprise me that he is not dead yet.

[11] Referred to in Letter 62 as Betsy Finlater.

Oct. 3. This goes off tomorrow. News have just arrived stating that Bubi's town was surrounded at midnight & a general massacre took place. The tribe is nearly destroyed. He may have 10 or 12 men left, not more. The Burolongs[12] were the perpetrators, & they shot their own commander in the dark. Thus my hopes respecting this tribe are gone.

[12] BaRolong, one of the main groups of Southern Tswana. They were by this time divided into several mutually independent tribes. The raid mentioned by D. L. was apparently made by a small party of those living at Motito (P. Lemue, letter in *Journal des Missions Évangeliques*, vol. 18 (1843), p. 283, dated 25.x.1842).

1843

8: To MR AND MRS N. LIVINGSTON

21 March 1843

Address: (Care of Revd. Dr Phillip, Cape Town) Mr Livingston, Almada St., Hamilton, Lanarkshire. *Postmark:* Hamilton, DE 12, 1843. [Wilson Collection; extract published in Blaikie, *Personal Life*, p. 54.]

Bakwain Country,
21st March 1843

My dear Parents,

I regret want of time prevented me writing you previous to commencing this journey,[1] because you may be anxious on my account before this has time to reach you. I am at present at the residence of a Bakwain chief called Sechele.[2] I spent Sunday last with him, & found him in a much better frame of mind for hearing the gospel than he was wont to be. He was one of those who attacked Sebegoe, & while beaten back by that chief he found that another tribe called Matibele[3] had in the mean time burned his town & taken everything he had, besides destroying many of the women & children. Yesterday a few women who were taken captive by the Matibele returned. They escaped by night & after travelling nearly two months, digging roots for subsistence

---

[1] D. L. had set out again for the Interior on 21 February.

[2] Owing to the MaTebele raid mentioned in Letter 7, Sechele and his people had moved eastwards from Shokwane to Chonwane (now known as "Secheli's Oude Stad", on the Letsororo stream, a tributary of the Ngotwane River, in the north-west corner of Marico District, Transvaal).

[3] The MaTebele (AmaNdebele), an offshoot from the Zulu kingdom in Northern Natal, had occupied the central and western portions of the Transvaal from about 1825 until 1837. They were then driven north of the Limpopo River, into what is now Matabeleland (S. Rhodesia), by successive attacks from Boer Voortrekkers and a large expeditionary force of Zulu. But they still continued to make sporadic raids on the tribes to the south of them in Bechuanaland.

by day & climbing some high rock for security by night, at
length appeared at their home. But the hardships have rendered them the mere skeletons of what the[y] were. Poor
creatures, this life is all their portion. It was affecting to hear
their tale, but it did not move in the least the feelings of their
fellows; they are "only women", & I don't believe a tear
would have been shed nor one pang of sorrow felt though
they had all perished, just because they are such.

I preached twice on Sunday to as many as could be collected together. I also preached to Sebegoe & his people on
Sunday week.[4] With the latter it was a more interesting
service, for he is a king indeed; his tribe is destroyed, but he
still keeps up as much barbarous dignity as if he were now
in all his glory. I told him I wanted a little milk for coffee.
He has but few cattle now, but he sent the largest pot of it
I ever saw, with an apology because he could not now feed
me as [he] was wont to entertain strangers. He was never
overcome by the Matibele, & is a regular general in his
tactics, & had it not been by the base deceit of Mahura he
would not have been overcome by any of the tribes near
Kuruman. I apprised him of his danger,[5] & he seems grateful, but says the reason why he did not take my advice was
entire ignorance of the power of guns. He had been so long
in the desert & he so earnestly desired to sow corn again,
his people too having decreased by disease so much there
was not a sufficiency for his immense herds of cattle, he
thought he might try to come out from his desert fastness.
He had been by Mr Moffat only once, & as Mr M. was
then ignorant of the language he does not seem to have
received any benefit from what may have been said.[6] When
I told him of Jesus & the resurrection he seemed quite
astonished, & during my addresses he frequently asked
questions; & on hearing that we observed the sabbath, he

[4] Sebego was then living close to the BaMalete at Rabogadi (roughly halfway
between the modern towns of Groot Marico and Zeerust, Western Transvaal).

[5] On his way back from the Shoshong Hills in 1842, D. L. had found messengers
from Sebego awaiting him at Bubi's village (Dithubaruba). He then gave them
the warning to which he refers (28.v.1842 MacLehose, 3.vii.1842 Freeman).

[6] Sebego had visited Moffat, then staying temporarily at Tswaing Pan (Moro-
kweng, 65 miles north of Motito), in May 1827. For Moffat's account of their
meeting, cf. *Apprenticeship at Kuruman*, ed. Schapera, 1951, pp. 254-7.

issued orders that no one should do anything on that day. This was something like what the Establishment like magistrates to do. May the Lord pour down his spirit on this dark country. It is pleasant to be able to make known the word of life in a foreign tongue, but I greatly need to be baptised by the Spirit, that the word may not be made ineffectual by my mode of presenting it to the mind.

Janet may be pleased to hear that I am become a poet, or rather poetaster, in Sicuana. Half a dozen of my hym[n]s were lately printed in a collection of the French bretheren.[7] One of them is a translation of "There is a fountain filled with blood", another "Jesus shall reign where'er the sun", another on "The earth shall be filled with the glory of the Lord, &c", another "Self-dedication", "Invitation to sinners", & another "The soul which loves God finds him everywhere".[8] Janet may try to make English ones on these latter subjects if she can, & Agnes will no doubt set her productions to music[9] on the same condition. I do not boast of having done this, but only mention it to let you know that I am getting a little better fitted for the great work of a missionary, & that your hearts may be drawn out to more prayer for the success of the gospel proclaimed in so feeble [a] way by my lips.[10]

I have received a letter at last from Charles. But only think of the impudence of the fellow, the first is a veritable *begging* letter. Let Mother excuse her little Benjamin if she can. And more than this, he asks what amount of salary I get!! Of course to make a few Yankee calculations on this subject. Waesucks[11] truly. But I suppose I must set it down to his head being turned by learning. I shall try & send him a little, but it will be, as you suggest, at your expense. I am quite unable to do as I wish this year on account of my clothes getting done, &c. If John could send you as much as

[7] The collection, a booklet of 32 pages entitled *Lihela tse li bokang Yehova, ki baruti bangue* ("Hymns that praise Jehovah, by some teachers", viz. P. Lemue, J. P. Pellissier, and D. L.), was published by the Mission Press, Kuruman, in 1843.

[8] ". . . others are on 'The earth being filled with the glory of the Lord', 'Self-dedication', 'Invitation to Sinners', 'The soul that loves God finds him everywhere' " (Blaikie).

[9] ". . . will doubtless set them to music" (Blaikie).

[10] ". . . proclaimed by my feeble lips" (Blaikie).

[11] An interjection meaning "alas".

take you over the Atlantic, I should engage to refund the half, as well as give Charles £5 a year or perhaps more.

Soon after this I shall send you £10, which will help to liquidate your score with Mr F[erguson], but as you have mentioned my name you must not give all that as coming from me. Give a portion, & then if you have any confidence left in yourself, as being able to keep it by you a few days, add to the former as if coming from yourself. I shall be sorry if you spend this sum in any other way than giving it towards the liquidation of the debt you mentioned. . . .[12]

I shall request a brother missionary, Rev. E. Williams of Hankey, who has now gone home on account of his health, to transmit the above amount to you. He has an affection of the throat which prevents him speaking. Was very anxious to come up to me, & wrote some letters to[o] stating he was then on the way. But as our winter was near, some medical men in the Colony gave opinions against his proceeding hither. He was then obliged to leave for England.[13] I shall request him to send you the money immediately. If he has it by him he will do so, if not he will wait till I send him a bill. I shall instruct him to send Mr Drummond a small bill to be spent in clothes & boots. I shall write him (Mr D.) at same time & send him my dimensions. Mr Turner has them, but it won't be proper to ask him.[14]

You must tell Mr D. that if he has anything stronger than common sailcloth he must send it. If not, the trowsers must be of the strongest sailcloth, no matter how rough it may be. I had two pairs sailcloth trowsers when I left 4 months ago, & before three months were done they were torn to shreds. Colour is nothing, & strength is everything. If Mr D.'s don't wear better than these sailcloth ones, I shall be obliged to take to leather, as M[ess]rs Hamilton & Moffat used to do. The thorns are shocking for tearing.[15] They are turned

[12] In the passage omitted (about 200 words), D. L. chides his father for disclosing to outsiders the expectation of a remittance from himself.

[13] Williams (2.7) arrived in England on 10 April 1843 (*Register*, p. 39).

[14] D. L. wrote to Drummond on 29.vii.1843, ordering various articles of clothing, and stating that he had sent £10 with Williams to pay for them (cf. Chamberlin, *Letters*, pp. 59–62). Mr Turner I have not been able to identify.

[15] "We don't need waterproofs, we require thorn-proofs only" (29.vii.1843 Drummond).

back like fish hooks, & never give up without being broken, tearing, or being carefully loosed out. This latter might always be done if we always walked slowly enough, but when running or riding on oxback there is seldom time to think of it untill the deed is done which exposes one's flesh. There is such a variety too, one would think Africa had got a larger share of the curse [of] thorns & briers &c than any other country.

I send also a small bill to Mr MacLehose to liquidate debt & get some books I need. You need not ask him anything about it. At least, I shall be obliged to you if you do not. Do you hear anything of Hugh Hall or Jas. Rankin? I sometimes think of Mr MacSkimming. Is he well? Kind remembrance to Mrs Aird.[16]

. . .[17] I don't know John's address & therefore can't write him. I believe he has removed somewhere else than Lanark,[18] but don't know whether I am right. Remember me to Wheelan & A. Brownlee. His letter I have yet to answer, & will soon. Also to Mrs A. & family, & J. Rankin's Do., & all others good bad & indifferent. Somebody told Janet to request me to write better. Is she wiser than Solomon then, who says that which is crooked cannot be made straight?[19] I have recieved Mrs McRobert's letter & answer it now.[20]

The Burgundy pitch plaster is for Janet.[21] The explanation of your medical man is nonsense. The reason of the uneasiness is a quantity of undigested food passing the stomach, distending the small intestine & preventing the

---

[16] William McSkimming was the master of a school at Blantyre which D. L. had attended (J. I. Macnair, *Livingstone the Liberator*, 1940, p. 36), and John Aird was a deacon of the Independent Church at Hamilton (*Correspondence between the . . . Congregational Churches*, 1845, p. 8). The other people mentioned I have not identified.

[17] Two lines heavily obliterated.

[18] A town in Ontario, Canada, about 40 miles south-west of Ottawa.

[19] Ecclesiastes 1: 15.

[20] Mrs John M'Robert, whose husband was pastor (1838–46) of the Congregational Church at Cambuslang, near Blantyre (Ross, *Congregational Independency in Scotland*, p. 247), "had promised, in the name of the congregation, £12 annually to support a native teacher" (Macnair, p. 79; cf. Annual Report of the LMS, 1843, p. lxxiii). For this D. L. was indebted to the good offices of MacLehose (20.vi.1843 MacLehose). D. L.'s letter to her is summarized in Blaikie, p. 56.

[21] Cf. Letter 9.

flow of bile, or it may be by air. The bile is absolutely necessary for the bowels.

[*No signature*]

9: To MRS N. LIVINGSTON

[*c.* 21 March 1843][1]

[Wilson Collection.]

My dear Mother,

I am very sorry to hear of the illness of sister Agnes. I hope she is now better, but if not you will do well to use some medicine in order to assist the healing of the sore on her neck, and I think very minute doses of corrosive sublimate as likely to produce that effect as any other. You know it is a virulent poison & must be taken care of. Father might purchase a scruple of it for 2d. or 3d. It is called the bichloride of mercury, & pronounced byklored, & is in little chrystals like common salt. If you put one of these chrystals or grains in a little water, say a spoonful, it tastes like lime water. I mention this, because chemists may think you intend to poison some one, & give you something else instead. Take as much as will stand on about an inch of the blade of a pen-knife, put it on a piece of window glass, & with a smooth chuckey stone[2] grind it to a very fine powder. Then mix that well with a spoonful of fine flour & form about a hundred pills of it. Of these let her take 3 or 4 a day, & intermit the use of them occasionally, taking them one week, then wait a day or so, & then commence again. If you can get a bit of sal ammoniac about the size of a pea & dissolve it in the rain water with which you form the flour into a mass for pills, it will prevent the sublimate from being decomposed by the food she may have taken. But this is not absolutely necessary.

You could make a salve for the sore by taking about a half inch of lunar caustic. Grind it on the glass as above

[1] The contents suggest that this letter was probably written about the same time as, and forwarded together with, No. 8.
[2] A small pebble.

untill it is a very fine powder. Then mix it with a large spoonful of hog's lard, taking up all the powder with a small bit of the lard first, then mixing it well in a teacup with the whole afterwards. A little spread on a small rag, & cut so that its edges don't touch the edge of the sore, may cause it to heal.

I had lately a case in the person of the daughter of a chief called Cornelius Kok[3] from a village named Campbell, which although of several years' standing was cured completely in less than two months by the above treatment. It increased my fame on that side of the country very much, & now I get patients from all parts of [it]. Many come even from the Orange River, although there they are close to the Colony doctors.[4] She was unable to walk on account of large ulcers on the legs, as well as others on the hand, but now she is quite well.

She ought to eat as much animal food as you can afford to give, avoiding vegetables or anything that distends the stomach or produces flatulence. If you make soup, make it with barley or rice & no greens, & let it be well boiled so that the barley be reduced to a pulp. She must eat little at a time & frequently. A large Burgundy pitch plaster, with a 7th part of its weight of blistering flies melted & mixed through it, ought to be worn over the whole stomach & situation of the uneasiness, and a broad flannel belt over the whole abdomen constantly. The pills you give the receipt for will do neither good nor harm with respect to the neck. They are simple aperients, but if taken constantly would salivate. I think I gave you a prescription for aperient pills. If you have it, & added a little quinine, if she is of a constipated habit then frequent use would be beneficial. In the attack the use of that man's pills to evacuate the contents of the bowels would be, in combination with warmth & an enema, useful in shortening the duration of the period of sickness. A voyage to America would cure her. I regret very much I cannot now send you the means of going.

[3] Chief, since 1824, of the Griquas at Campbell, an LMS outstation about 30 miles east of Griquatown by road.

[4] The Griqua settlement at Philippolis, to which D. L. is probably referring, was more than 250 miles south-east of Kuruman, and approximately 35 miles by wagon road from Colesberg, the nearest village in the Cape Colony.

If Mr Williams has the money (£10) he will send it immediately.

You must not think I am angry because Father told Mr F[erguson] he should get a lift from me. It was a pity, but it can't be helped now. I felt sorry when I knew it, but am not now. I don't now know John's address & therefore can't write him, but I shall be obliged to you if you tell him, if he gives you as much as take you all over I shall engage in the course of a few years to refund whatever he may require of me, whether the half or the whole. I shall do it through the American consul at the Cape. At present I am dreadfully bare both with respect to clothes & books, &c. I send a bill of £30 to Mr Williams in a few months hence, 10 of which will go to you. I shall request him to get my clothes of Mr Drummond. It will look much better for your passage money to come from John than from me.

Although this sheet is addressed to you, I have had no space to speak to you in particular, & can only assure you of my unabated affection.

[*No signature*]

10: To MR N. LIVINGSTON

[*c.* 6 August 1843][1]

Address: (Care of Revd. Dr Phillip, Cape Town) Mr Livingston, Almada St., Hamilton, Lanarkshire, N.B. *Postmark:* Hamilton, DE 12, 1843. [Wilson Collection.]

. . . I never hear from Mr Taylor, & I don't know where to address him. You say he has gone to a Mrs Connel.[2] Where she lives I don't know. I have told Mr Fergusson that I have sent you an extract from your letter of April / 39. You must give him the whole of the extract & whatever else, perhaps the whole, of mine. A sight of it while you

[1] The first portion of this letter is missing. Its date is fixed approximately by the reference in the opening paragraph to D. L.'s imminent departure for Mabotsa, which occurred early in August (30.x.1843 Tidman).

[2] Possibly Mrs Ann Connell, a straw hat maker, of Glassford Street, Glasgow (Pigot, p. 546); she is listed in the annual reports of the LMS for this period as a "life member".

stood by would be better than a copy.[3] Janet's letter is very good. I shall answer it as soon as I can. I write the cover of your letter on Sabbath, & tomorrow morning I shall set off for the Bakhatla in company with Mr Edwards.

With respect to the doses of the medicines, it must have been two or three times a day. I don't remember what they were. If of corrosive sublimate, I meant it should be taken at least so often. Your complaint seems to be what is called follicular gastric dyspepsia, and if you wish to get quit of it you must avoid all vegetables. Take solid food chiefly, avoiding all fat & greasy aliment. Take all your meals warm, never twice cooked, never so much as to distend the stomack. Give up doses of sweet milk, fish, fruit, cheese, eggs. Your food ought to be cooked thoroughly, & when taken well chewed. The lean of animal food is good for you with stale bread, but taken in small quantities & frequently. Avoid much of any fluid. A cup of coffee after dinner will help you. Brush your skin with any hard rough substance, as coarse flannen[4] or towel, every night & morning, & take an aperient pill of equal parts of rhubarb, aloes & galbanum frequently, perhaps every other day. If you buy a drachm of each of these, grind them down to powder with two stones, add two teaspoonfulls of powdered cinnamon & 2 of powdered ipecacuhan (or one only if they make you sick), you can make more than a hundred pills. Take according to their effect. Gentle opening is all that is required. Perhaps biuscuits made without any fat or butter would be good for you in travelling, or oatmeal cakes with a little bit of lean meat. But you ought never to drink before eating. If you attend to these means, you will very likely get quit of a very troublesome form of indigestion. If that does not do, try the

---

[3] On 28.vii.1843 D. L. wrote to Ferguson: "I am very sorry to hear of some disagreable circumstances which have transpired, and that Mr Moir has thought proper to implicate me in the affair. My memory does not serve me either positively to contradict or affirm. But my father having been my only informant on the subject, I have sent an extract from his letter to him at the time it happened, which will completely exculpate him." The reference is to some controversy connected with the church at Hamilton; Moir apparently maintained that D. L. had told him, in London in 1839, "that my father put his name to a note of censure which in his heart he did not approve". Moir's pastorate of the church had terminated in that year (Ross, *Congregational Independency in Scotland*, p. 251).

[4] "The name invariably given by the vulgar to flannel" (Jamieson).

tincture of the muriate of iron in doses of ten drops three times a day in a little warm water, increasing the dose weekly untill you get up to 40 drops.

Kind regards to Wheelan. How is Elizabeth Finlay, alias Mrs Mason? Kind regards to her. My Christian salutation to Thomas Burke, & to John & Mrs Todd. How is Mrs Crawford, Aunt Margaret, C. Menzies,[5] everybody to whom I either might, could, would, or should, send greetings?

[*No signature*]

11: To JANET LIVINGSTON

21 August 1843

Address: (Care of Revd. Dr Phillip, Cape Town) Mr Livingston, Almada St., Hamilton, Lanarkshire, N.B. *For J. L. Postmark:* Hamilton, FE 7, 1844. [Wilson Collection; extracts published in Blaikie, *Personal Life*, p. 63.]

In sight of the Hills of the Bakhatla,[1]
August 21, 1843

My dear Sister,

I recieved your first a little before setting out on this journey[2] & liked it very well. It was infinitely better than a slush of poetry you once sent,[3] for that came upon me as if I had fallen under a cataract of cold water gruel. I could not answer it then, as I was busy in making preparations,

[5] "Aunt Margaret" probably refers to the sister of D. L.'s father (cf. Campbell, p. 29). Thomas Burke, of Blantyre, is mentioned in *Travels*, p. 7 n., as "an old Forty-second Peninsula soldier, who has been incessant and never weary in good works for about forty years" (cf. also Blaikie, pp. 16 f.). The other persons mentioned I have not identified.

[1] The "Bakhatla" (BaKgatla-baMmanaana), an Eastern Tswana tribe, were then living about 30 miles north-west of the present town of Zeerust, in the neighbourhood of what is now known as Gopanestad (in Moilwa Reserve, Marico District, Transvaal); the locality is described as a plain surrounded by a number of hills (cf. P. L. Breutz, *The Tribes of Marico District*, 1953, pp. 24, 90).

[2] "We left [Kuruman] in the beginning of August, and after a fortnight spent in the journey arrived in safety among the Bakhatla" (30.x.1843 Tidman). Although D. L. does not mention it in the present letter, he was travelling together with Edwards, to start a mission among the BaKgatla.

[3] Cf. Letter 4.

but begin now in order to provoke you to write me such another.

We are in company with a party of hunters. Two of them are gentlemen from India, & one a son of a planter from the West Indies. As he is the greatest fool of the three, I shall tell you of his adventures first.[4] He came to the Colony last year, and determined to have a tour in the Interior. He purchased 18 horses, but when he came to the Modder River[5] every one of them died. He then set out for Colesberg,[6] bought twelve more. These went the same road by means of a peculiar sickness which in this country attacks that animal.[7] He then bought a number more, & with these proceeded to hunt. The Boors to the Eastward of this got a hold of him & made him pay a tax. Six of them then went with him & compelled him to feed them. He did not reach beyond the latitude of the Bakwains, & his expedition cost him between 2 & £3,000. A fool & his money is soon parted. But it was money got from slave labour, & what better can be expected? He cries out bitterly against the emancipation of the slaves in the West Indies. Poor fellow, if he goes on as he has done he will one day have as little connection with those islands as myself. He intends soon to leave this country & go to Ceylon to enter into some coffee speculation there.

Well, the next in our list is a Mr Pringle, a Scotchman from Tinevelly, E. Indies.[8] He is a Collector, which is a most lucrative situation, as they are now in the places of the

[4] This man, nowhere named by D. L., was probably Andrew Hudson Bain (20.6), who on 9.vi.1843 wrote to Waterboer that Pringle, Steele, and he, were going "on a shooting excursion to Moselikatse's land", and needed help to cross the Orange River, then in flood (quoted in D. Arnot and F. H. S. Orpen, *The Land Question of Griqualand West*, 1875, p. 18).

[5] Flowing westward through the Orange Free State, the Modder is a tributary of the Riet, which in turn joins the Vaal in Lat. 29° S., near Douglas.

[6] A village about 290 miles north of Port Elizabeth and 300 miles southeast of Kuruman; it was at that time the centre in the Cape Colony nearest to Bechuanaland.

[7] "The African horsesickness . . . occurs in the region of summer rainfall . . . it appears after the rains begin and is rife from January through April . . . It is an acute, febrile, infectious disease of equines that is peculiar to Africa, but it is not directly contagious. It affects horses severely, mules and zebras mildly, and donkeys almost never" (E. C. Tabler, *The Far Interior*, 1955, p. 81).

[8] Probably John Robert Pringle, "head assistant to the Collector and Magistrate of Tinevelly 1841–6", died 1847 (C. Prinsep, *Civil Servants of the Madras Presidency from 1741 to 1858*, 1885, p. 117).

Rajahs of old. He came[9] to Africa on account of rheumatism in his knee, & is come up here merely for the sake of killing game. The next, Captain Steele of the Coldstream Gaurds & aidecamp to the Governor of Madras,[10] is come on the same errand. He was only a month in India when attacked with cholera. He & Pringle have spent one thousand pounds in the journey up, by purchasing horses, waggons, provisions, &c &c., & all they will take away will be a few skins & heads of animals. The Captn. is the politest of the whole, well versed in the classics & possessed of much general knowledge. All are men of the world, & would travel on Sundays if we were not with them. When will the time come when men will spend thousands in the cause of Missions? It will come. The silver & the gold are the Lord's, & He will yet bring it to pass that men will acknowledge whose right it is.

They have many servants: their own body-servants (natives of India), about a dozen Hottentots, & an Englishman to superintend them. Yet with all their retinue they are not so well off as ourselves. We being acquainted with the country get on quite smoothly. When we arrive at the spot where we intend to spend the night, all hands immediately unyoke the oxen. Then one or two of the people collect wood, one of us strikes up a fire, another gets out the water bucket & fills the kettle, a piece of meat is thrown on the fire, & if we have biscuits we are at our coffee in less than half an hour after arriving. The same operation is gone through in the morning, & then we are ready for starting away accross the plains. We never get tired of this sort of food. Although sometimes we have coffee with sugar, the thought that very likely before the journey is done we shall have no coffee at all makes all pleasant so long as it lasts. We have usually but two meals a day. This makes the third very pleasant when we get [it], & the two better than they should otherwise be.

[9] MS. has "come".

[10] (Sir) Thomas Montague Steele (1820–90); "aide-de-camp to governor of Madras, 1842–8; military secretary in Crimea, 1854–5; . . . general, 1877; commander-in-chief in Ireland, 1880–5" (*D.N.B.*). He became and remained very friendly with D. L., and it was through him that the discovery of L. Ngami was communicated to the Royal Geographical Society in 1850; he was also one of the pall-bearers at D. L.'s funeral in Westminster Abbey.

Our rich Indian friends sit or stand shivering at their fires for two or three hours before they get their trash ready, & are glad of a cup of coffee from us occasionally. If you were here you might see us sitting with these big wigs on stones & handing each other black coffee & lumps of beef, & hear them saying we get on much more comfortably than they. I believe it is quite true, for at present the weather, which to you would feel delightfully warm, is to us & them bitterly cold. They get up a splendid tent, their Hottentots quarrelling all the time—one refuses to go for water, another for wood, another to kindle a fire, one has lost a horse during the day, 4 or 5 must go & seek it, &c &c. The whole of the time these disputes are going on, the gents are standing shivering or scolding, or trying themselves to get a little caloric out of the embers, and no doubt they think us a pair of hair-brained enthusiasts. Their object in coming up to this part of the country is simply to kill animals. They frequently do so, & then leave their carcases to be destroyed by the vultures. They are enthusiastic hunters. We have a nobler subject on which to be enthusiastic. We shall part with them in a day or two.

I mentioned to you that Jan Bloom, the chief of a party of Corranas, had been visited when I went to the Yellow River with Mr Edwards.[11] He afterwards came to me at Kuruman to be cured of indigestion. He thought he had been bewitched, & wished me to relieve him of the poison which had been inserted into his system by some witch. He was relieved by the means employed, & came to me a few weeks [ago] to thank me for my medicine. He said he had tried a great many doctors, but none of them could master witchcraft in him but myself. It was all in vain I told him no one could bewitch. He firmly believes it, & he will believe it. During his stay at K[uruman] news came that one of his people had been killed by a Motchuana. He left us like a

[11] The Korana ("Corranas") were a people of Hottentot stock, then living in scattered groups along the Vaal ("Yellow") River to the east and south-east of Kuruman. Jan Bloom (or Bloem), son by a Korana woman of a white renegade from Cape Town, was chief of the Springbok tribe, settled in the vicinity of the present town of Barkly West. Like his father, after whom he was named, he was a notorious freebooter. D. L. may have visited him in the latter half of 1842, when helping Edwards to build "a small chapel . . . at one of the outstations" (24.vi.1843 Tidman).

raging lion, but I hope his wrath will cool before he gets home. Mosilikatze[12] thought Jan's mother must have been very clever indeed, nearly equal to his own, she has produced such a desperate fighter.

To your question concerning Bubi, whether he fought or not he was guilty in the affair, for he encouraged Sechele to fight & looked on at the battle. This was policy in him. He wanted Sebegwe to beat his superior in order that he himself might thereby obtain peace.[13] As soon as Bubi saw that Sechele was beat, he retired. He however gave Sebegwe all the cattle which he had in charge, but this was before he lost his own. He seemed displeased when I told him I could not come to live with him, & thought that I had promised & decieved him. I had only promised a teacher, viz. Pomore, but he knows very well no teacher could now live with him where he is now living.[14] There is no goodness among them unless it is implanted by the gospel. I should not be the least surprised to hear of treachery from any of them, they have no fear of God before their eyes. My waggon remained with him quite safely, although he knew I should be a month absent.[15]

One of the three poor fellows who accompanied me to the Interior (after leaving the waggon) died after coming home. Poor Sehamy,[16] where art thou now? Where lodges thy soul tonight? Didst thou think of what I told thee as thou turnedst from side to side in distress? I could now do anything for thee. I could weep for thy soul. But now nothing

[12] Moselekatse (the Tswana version of Mzilikazi) was chief of the MaTebele, 1822–68. There is a good account of his adventurous and bloodstained career in A. T. Bryant, *Olden Times in Zululand and Natal*, 1929, pp. 417–45; cf. also the works of such contemporary observers as Moffat, A. Smith, W. C. Harris, and others.

[13] Sechele, after becoming chief of the BaKwena, had tried without success to reunite the tribe by subjugating Bubi's section. The "battle" mentioned was his attack upon Sebego (cf. Letter 7).

[14] After being raided by the BaRolong (cf. Letter 7), Bubi's people had moved from Dithubaruba (*Travels*, p. 10). D. L. does not name their new residence, but according to local tradition it was in another part of the Dithejwane Hills (cf. Schapera, *Ditirafalô tsa Merafe ya BaTswana*, 1940, p. 50).

[15] This was in the early half of 1843, when D. L.'s servants, owing to fear of the MaTebele, refused to go with him to Shoshong, and he had to make that portion of the journey, "more than 200 miles", on ox-back (24.vi.1843 Tidman, 30.vi.1843 Bennett).

[16] Seitlhamo; he was one of Bubi's people (20.vi.1843 MacLehose).

can be done. Thy fate is fixed. O, am I guilty of the blood of
thy soul, my poor dear Sehamy? If so, how shall I look upon
thee in the Judgement? But I told thee of a saviour. O, didst
thou think of Him, did He lead thee through the dark
valley, did He comfort as He only can? Help me, O Lord
Jesus, to be faithful to every one. O remember me, & let me
not be guilty of the blood of souls.

This poor young man was the leader of the party. He
governed the other two, & most attentive he was to me. He
anticipated my every want. He kept the water calabash at his
head at night, & if I wakened he was ready to give me a
draught immediately. When the meat was boiled he secured
the best portion for me, the best place for sleeping, the best
of everything. O where is he now? He became ill after
leaving a certain tribe,[17] & believed he had been poisoned.
Another of the party & he eat of a certain dish given them
by a woman whom they had displeased, & having met this
man yesterday he said, "Sehamy is gone to Heaven, & I am
almost dead by the poison given us by that woman". I don't
believe they took any poison, but they do, & their imagina-
tions are dreadfully excited when they entertain that belief.
The latter, poor fellow, ran away from the Bakwain country
when S. died & came to Khatleng.[18] He thinks he is more
secure here than he was there, but death will find him. O
that he may be prepared for it.

We have been with the Bakhatla a few days now. Every
thing has been as well as we could have wished. The Lord
has given us favour in the eyes of the heathen. But we have a
mighty work before us. We have been recieved most kindly.
Have had the choice of a new location for a settlement. The
villages (8 in number) will remove to it shortly. It is pretty,
but will be quite a frying pan, for it is situated in what you
poetical ladies would call an amphitheatre of mountains. The
Kurrichane[19] lies about thirty miles to the S.E. of it, &

[17] Elsewhere identified by D. L. as the MaKalaka (17.ix.1844 Sunday school
children, Southampton).

[18] A locative form, meaning "the country (or village) of the BaKgatla".

[19] Kaditshwene, formerly the chief settlement of the BaHurutshe; visited by John
Campbell in 1820 and described in his *Travels in South Africa*, 1822, vol. i, pp. 222 ff.;
situated on the present farm Bloemfontein 223, Marico District, Transvaal, about
28 miles north-east of Zeerust.

scarcely visible owing to the intervening mountains. Where the people now are, they can be seen, but we go a little way to the North among mountains not mentioned in any map I have seen. Their form is as follows:

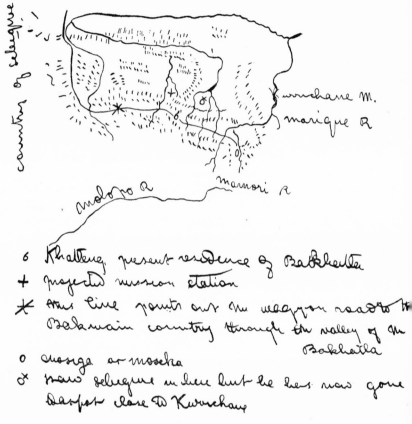

6 Khatteng, present residence of Bakhatla
+ projected mission station
✳ this line points out the waggon road to the Bakwain country through the valley of the Bakhatla
o chonga or moseka
♂ was sebegwe in here but he has now gone Deeper close to Kurechane

I have not yet taken the latitude or longitude, but it is not much more than half a degree West of Moseka, the for[mer] location of the French, American, & Church of England Societies' miss[ionar]ies.[20] It abounds with streams, & the mountains are covered with wood to their tops.

[20] Mosega, now known as Sendelingspos (about 10 miles south of Zeerust), had been successively occupied as a mission station by the Paris Evangelical Missionary Society (1832), American Board of Commissioners for Foreign Missions (1836–7), and Church Missionary Society (1839–40).

11: TO JANET LIVINGSTON

The woody summits wild & high
Heave up their "hurdies" [21] to the sky;
Their arms extended down below
Try to obstruct the river's flow,
and laughingly almost say phooh
To all our puny picks can do.

There now you have poetry made when mending my pen, and about as good as the stuff you sent me, only the fellow who strung your verses for you had a better subject than I.

You must not send such things as old caps. Do you think a Motchuana would wear them? No, they are not the fashion. A handkercheif tied round the head is all the go in this country. At Kuruman the ladies, as they have all short hair, put on three, fo[u]r, or five; one or two are put where the knot of hair should be, & then the others are wrapped round so that no part of the forehead or ears are seen. The whole has very much the shape of the head of a horse. In here they are very fond of having a handkercheif in order to wrap round the head when they go out to hunt, that the game may when they see it stand & stare at the foreigner who has come amongst them.

You must not collect any money for me. If any one offers it you can take it for the Society & give it to your collector, but for me individually you must not recieve a penny. Anything you have to spare send it to Charles, not to me, as it costs the Society more than the value of what you send. The seeds I shall be glad of; all sorts if they are sealed up in tin— the dentelion,[22] firs, acorns, rhubarb, or any medicinal plant, the crocus, the henbane. I saw agrimony growing on the banks of our stream yesterday.

The new village will be called Mabotsa (a marriage feast), that being the name of the hill which is immediately behind it Southwards.[23] May the Lord favour us so that many from

---

[21] Buttocks, loins.
[22] "The vulgar name in Scotland for the herb dandelion" (Jamieson).
[23] Mabotsa is about one mile south of Gopanestad (11.1). The site of the mission station was described more fully by D. L. as "that parcel of land which is bounded on the South-East and North-East by the stream Tlomesho, on the North and North-West by the stream Manuane [Maanwane], on the South and South-West by the watercourse winding along the bottom of the hill Mabotsa, extending thence

thence shall be admitted to the marriage Supper of the Lamb.

29 Septr. I returned to Lattakoo[24] 2 days ago, & found a letter from Mrs Pyne announcing the deaths of three of my acquaintances.[25] O teach me to number my days. Also one (No. 2) from Father. I have sent home a bill to Mr Williams, late of Hankey, £10 of which he is to give to you, & £10 to Mr Drummond for clothes. If this reaches [you] before he has prepared the clothes, get the £10 from him, add to the other, & try if you can't emigrate. I shall try & do without clothes from him till next year. I have got some sail cloth from these Indian hunters which will make excellent jackets. This is all I can say at present.

If at any time an opportunity of sending occurs, you may let me have the Weekly Visitors[26] in which were some articles on botany. I remember having seen something there which I wish to see again. Agnes should not take the corros. sublimate very long. The iodine will do better. Love to Mother, & to that old wretch . . .[27]

Yours ever,
D. Livingston

I shall answer Mrs Pyne's letter as soon as I can.

Explain to Mr Drummond how it stands with you. I send Charles £5 just now. Not a word from these Yankee niggers[28] yet.

D. L.

Eastward to a point where the above-named streams meet . . . The land is about a mile & a half in breadth and two in length" (30.x.1843 Tidman).

[24] "New Lattakoo", the early name of the mission station at Kuruman, to which the BaTlhaping had moved in 1817 from "Old Lattakoo" (Dithakong), about 45 miles to the north-east.

[25] "Salome and Miss Marshall and Radford all gone" (9.x.1843 Prentice). Salome was the daughter of Rev. R. Cecil (D. L.'s tutor at Ongar), in whose home Miss Marshall had also lived.

[26] *The Weekly Visitor* (1833–5), continued as *The Visitor, or Monthly Instructor*; published in London by the Religious Tract Society.

[27] Name obliterated.

[28] His brothers John and Charles, then living in Canada and the United States respectively.

12: To MR AND MRS N. LIVINGSTON
16 December 1843

Address: (Care of Revd. Dr Phillip, Cape Town) Mr Livingston, Almada St., Hamilton, Lanarkshire, N.B. *Postmark:* Hamilton, AP 8, 1844. [Wilson Collection.]

Kuruman
16 Decr. 1843

My dear Parents,

I recieved the boxes you sent by Mr Moffat a few days ago,[1] and have to inform you that a bill of which I advised you was not forwarded at the time I expected. It however will now go, & go to Mr Pyne, who will transmit the sums to the different individuals. The reason of the delay I need not mention, as it is connected with the character of Mr Williams.[2]

I am sorry you sent so many things. It would have been much better had you kept the money for your own use. What on earth induced you to send large buckling combs to people who have no hair to buckle? The Bechuanas have all short curly hair, not more than an inch in length. If you get any more, bury them in the garden, as I shall do today, for they are of no earthly use; also pincushions & any other nonsense, bury them rather than send stuff. For the other articles I feel much obliged. I am only sorry you send when you have nothing to spare. If you can send to Charles it will be better bestowed. The caps & Janet's shawl I give to Mrs Bartlett.[3] The straw hat won't look [well] on my head. . . .[4] If any one else asks leave to write to me, it will be better

[1] After being in England since June 1839, the Moffats had recently returned, reaching Kuruman on 13 December (Moffat to Tidman 24.ii.1844; cf. *LMS Chronicle*, vol. 8 (1844), p. 152, and J. S. Moffat, *The Lives of Robert and Mary Moffat*, 1885, p. 245).

[2] D. L.'s available correspondence throws no further light on this allusion.

[3] Wife of John Bartlett, a former LMS missionary living at Campbell.

[4] One sentence (18 words) omitted, in which D. L. refers ungraciously to the person, not a relative, who had sent the straw hat. Methuen mentions seeing Sechele at Mabotsa in August 1844, "a distinguished visitor . . . wearing a straw hat" (*Life in the Wilderness*, 1848 ed., p. 155). Was this how D. L. got rid of an unwanted embarrassment?

to say that I am public property and can be addressed by any one. I can then answer their letters or not as I like. My address is South Africa. Give it always in a general way. I never wear a hat; a common midshipman's cap covers my head, & I leave my complexion to take care of itself.

I write this in a great hurry, as we are packing up to go off for the formation of our new mission. I have not had time to read all my letters yet, as I must write back by the individuals who came & go back again to the Colony.

I went a good way to meet Mr Moffat.[5] He does not seem at all spoiled by the honours which have been heaped on him at home. We hope the work will recieve a new impulse by the arrival of the newcomers. May the Spirit be poured out, & cause the wilderness and solitary place to be glad & blossom as the rose.

Mother's cakes were like wormwood to the taste, but I must not say so lest it should offend. Will cakes keep well at home for a twelvemonth? Ought they to be sent to a warm climate where they very soon become like . . .?[6] I ask these questions only, I don't say send no more. I am very much obliged to Mother for her towels, handkerchiefs, &c &c, all which I cannot at present enumerate, as I have not got time to look yet. My kind love to her, & may the Lord bless her & keep her near to himself.

Many of the Bechuanas met Mr & Mrs Moffat with tears of joy. One poor Bushman who has been brought up by him wept aloud when he approached him; and as I had gone to meet him, I recieved many thanks for bringing him. They had believed he should never return. He is not, as I was informed by some who knew him, in the least opposed to Native agency.[7] He is a warm friend to them, but his character has been sadly traduced by many who ought to have known better. He told me the reason of the slander brought against him was his having got an unworthy

[5] D. L. rode on horseback about 150 miles from Kuruman, meeting the Moffats somewhere between the Vaal River and Philippolis (J. S. Moffat, *op. cit.*, pp. 243, 245). Campbell (p. 97), Macnair (p. 86), and Seaver (p. 78) all say, mistakenly, that this was in January (1844).

[6] One word undecipherably obliterated.

[7] The employment of Natives as evangelists or "teachers", especially at out-stations.

character turned out of that office. He has been sadly slandered by some in other & more tender points. This he must expect, for nearly all great men have their slander[er]s & traducers. He is truly a good man, & will shine when all his enemies are forgotten. Mrs Moffat is [a] good motherly woman. She takes a kind interest not only over her own family, but seems to consider Mr & Mrs Edwards & Mr Hamilton as her children too.

Inglis[8] I suspect won't do for Africa. His heart is in Scotland, and he ought never to have been out of it. But I have not yet seen him, as he has gone to Griqua Town instead of coming here. If he is not a blessing he will be a curse. Mokoteri[9] is likely to prove the latter from un-bear[able] pride & vanity fostered by the good people in Engl[and].[10]

All is quiet in the Interior. I have thought that tartan will make good jackets. Let me have some. If so, you can tell Mr Drummond I mean . . .[11]

I shall answer all letters as soon as I can, Janet's & everybody's. Give thanks to everybody, & greetings to all who deserve them. You know I write this in great haste.

Yours affectionately,
David Livingston

Thank Mr Naismith for the boots; they fit exactly. I shall write him. No letter from either Samuel or John Nai-smith, Jun., nor yet from Mr Drummond.

[8] Walter Inglis (1815–84), born in Scotland, joined the LMS in 1838, and after preliminary studies at Ongar, Glasgow, and London, was appointed to the Bechu-analand mission; accompanied the Moffats from England; expelled by the Boers in 1852 from his station at Mathebe; subsequently left the LMS and became a minister in Canada (*Register*, p. 56; W. Cochrane, *Memoirs and Remains of the Reverend Walter Inglis*, Toronto, 1887). D. L., very friendly with him as a fellow-student, had looked forward eagerly to having him as a companion in the mission field (8.xii.1841 MacLehose, 7.iv.1842 Mrs Sewell, 30.x.1843 Tidman).

[9] A Native youth whom the Moffats had taken as a servant to England, where some LMS supporters paid him far more attention than his conduct or position justified. The Directors hoped that on his return to S. Africa he would be employed as a "teacher". D. L. had met him when they lodged together at Mrs Sewell's.

[10] Paper slightly torn at seal.

[11] Four lines heavily obliterated.

1844

13: To ROBERT MOFFAT

15 February 1844

Address: Revd. R. Moffat, Kuruman. [Bruce Collection.]

Mabotsa,
Feby. 15, 1844

My dear Sir,

I am in very different circumstances now from those in which I expected to have addressed [you] from our new station.[1] The lions here are very numerous & very troublesome, and besides having attacked us here & destroyed some of the cattle of our people, one of them destroyed 9 sheep & goats in broad daylight on a little eminence opposite our hut last Wendensday.[2] The natives came screaming to us as we were engaged in the watercourse,[3] and as all operations were immediately suspended I very imprudently ventured accross the valley in order to encourage them to destroy him. This very nearly cost me my life, for after he was wounded he rushed down, bit Mabalwe[4]

---

[1] D. L. and Edwards had left again for Mabotsa after attending the first meeting of the LMS District Committee at Kuruman on 6 January.

[2] Since 15 February was a Thursday, "last Wednesday" was either the 14th or, more probably in the circumstances, the 7th. Moffat, reporting to the Directors of the LMS, wrote in the postscript of a letter dated 24.ii.1844: "The event transpired on the 16 of February". The date of D. L.'s letter makes that impossible, though "16" may be a slip for "14". In any event, the information here given dispels Macnair's vision of D. L. riding to the Vaal River to meet the Moffat family, "his arm still probably in a sling—a romantic invalid" (*Livingstone*, p. 86; cf. Campbell, p. 97). Chamberlin, incidentally, has "April, 1844" as the date of the "encounter with the lion" (*Letters*, p. xxv).

[3] The irrigation canal for the mission gardens at Mabotsa.

[4] Mebalwe Molehane, a member of "a small tribe of Balala [BaKgalagadi] called Bachaine [BaTshwene]", which had settled at Kuruman (24.viii.1850 Freeman). After being baptized, as "David", he became a deacon of the local church, and went as a "teacher" with D. L. when the mission at Mabotsa was started, his salary

badly on the thigh, another Native on the shoulder, &
myself on the arm. The humerus is splintered, & his teeth
have produced deep wounds which may trouble me for a
long time. Had it been directly in the way of duty I should
not have cared for the pains, but I have not that consideration to comfort myself by. It was, too, so contrary to my
regular rules of acting I don't know what induced me to go.
However, I have great cause for thankfulness that I escaped
with my life. He shook me as a cat does a mouse, & had
the mercy of the Lord not prevented could easily have torn
me to peices.[5]

I am sorry this event has happened now, for it gives our
friends the Edwards trouble which various circumstances
render them ill able to bear. If you are writing to the Directors, perhaps you might give them the substance of the above
account. I don't know what they will think of me after this,
but it seems to me we ought to tell them our misfortunes,
and the causes of them too, faithfully.

Before I met with this misfortune, I thought of requesting to purchase from you an adze, large handsaw (the one I
have is very small), a common axe or two, with any other
tools either smithy or carpenter's you can spare. I think I
may still request them, & as it is fortunately the left arm
that is injured so, I shall be able to work with the right
while that is still weak.

You know I have a brother in America. He is partly
dependant on me, & as in the transmission of small sums
frequent failures through the dishonesty of the American
post office have taken place, if you are acquainted with any
safe mode of transmission and would send him £10 of the
enclosed £20 you would relieve my mind of a great deal
[of] anxiety, and I think do good, for I believe the chief
desire of the poor young fellow is to spread the knowledge
of the Redeemer among men. His address is: Charles
Livingston, student, Oberlin College, Lorain County, Ohio,
U.S. Please excuse my venturing thus to trouble you.

of £12 per annum being provided by Mrs M'Robert (cf. 8.20). He subsequently
gave the LMS many years of faithful service, and was still alive at Kuruman in
1882 (*Journals of Elizabeth Lees Price*, ed. Una Long, 1956, pp. 548 and *passim*).
 [5] This is D. L.'s earliest version of the famous incident so graphically described in
Travels, pp. 11-13.

The other ten pounds please let remain in your hands for tools & anything else you may send. If you are about to send for beads, a lot of any kind would much oblige me. Have you seen that box for me which is marked "Beads"? Perhaps it was a mistake.

Please present my Christian regards to Mrs M., Mary, Ann,[6] &c, & believe me

Yours affectionately,
D. Livingston

The reason I have requested you to write the Directors is inability on my part, & I don't wish them to hear from a less authentic source.

14: To MR AND MRS N. LIVINGSTON

27 April 1844

Address: (Care of Revd. Dr Phillip, Cape Town) Mr Livingston, Almada St., Hamilton, Lanarkshire, N.B. *Postmark:* Hamilton, JA 14, 1845. [Wilson Collection; extract published in Blaikie, *Personal Life*, pp. 68 f.]

Mabotsa,
27th April 1844[1]

My dear Parents,

You may not have for some time past recieved any letters from me. But this is not to be wondered at, for I am not now at Kuruman, where opportunities occurred comparatively often for their transmission. Here we are almost entirely dependant on the arrival & departure of hunters from the South, and as they come only during the winter season[2] you must not expect to hear from me so often as you have in times past.

---

[6] Mary (1821–62) and Ann (1823–88) were the two eldest children of the Moffats.

[1] Seaver, arguing that D. L.'s injury from the lion was not as serious as some have maintained, says: "we find Livingstone writing to his parents *from Kuruman* on 27 April" (*David Livingstone*, p. 80; italics in original). But the heading "Mabotsa" is unmistakable, and further evidence of Seaver's mistake is provided in the second sentence of the letter.

[2] The winter season in S. Africa is from June to August.

We arrived here, I believe, in February last,[3] and began immediately to prepare for a permanent residence by leading out the water for irrigation. During this period we were much troubled by lions destroying cattle &c during the night. This always put a stop to our operations, for all the people left off work next morning after an attack in order to hunt them. At last one of the lions destroyed 9 sheep in broad daylight on a hill just opposite our house. All the people immediately ran over to it, & contrary to my custom I imprudently went with them in order to see how they acted & encourage them to destroy him. They surrounded him several times, but he managed to break through the circle. I then got tired, & coming home had to come near to the end of the hill. They were then close upon the lion & had wounded him.[4] He rushed out from the bushes which concealed him from view, & bit me in the arm so as to break the bone. It is now nearly well however, feeling weak only from being confined in one position so long. And I ought to praise Him who delivered me from so great danger to life. I hope I shall never forget His mercy. You need not be sorry for me, for long before this reaches you it will be quite as strong as ever it was. Gratitude is the only feeling we ought to have in remembering the event. I don't think you ought to make any talk of this to any one.[5] I don't like to be talked about. . . . However, you are not to blame for all the nonsense which other people may attach to your words.[6]

I lately suffered severely by Inglis putting another interpretation to my words that I meant to convey. But this same fellow has shewn himself the meanest Scotchman in all South Africa, & the sooner he goes home to Scotland the

[3] "We came here in February last" (11.v.1844 Parker); "on arriving in January of last year" (Edwards to Tidman, 28.i.1845). Since D. L. and Edwards left for Mabotsa "immediately after" the Committee meeting on 6 January (Moffat to Tidman, 24.ii.1844), and the journey normally took about a fortnight, the date given by Edwards seems the more likely.

[4] In *Travels*, p. 12, D. L. states that he himself had wounded the lion. Methuen, who met him at Kuruman in July 1844, says: "his arm had been broken and much lacerated by a lion which he had assisted in destroying" (*Life in the Wilderness*, p. 102).

[5] "Do not mention this to any one" (Blaikie). In the MS., the words "make any talk of" have been deleted, and "mention" written in above, but not by D. L.

[6] In the passage omitted (about 75 words), D. L. refers to a statement of his father's quoted by a correspondent (the sender of the straw hat (cf. Letter 12)).

better. He said to his wife once in the hearing of others, "Margaret, if we don't make a living of it here we must just go home"! ! And he has such a bad opinion of us all, he says it would have been much better had there never been a missionary sent out to Africa. He has a wonderful facility in dabbling into all the scandals circulated concerning missionaries & treasuring them all up in his mind. Has become odiously spiritually proud. Intercourse with some of the older missionaries, to whom & their children who have enjoyed no educational advantages he uniformly puts questions on out of the way questions in theology, metaphysics, &c, has made him, if he had it not before, ridiculously intellectually proud. An odious character, but from all I saw of him I fear the true one. Not one of the missionaries who assembled in Committee at Kuruman[7] would associate with him.

In a confidential letter I wrote him, I cautioned him against listening to the tales which are circulated against missionaries in the Colony. (These are exactly such as I have heard enemies to the cause of Christ in Scotland retail with glee against ministers—private character, treatment of servants, &c.) And as they are sometimes mentioned by missionaries &c, I told him not to believe them, even though from Mrs Moffat. He took this confidential letter, read it to us all, & tried to fix the blame of his prejudices on me. But this was not untill he had in vain attempted to fix it on Mr & Mrs M., Mr & Mrs Ashton,[8] & several missionaries in the Colony. They all, however, saw through his meanness in betraying confidence, & his miserable attempt to place me in the position which he himself occupied, & told him so plainly.

He says he will write home to Drs Wardlaw, Brown of Edin[burgh], Paterson, & I suppose Heugh,[9] & give our

[7] The first meeting of the newly-formed "District Committee of the Griqua and Bechuana Missions" was held at Kuruman on 6 January 1844.

[8] William Ashton (1817–97), born in England, came to S. Africa together with Moffat and Inglis in 1843; served at Kuruman (with several breaks) until 1864, and then at various other stations, with a second spell at Kuruman 1871–6 (*Register*, p. 56).

[9] Ralph Wardlaw (1779–1853), John Brown (1784–1858), John Paterson (1776–1855), and Hugh Heugh (1782–1846), were all prominent Scottish clergymen and

characters. Mine won't be white. For when the Committee met, & he wished to meet not as a member but spectator, I moved that he should immediately retire, as there is an express regulation against any such proceeding. This was unanimously agreed to.[10] He thinks it was revenge on my part, but we all wished, as there was private business to be transacted, no tale-bearer should look into it with jaundiced eye.

He objects to Committees because he is an Independant.[11] As missionaries of the London Miss. Soc. we are neither Independants, Presbyterians, nor Episcopalians. A Committee is often necessary to prevent wasteful expenditure of the Society's money, as individual missionaries are not generally capable of judging how much ought to be expended on their stations, & whether their stations in the changing circumstances of the country ought to be continued as such. The Directors can't judge in these & many other cases without reports from something of the sort, for each person loves his own station & wishes it to be advanced by every means, & when it is almost useless to the general cause his local attachments prevent his discerning this. The Committees of missionaries are as much like Congregational Unions as it is possible in their very different spheres to be. This is all private. It must on no account be communicated to any one unless they introduce the subject.

We have got the water led out & our hut put into a good state for dwelling in it. The people are still at some distance from us, which is a hindrance to missionary work. The harvest prevents their immediate[12] removal, but it will take place in the course of next month. We are however getting acquainted with them, as we have many visitors constantly & we visit them statedly. They have all behaved well

Directors of the LMS. Wardlaw had been one of Inglis's theological tutors at Glasgow, and Brown presided at his ordination in 1842, when Paterson was also among those officiating (Cochrane, *Walter Inglis*, pp. 30, 39, 59).

[10] The minutes of the Committee meeting state that Inglis "declined to sit as a member", but do not record the motion to which D. L. refers (Ross to Directors LMS, 20.i.1844).

[11] According to the minutes, Inglis in refusing to join the Committee stated merely that he wished first to consider carefully the rules of its constitution. He did in fact later join, and was present at the second and various subsequent meetings.

[12] MS. has "immediately".

towards us yet; there is no stealing, and all treat us with respect. The treatment of the first missionaries by the Batlapi[13] was very different. They are a proud set, and hindered by their pride more than by anything else from recieving the gospel. Here if they were formerly proud it has in some measure been subdued by the scourge of war. May they have the wisdom bestowed upon them to recieve that which alone exalteth a nation.

. . . Are John & he[14] well? The niggers never write to tell. . . .

Have you read Mr Moffat's work? It is excellent, and to us who know all the localities [and] many of the persons described it is peculiarly interesting. The person who stole Mr Hamilton's loaf and many things besides was leader to my waggon in coming in here, and is now a deacon in the church. The man who stole the goats was standing at our door about the time I was reading the account, and is so altered in appearance I could not have guessed that it was he. There is nothing ferocious about his looks now; he seems a quiet inoffensive good man.[15] The gospel has always a great effect on their features. Mr M. seems in no way spoiled by his visit home, and I suppose it has done good to the cause.

Here we are kindly treated by the Natives of all the tribes who come to see us. Sebegwe came to see us immediately after our arrival, with a retinue of about 40. But his power is completely gone. I should have returned his visit before this had I not been disabled. However, I hope soon to go to the surrounding villages, of which there are many to the Eastward. Sebegwe lives a little to the South of Kurreechane.[16] The range you see marked in the map so

[13] BaTlhaping, one of the main groups of Southern Tswana tribes, among whom the mission at Kuruman was started. Their attitude to the early missionaries, during the years 1820–8, is described in detail in Moffat's *Missionary Labours*, and in his journals and letters (*Apprenticeship at Kuruman*, ed. Schapera).

[14] D. L.'s younger brother Charles. The dots represent passages of seven and two lines respectively that have been heavily obliterated.

[15] The theft of the loaf is described in *Missionary Labours*, pp. 240 f.; the other incident I have not traced, though Moffat (p. 289) mentions thefts of an ox and of sheep. He does not identify the thieves, by name or otherwise, but D. L.'s description suggests that it was Mebalwe who had taken the bread.

[16] See above, 8.4.

is somewhat long, but there is one conical hill in it which gives explanation to the whole name. It means a little baboon, & the Natives below being much plagued by baboons spoiling their gardens say, "By it we are vexed", or Karechuenya. It may also be translated, "A vexation by or near us", viz. the whole range, on account of the depredations of the baboons.[17] These animals always inhabit rocks.

We have got our hut fixed in a beautiful valley. But it seems the nearer we come to Egypt we get more into the region of flies, fleas, puleys,[18] moths, vermin of all sorts, which eat everything except iron & glass &c. On complaining to a Native about the superabundance of these animals he said, "O we have always plenty of these, but you have more than ordinary just now because they come to greet strangers".

I got the letter in which Janet writes a small peice at the end, and I believe another which I answered. Mr M. remembered having seen you in Glasgow,[19] but was so worried he could not speak to many to whom he wished. We have had no news from the South & of course from the rest of the world since we came here. We expect however to get some old newspapers, letters, &c, some time next month. My love to Mother, Janet & Agnes.

It seems I must not jibe any about the ———.[20] There is one on the tip of my tongue, but I swallow it.

[No signature]

[17] "Kurreechane" was Campbell's rendering of the name Kaditshwene (11.19). D. L., apparently misled by the spelling, wrongly suggests that it is derived from *ka-rea-tshwenggwa*, "since we are troubled". The "conical hill" is Tshwenyane, which he correctly translates "little baboon"; it is located, very close to Kaditshwene, "on the farm Mezeg 139, 'Waterval', around the post office Enzelsberg" (Breutz, *Tribes of Marico District*, p. 93).

[18] "Poolies", lice. In the MS., D. L. added the letters "oo" above the "u" of "puleys".

[19] Moffat was at Glasgow at the end of October 1842, when he addressed a meeting in the City Hall attended "by at least 7,000 persons" (*LMS Chronicle*, vol. 6, 1842, p. 190).

[20] Dash in MS.

15: To JANET LIVINGSTON

21 May 1844

Address: (Care of Revd. Dr Phillip, Cape Town) Miss J. Livingston, Almada St., Hamilton, Lanarkshire, N.B. *Postmark:* Hamilton, JA 14, 1845. [Wilson Collection.]

Mabotsa,
21st May 1844

My dear Sister,

I have just now recieved a letter dated Octr /43 written partly by you & partly by Father, and having written Agnes some time ago I now address this to you. I believe I got one dated Newyearsday of that year, but none of the others mentioned as coming from John & Charles. I have written them both repeatedly, & recieving no answer I have concluded to write no more, for it seems of no use. The Yankees are a miserable set of people. Their post office ought to be called the den of thieves. And as Sidney Smith tells them, they ought to call their public works by such names as Crafty Canal, Rogues' Railway, Swindling Swamp. He refers to the act of repudiation by the State of Pennsylvania &c, and says they are always talking of the virtue & honour of the United States, they soar above others in what they say & sink below all nations in what they do.[1] If Charles & John write & I recieve their letters I shall begin again, but I am tired [of] writing in order that my letters may be distroyed by drab-coloured Yankee swindlers. You may tell them to direct their letters straight to the Cape & not by way of Mrs Sewell, as it is as likely they will come safely by that way as by the other. These two however may come yet, as the last parcel I had from Mrs Sewell was given to Mr Moffat some time before he sailed in January /43.

Father mentions that he had invited Charles to some

---

[1] Sydney Smith (1771–1845) was the famous English divine and wit. His "Humble Petition . . . to the House of Congress of Washington", and two supplementary letters, were originally published in the *Morning Chronicle,* 1843 (18 May, 3 November, 22 November), and are reprinted together in his collected works under the title "Letters, etc., on American Debts". The reference to public works occurs in the letter of 3 November.

school got up in Kilmarnock.[2] The motive for this invitation is above my comprehension. I am glad however Charles had the good sense to decline. Hunger & Independancy is much more honourable than comfortable dependancy. Would it not be as well to send your half sovreigns to Mr F[erguson] as to the post office sharks of America? If you could raise as much as send out Agnes, & yourself perhaps go to take care of her, it would very likely be very beneficial for her health, & you would soon save as much there as pay for a cabin passage for Father & Mother. I think you ought to try something of the sort. If John could advance as much as take you all out it would be well. I have found a safe conveyance for money to Charles. Have sent him £10 this year, & will remit the same sum yearly if spared so long as he continues in America. If he leaves it for the Kilmarnock school you speak of, I won't send him a farthing. Perhaps you are now grown rich enough to support him at it. He had better have blistered heels[3] & education in a regular way than have a half course & sound ones.

I got one letter from Mrs McRobert & answered by three. I expect one in return from her now.

Father & yourself seem very anxious that I should hear the sermons you do. That is a very good wish. But as it is without the shadow of a shade of probability I ever shall hear them, instead of looking at each other & saying, "O, I wish David heard that sermon", I would suggest the turning of your heads from each other to some of the surrounding inhabitants who know not the gospel. Private Christians are not exempted from the duty of bringing sinners to the Saviour. Their lives are to be consecrated to the glory of God as well as those of ministers & missionaries. You hear fine sermons no doubt, but do they enter into your heads & come out again for the good of those who are not so favoured? Try what you can do, & don't content yourselves by listening & admiring & doing nothing. Some content themselves by the excuse of humility on account of inability, but should any one tell them they were not able to connect two ideas together so as to tell a plain

[2] A town 21 miles south-west of Glasgow.
[3] MS. has "heals".

99

story their humility would have some bristles standing straight up on its back.

Father gives me some instructions in every letter how to preach, & they are very good when we think of people in Scotland, who are comparatively well informed on the doctrines of the gospel. But we don't preach to Scotchmen. We preach to men who don't know but they are beasts who have no idea of God as a personal agent, or of sin as evil otherwise than as an offence against each other, which may or may not be punished by the party offended. Their consciences are seared & moral conceptions all blunted. Their memories retain scarcely anything we tell them, & so low have they sunk the plainest text in the whole Bible cannot be understood by them. You may think me heretical, & that I ought to preach, as Father says, "that the remedy is as extensive as the disease. Christ loved *you* & gave himself for *you*". Now what is most needed in Scotland is least needed here. We don't need to make the extent of the atonement the main theme. The atonement itself is our theme. When we come to a people who know nothing of "generals" nor of a "limited atonement", our coming is to *them*. They perfectly understand it. We speak to them as men. We talk of this atonement as provided for them, & that our only object in visiting them is to tell them the good news; & when we speak to them thus it never enters their heads to imagine, like the wise people in Scotland, that we are speaking to somebody else than those to whom we are pointing & looking & putting questions.

Suppose we take the text, "God so loved the world, &c",[4] & this is a very common text for missionaries, & has been preached from thousands of times, & not a single conversion follow it, & that simply because it was not understood. A sensible preacher in Scotland would speak of the wonderful love of God, how little deserving men were of His love, the nature of the atonement provided, its freeness, fullness, &c &c., and where he knew people had been led astray by general dealing would apply it to each individual, by shewing how each constituted a portion of the world,

---

[4] "For God so loved the world, that he gave his only begotten Son, that whosoever believeth in him should not perish, but have everlasting life" (John 3: 16).

&c &c, quoting other passages to prove it; & very likely good would be done, for his auditors would understand him. Let the same sermon be preached here, & as much good would be done by an address in Greek.

This I think you will understand when I tell you how we are obliged to do. I say obliged, for I should be delighted were the Bakhatla so far advanced as to be able to understand such sermons as you hear. Taking the same text, we have to begin the address by telling that there is a God, that He not merely exists but that they are related to him, that he knows them all, knows all their actions &c; & then it is absolutely necessary to explain to them what they are, not only as men but as sinners, that they have souls or rather that the soul is the man, its future existence &c., what sin is, what the atonement for that is, &c &c., the manner by which men may be made partakers of the benefits of that atonement.

But I need not go through all the process we must take to explain the simplest text in the Bible. If you look at the sermons of the apostles in the Acts, you will see that to different people their address was different in order to make the truth profitable. The Jew was addressed differently from the Gentile, and though the object & the truths were the same, Gentiles of different localities were addressed differently. I know a missionary who translated some English sermons into Sitchuana & read them to the people of Kuruman; they although comparatively enlightened said, "We don't understand that man, what does he mean?"

We have now got our house finished and watercourse prepared for gardens. The people are still at a distance from us, but begin to remove to our locality tomorrow. We are kindly treated, & I am through the mercy of God now quite restored to health. My arm has got quite strong, so that I can work with it. We have to build a meeting house next, but I intend to itinerate to the surrounding localities in the mean time. You can't comprehend how degraded they are in their conceptions & in everything. We have therefore great cause to plead for the wisdom which will enable us to win their souls to Jesus. And we need much grace to uphold us in our work, lest we grow weary of their obstinacy & stupidity. All that we need may the great head of the church grant to us for His own glory.

If you have got the seeds I mentioned something about, they could be put into a box (of tin) of the exact size of the Evangelical Magazine[5] & about 2 inches or 3 but not [more] in depth. Mr McLehose would enclose it in the first parcel of magazines he sends & it would come safely. But you must not send anything else. I get the Eclectic & Medical Reviews[6] in small parcels by the way of the Mission House[7] regularly, but you must not send anything else by that means. Letters in parcels I dislike very much.

I have got Fergus's letter & answered it. Nothing from Charles nor John. They are I suppose being Yankified. But we shall see.

June 8th. I am through Divine mercy getting quite strong. My love to you all. Tell Charles to write by Cape of Good Hope, care of Dr Phillip.

[*No signature*]

16: To MARY MOFFAT

1 August 1844

Address: Miss Moffat, Kuruman. [Bruce Collection; extract published in Blaikie, *Personal Life*, p. 71.]

Motito
1st August 1844

My dearest Mary,

We arrived here last night, and intend leaving in the afternoon.[1] But though my visit is short I must make it long

---

[5] *The Evangelical Magazine and Missionary Chronicle*, published monthly in London since 1793; highly sympathetic to the work of the LMS, whose *Chronicle* was for many years issued as a supplement with each number; edited by John Morison 1827–57. Its page measures 8·5 by 5·4 inches.

[6] *The Eclectic Review* was a monthly journal published in London since 1805, and widely read by nonconformists; *The British and Foreign Medical Review* was a quarterly "journal of practical medicine and surgery", published in London since 1836.

[7] The London headquarters of the LMS, in Blomfield Street, Finsbury Circus.

[1] D. L. had arrived at Kuruman from Mabotsa about 8 July (Methuen, *Life in the Wilderness*, p. 102), and therefore could not have stayed more than three weeks

enough for a few lines to you, and though they shew nothing else they will at least demonstrate that distance does not affect my desire to please you. The Motito friends[2] know of our affection for each other, and seem pleased, as indeed every one else ought to be when we are. You must not forget your promise to visit them after the Daumas'[3] have gone. It is probable you will see them (the D.'s) at Kuruman, so you will know how to act. I have not mentioned your intention to them, as the time is still distant.

Will you be so kind as mention an iron bedstead to your father? I forgot to request him to order it, or rather I was ashamed to do so, as I had asked him to put himself to trouble with respect to so many things. You must put him in remembrance about writing to Colesberg about the licence.[4] If he forgets, then we shall make it legal ourselves. What right or portion has the State church in me? None whatever. If they don't grant it willingly, let them keep their licence. We shall licence ourselves.

We came away without our coffee pot. But it was very good out of the large baking one. All however is now right, and with the Divine blessing we shall go on well. Two waggons from Daniel's Kuil or Tsantsibane,[5] I forget which, have been waiting here for us. One of them takes a large box of trees for me, & to the other I shall give another part of my load, so our passage in may be speedier than I anticipated. We go by the Westward route, as it is shorter though a little more sandy, so you need not be surprised though no one (coming out by the old route) sees me. Don't forget to write a long letter, the longer the better, although it may contain nonsense.

And now, my dearest, farewell. May God bless you. Let your affection be towards Him much more than towards

(Motito was two days' journey from Kuruman). During that time he had become engaged to Moffat's eldest daughter Mary.

[2] The French missionaries Prosper Lemue (1804–70) and Jean Lauga (1811–87); they were both married.

[3] François Daumas (1812–71), a missionary in Basutoland, was married to a sister of Mrs Lemue (T. Jousse, *La Mission Française au Sud de l'Afrique*, 1889, vol. i, p. 166).

[4] Colesberg was at that time the Colonial government centre nearest to Kuruman.

[5] Griqua settlements, respectively about 55 miles south, and 65 miles south-south-west, of Kuruman.

me, and kept by His mighty power & grace I hope I shall never give you cause to regret that you have given me a part. Whatever friendship we feel towards each other, let us always look to Jesus as our common friend and guide, & may He shield you with his everlasting arm from every evil.

Believe me,

Yours ever sincerely & affectionately,
David Livingston

17. To MARY MOFFAT

12 September 1844

Address: Miss Moffat, Kuruman. [Bruce Collection; published in part in Blaikie, *Personal Life*, pp. 71 f.]

Mabotsa
12 Septr. 1844[1]

My dear Mary,

As I have no hope of prevailing on Baba[2] to remain longer than the 16th currt., I begin to address you, in order that I may not be obliged at last to send only a hurried note. And first of all I must tell you of the progress I have made in architecture. The walls are nearly finished, although the dimensions are 52 feet by 20 outside, or about the same size as that in which you now reside. I began with stone, but when it was breast high I was obliged to desist from my purpose to build it entirely of that material by an accident which, slight as it was, put a stop to my operations in that line. A stone falling was stupidly, or rather instinctively, caught by me in its fall by the left hand, & it nearly broke my arm over again.[3] It swelled very much, and I fevered so much I was glad of a fire, although the weather was quite

[1] D. L. had arrived back in Mabotsa on the evening of 13 August (Methuen, *Life in the Wilderness*, p. 155).

[2] "A Griqua trader, and celebrated sportsman" (Methuen, p. 193), who had previously acted as interpreter to several European expeditions into the Interior. He is often mentioned in the writings of Andrew Smith, W. C. Harris, and Moffat.

[3] On 9.v.1844 D. L. had written to Tidman (from Mabotsa): "... the whole has healed well beyond my most sanguine expectation, and the bone is perfectly straight and firm".

warm. I expected bursting & discharge, but Baba bound it up nicely with splints, gum, white of egg, & sugar of lead, and a few days' rest put all to rights. I then commenced mud architecture,[4] and six days have brought the walls up a little more than six feet. If you will not laugh at my drawing, I shall give you the plan.

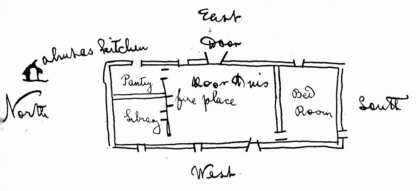

There is a fireplace in the study or library, whichever you may call it. The walls will be finished long before you recieve this, & I suppose the roof too. But I have still the wood of the roof to seek. It is not however far off, and as Mr E[dwards] & I, with the Kurumanites,[5] got on the roof of the school in a week, I hope this will not be more than a fortnight or three weeks. Baba has been most useful to me in making door & window frames. Indeed, if he had not turned out I should not have been so far advanced as I am. Mr E.'s finger is the cause in part of my having had no aid from him.[6] But all will come right at last. It is pretty hard work, and almost enough to drive love out of my head. But it is not situated there; it is in my heart, and won't come out unless you behave so as to quench it.

[4] "commenced my architecture" (Blaikie).
[5] Native converts from Kuruman, who had come to help D. L. and Edwards establish the mission station at Mabotsa.
[6] "When he [D. L.] returned from a visit to Kuruman, I had got up the walls of a building 40 by 18 for a school room & collected the wood for roofing & thatch. Three men he brought with him from Kuruman & two already here assisted me 4½ days to put on the roof. That assistance was very timely, having just had the end of my right finger crushed off by removing a large stone out of the way of the waggon" (Edwards to Tidman, 28.i.1845).

If you wonder why I have built such a large house for only two people, you must be content with the explanation that it is necessary on account of greater heat; and that we have nothing to put into it is no matter, for I shall think it furnished when you are here.

You need not send the starch I mentioned. I shall make the other preparations mentioned above do all the needful. Are my "inexpressibles" ready? I shall be out of that essential article of clothing by the time I come, & I don't admire the Bechuana trowsers. Don't forget to set Dinah[7] to them directly if they are not yet made.

You must try & get a maid of some sort to come with you, although it is only old Mojimañ. You can't do without some one, & Bakhatla can't be had for either love or money. Mebaloe's wife will do all she can for you, but that is not sufficient. Besides, if there is only one she soon becomes saucy. Mrs E. & Mapoleane[8] quarreled during my absence. I don't know who was wrong, but it was about meat which had been killed for them. I hope as little of that will occur to us as can be.

You must excuse soiled paper. My hands won't wash clean after dabbling in mud all day. And although the above does not contain evidence of it, you are as dear to me as ever, & will be so long as our lives are spared.

I am still your most affectionate,

D. Livingston

I expect to get a Mokhatla[9] to go along with Baba.

D. L.

18: To MARY MOFFAT

[October 1844][1]

[Original not located; copied from Blaikie, *Personal Life*, p. 72.]

As I am favoured with another opportunity to Kuruman, I gladly embrace it, and wish I could embrace you at the

[7] Like Mojimang, mentioned in the next sentence, she was probably a Native servant in the Moffat household.

[8] Mebalwe's wife.   [9] Sing. of BaKgatla.

[1] Blaikie, p. 72, says that this letter was written "a few weeks later" than No. 17.

same time; but as I cannot, I must do the next best to it, and while I give you the good news that our work is making progress, and of course the time of our separation becoming beautifully less, I am happy in the hope that, by the messenger who now goes, I shall receive the good news that you are well and happy, and remembering me with some of that affection which we bear to each other. . . .

All goes on pretty well here; the school is sometimes well, sometimes ill attended. I begin to like it, and I once believed I could never have any pleasure in such employment. I had a great objection to school-keeping, but I find in that, as in almost everything else I set myself to as a matter of duty, I soon became enamoured of it. A boy came three times last week, and on the third time could act as monitor to the rest through a great portion of the alphabet. He is a real Mokhatla, but I have lost sight of him again. If I get them on a little I shall translate some of your infant-school hymns into Sichuana rhyme, and you may yet, if you have time, teach them the tunes to them. I, poor mortal, am as mute as a fish in regard to singing, and Mr Inglis says I have not a bit of imagination. Mebalwe teaches them the alphabet in the "auld lang syne" tune[2] sometimes, and I heard it sung by some youths in the gardens yesterday—a great improvement over their old see-saw tunes indeed. Sometimes we have twenty, sometimes two, sometimes none at all.

Give my love to A.,[3] and tell her to be sure to keep my lecture warm. She must not be vexed with herself that she was not more frank to me. If she is now pleased all is right. I have sisters, and know all of you have your failings, but I won't love you less for these. And to mother, too, give my kindest salutation. I suppose I shall get a lecture from her too about the largeness of the house. If there are too many windows she can just let me know. I could build them all up in two days, and let the light come down the chimney,

[2] In *Missionary Labours*, pp. 600 f., Moffat describes how on one of his itinerating excursions, towards the end of 1836, he was persuaded to teach some youngsters "the A B C with music . . . The tune of 'Auld lang syne' was pitched to A B C, each succeeding round was joined by succeeding voices till every tongue was vocal, and every countenance beamed with heartfelt satisfaction."

[3] Presumably Mary's younger sister Ann.

if that would please. I'll do anything for peace, except fighting for it. And now I must again, my dear, dear Mary, bid you good-bye. Accept my expressions as literally true when I say, I am your most affectionate and still confiding lover,

D. Livingston

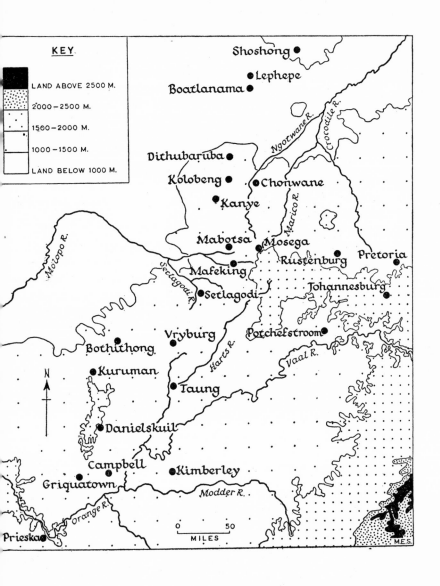

KEY.

LAND ABOVE 2500 M.

2000 – 2500 M.

1500 – 2000 M.

1000 – 1500 M.

LAND BELOW 1000 M.

Shoshong

Lephepe

Boatlanama

Dithubaruba

Kolobeng

Chonwane

Kanye

Mabotsa

Mosega

Rustenburg

Pretoria

Mafeking

Johannesburg

Setlagodi

Vryburg

Potchefstroom

Bothithong

Kuruman

Taung

Danielskuil

Campbell

Kimberley

Griquatown

Modder R.

Prieska

MILES

0   50

Molopo R.

Ngotwane R.

Crocodile R.

Marico R.

Setlagoai R.

Harts R.

Vaal R.

Orange R.

N

M.E.S.

1845

1 April 1845[1]

Address: [Revd.] R. Moffat, K[uruman]. [Wellcome Historical Medical Library, 68213.]

. . . Richardson's dictionary,[2] the hamper in which the apples were, and sail cloth bag in which the bed was rolled up. If anything else was to go back we have forgot, but should it occur to us we shall return it by first opportunity. If Mr Hume could sell us one of his mills we should be glad, for we have both wheat & maize we could grind. We have excellent potatoes, but a worm plagues them & kills large plants. What will destroy them?

Cornelius[3] came & spoke to me about his soul on Saturday last. He seemed much affected. I wished he had gone out straight to you. When he does come you will remember him. . . .[4]

I enclose a letter for Robert[5] which I wrote on the Molopo.[6] If it will do, address it. If not, tell me & I shall try & write a better. I leave my answer to Mr Edwards's

---

[1] The first part of this letter is missing. Its date is fixed by Moffat's endorsement: "Livingston, Mabotsa 1st April 1845". The Livingstones had reached Mabotsa in the last week of March.

[2] Possibly *A New Dictionary of the English Language,* by Charles Richardson, 1836–7; one volume ed., 1839.

[3] The name suggests that he was a Griqua. I cannot identify him more precisely, though in 1854 the Moffats were employing a wagon-driver who may have been the same man (*Journals of Elizabeth Price,* ed. Una Long, pp. 55, 61).

[4] Bottom of page cut away, possibly for the autograph. The remainder of the Letter is on the back.

[5] Moffat's eldest son (1825–62). He was then studying in England, where he had been left when his parents returned to Africa.

[6] A river rising near Mafeking and flowing westward, though nowadays almost perennially dry over most of its course. It constitutes the southern boundary of the Bechuanaland Protectorate.

letter open.[7] The other to the Directors was written on the Molopo & may be sent off immediately.[8] If you think it ought to be sent now, they may both go together.

20: To ROBERT MOFFAT

12 May 1845

Address: Revd. R. Moffat, Kuruman. [Bruce Collection.]

Mabotsa,
12 May 1845

My dear Father,

We recieved your very welcome letter by the Bakhatla who went out with Mosi,[1] & felt very thankful for it, for we were very anxious to hear what you thought after perusing my long epistle on the disagreable subject.[2] We hope to have an opportunity soon, so I begin to answer what is answerable & let you know how we get on.

Your question about the Boerish peace makers is easily settled. The Interior is not yet pacified. Bube intends, it is currently reported, to remove to a spot not very distant from this. He sent me word that he intends coming for the purpose of asking land next week, & the reason is, he fears the Matibele will come out during this winter. Sekhomi[3] has stolen some sheep from Mosilikatse this year, & he killed 23 of his people last year when they came to ask tribute. All are now dreading Mosilikatse's resentment. Sechele told me he would remove instantly to a fountain

[7] This was in reference to various charges made against D. L. by Edwards (of which details are given below, in Letter 22).

[8] Dated "Banks of the Molopo, 23 March 1845", this letter (published in part by Chamberlin, pp. 78–82) describes the mission station at Mabotsa and some customs of the BaKgatla. Enclosed with it was a drawing of Mabotsa, by A. H. Bain, which was reproduced in the *LMS Chronicle*, vol. 10 (1846), p. 65.

[1] Mmusi. Moffat in 1827 had a wagon-driver of that name (*Apprenticeship at Kuruman*, pp. 238 ff.), but whether he was the man referred to here is uncertain; the name is fairly common among the Tswana.

[2] The "answer to Mr Edwards's letter" mentioned in No. 19.

[3] Sekgoma I, chief (1834–75, with two breaks) of the BaNgwato ("Bamangwato"), then living at Shoshong. He was the father of the well-known Christian chief Khama.

called Koloben[4] in hopes of getting a missionary, if it were not for that same fear. And two years ago when the Matibele attacked in succession the Bamangwato, Bakwains & Wanketze of Sebegoe, the Boers heard the news *and fled*. They would do so again this year. Sechele went with large presents of ivory to Hendrik Potkeiter,[5] the commandant of the Boers, to entreat their assistance for the recovery of his cattle. Instead of *pacifying* the poor fellow as he wished, they told Mr Bain[6] that the Caffres had come with tribute to them. Catch Sechele going back again with his ivory while Mr Hume lives. Not a single fray has been prevented by the Boers, & the notion that they drove away Mosilikatse I believe now to be very questionable. The Zoolahs were the cause of his flight, & not the paltry attack of Mosega.[7] Ask the people of Sechele how they like the Boers, & they will tell you that rather than come near them again they will desert their chief.

I began a meeting for the purpose of trying to interest the people in our meetings in general, & have continued talking on different subjects calculated to engage their attention, but have not met the success I expected. Our own people are the chief attendants, and they seem to enjoy what is told them. The hearts of the Bakhatla must be changed before anything can be made of them, that is the first thing I see, and I shall attend to it as the everything.

My mind has been taken up with the affair of Edwards to an extent far exceeding my wishes. I think of it when I ought to be meditating on better things. But I hope I may not indulge in any improper spirit towards him. I have felt less anxious than I expected I should be when told I should have a Committee held over me. By the way, I may ask if he will be allowed to speak or contradict without my

---

[4] Kolobeng, about 40 miles north-west of Chonwane. Sechele did in fact move there in 1847.

[5] Andries Hendrik Potgieter, 1792–1852, Voortrekker leader and subsequently Chief Commandant of the Boers in the Transvaal.

[6] Andrew Hudson Bain (cf. 11.4). In 1844 he had again been in the Interior, with Methuen, visiting both Mabotsa and Chonwane. He settled in the Orange Free State, where he became a prominent public figure, being appointed to the Legislative Council in 1851 (during the period of British rule).

[7] Cf. above, 8.3. The Boers under Potgieter had attacked and defeated the MaTebele at Mosega in January 1837.

presence? I concieve as I speak by writing he ought, although there,[8] to do the same, & then let the bretheren judge. I don't know what he will say after he could speak about my shabby treatment when he offered *to build the house*, & no such offer was ever made.

Another affair I wish to mention to you as I feel rather at a loss how to act in it. If I were not already involved with Mr E. I should see my path clear. But as it is I fear I may act more from an improper spirit than from a wish to prevent the degradation of the missionary character. Some time last year Mr E. told me that, having been at Bube's, a brother of the latter offered him a large tusk for a musket he had with him, but he (Mr E.) had declined. The same man came here a short time before Mr E. left for Kuruman, & came to me & asked if I should give him a cow for a large tusk. I replied, "No, I am not a trader." He said, "Yes, I know you are not a trader, but Edwards helped me with a gun & I helped him with a tusk." Mr E. was that day down on a visit to the Bahurutse,[9] & having come home in the evening the man left on the day following, and I neither asked nor heard any more about it untill the return of Mr Milligan[10] from Bube's. Mr E.'s man went with Mr M. to Bube's to purchase karosses for Mrs E. (I suppose for carpets), and Mr M. said to me, "O, Mr Edwards has turned trader now; his man brought a fine large tusk" (*this is No. 2*) "from the Bakwains for him." If it were not for our difference I should ask an explanation from Mr E., and caution him against appearing to degrade the missionary character. He has been purchasing oxen ever since we came here, but he always mentioned his journey

[8] In April, shortly after D. L.'s return to Mabotsa, Edwards had gone to the South, intending to lay his complaints before "a Committee of the bretheren". He was now living, not at Kuruman, but with the French missionaries at Motito, where Cumming met him on 17 May (*A Hunter's Life*, vol. i, p. 199; cf. 15.viii.1845 Watt, 17.x.1845 Tidman).

[9] Traditionally the senior group of Tswana. Formerly settled at Kaditshwene, most of them had fled to the South from the MaTebele, but there were still a few small groups (the people mentioned here) in the vicinity of Pôwê, about 8 miles south-east of Mabotsa.

[10] Apparently one of the several Europeans who at that time used to go on trading expeditions from the Cape Colony into the Interior; I have found no reference to him by any other writer.

to the Colony as the reason, and of course that journey does require many.[11]

I shall not feel surprised although I hear that Mr E. has made overtures to Mr Ashton to supplant me here. Many things have recently come back to my recollection which had entirely escaped me, and why they should have vanished from my mind I cannot concieve. But now when I put them together I see the reason of Mr E. running to a Committee. He wishes to have me out of this altogether, & he thinks Mr Ashton a more likely subject for him to twist round his finger. When Mrs Moffat wrote from Bethelsdorp[12] she omitted mentioning anything about the young bretheren. When I returned to the house[13] this was the first piece of news I got; and Mrs E. having conjectured that there must be some difference among them, "A very good thing indeed", remarked Mr E., "if there is, Moffat will not have it all his own way"; and again on a subsequent occasion, I think after your arrival but I am not sure, perhaps after my return from meeting you, "I think Ashton is a man of independant mind & won't be led by the nose by Moffat"; and then when I returned from seeing Mary, I was asked if I should not like to live with my father-in-law. I thought the question very impudent & simply said, "No"; & then among a number of fishing pumping questions put to Mary, such as "You & Mrs Ashton must be very intimate", & if Ashton was to remain at the Kuruman—these things had all vanished from my mind. But in thinking over the other affair, a connecting link I recieved from one of Mr E.'s intimate friends came back with great vividness. "I advise you", said he, "to be as little dependant on Kuruman as possible; we have all been too much so." Now I may be wrong, but my close connection with Kuruman seems to have had

[11] Edwards wrote to Tidman on 28.i.1845 that he intended to visit Grahamstown "next October" for domestic reasons, "a very troublesome & expensive journey which I shall undertake very reluctantly".

[12] The Moffats reached Bethelsdorp in June 1843 and left for Kuruman on 10 October, having had to await the ship that was bringing their goods to Port Elizabeth (Moffat to Tidman, 24.ii.1844). The "young bretheren" were Ashton and Inglis, who had accompanied them from England.

[13] Presumably in September 1843, when D. L. and Edwards returned from Mabotsa to Kuruman, where D. L. stayed in Edwards's house.

some influence, as well as my "dishonest, dishonourable, unchristian & shabby conduct." [14]

The plough is in process of resuscitation, and though Mr E. consigned it to "old iron" I feel sanguine it will soon be of more use than that material. Not having the instruments for boring or drilling holes for rivets I have taken the essential portions & let them into a log of murutu[15] of

this shape ▭. The different portions are firmly

screwed to it, & tomorrow we shall put in a new beam of white ash, much thicker than the old, but with the old wheel & coulter irons. Mr Milligan gave me an idea of the shape, or I should have gone wrong altogether. I had the handles in when he came, & as I was doing it simply from my recollection of the shape of a plough, I have the centre of the handles right in the centre of the plough, & not chiefly on the furrow side as it ought to be. Will you send the iron which runs from the handles to the beam, which you shewed me in the printing office?[16] The one you made is entirely gone.

We have been favoured with Mr Greig's[17] presence more than agreable. We escaped from him only once, & that was by getting all ready & starting for Sechele's as soon as he made his appearance from the other side. He was nearly quits with us, for he said he would come to meet us. We went round by another way. But our gent. very soon came back to see if we had not arrived. I thought of going off to Bube, but he is determined to accompany us, so I gave that up & now think of going Eastward to the son of Sebegoe.[18] I could easily be plain with him & get quit of his very

[14] "I was totally unprepared for our first interview, which was begun by Mr Edwards in the following words: 'Your conduct has been dishonest, dishonourable and mischievous, at least that is my opinion'.... Having in his presence taken note of these and other denuntiations . . ." (17.x.1845 Tidman; cf. below, Letter 22). "His [Edwards's] wife wrote to my mother-in-law to let her know how 'shabby, ungentlemanly and unchristian' a son-in-law she had got" (23.v.1845 Watt).

[15] *Modutu*, the Tswana name for *Celtis africana*, a species of white-wood tree.

[16] A mission press had been established at Kuruman in 1831 (Moffat, *Missionary Labours*, pp. 563 f.).

[17] Evidently also an itinerant trader.

[18] Sebego had died near Kuruman in November 1844 and been succeeded by his son Senthufe.

insipid company, but for one consideration. Before we had been many days here, he made some remarks which made me believe Mr E. had been reciting to him the burden of his song; for instance, "Mr Edwards is a man of a very peculiar temper", "very difficult to get on with, I should think", "he tells me he did the most of the work of the church at Kuruman, at least all the woodwork". To these remarks I only replied that as Mr Hamilton & Moffat were there it is not very likely they would be idle, & avoided saying a word about Edwards. But believing that Edwards had given, as Mrs E. would say, "the other side of my character", I rather submit to be half eaten up by Mr G. than that he should have anything to say against us.

If we could by any possibility get a secondhand mill un- till our own comes, we should get on well, whoever comes accross us. We have maize, & the large box which contained the drawers nearly full of wheat. We are inundated with pumpkins. I got two sheep for gun mending, thanks to you, and two karrosses (debt), which I shall send as soon as I get as payment for the steel. The people believe that having married your daughter I must know as much about the business as yourself. The goodness of the steel confirms their opinion. When putting on a plate for Sechele last week, I soldered it very well with powdered glass instead of the borax you use. But in hardening again the libi[19] were not warm enough, so I took it to the bellows & the copper came all out again. I tried it again with other copper no fewer than four times, & it always ran anywhere but where I wanted it. In dispair I put in some white lead. What must I do if I make the same mistake again?

The old files you gave me I case-hardened, & find they supply the place of the fine large coarse-teethed one you gave & which I got spoiled by lending to Paulus.[20] If you

[19] Tswana *dibi*, cakes of dry cowdung used as fuel.

[20] More commonly known as Paul, and sometimes as Paulo. "Of the same family" as Mebalwe, he was one of Moffat's earliest converts and the "oldest deacon" of the church at Kuruman; in 1834 he was already being employed as a catechist (17.iii.1847 Tidman; Moffat, *op. cit.*, p. 589). Early in 1845 he went to Mabotsa "for the purpose of spreading the knowledge of the gospel among his countrymen" (17.x.1845 Tidman). D. L.'s attempts to find a suitable location for him are described in later letters. There is much information about his mission work after D. L.'s departure

have any others from Mr Hamilton's burned house[21] which you don't care about, I shall feel thankful for one or two, either to harden or make taps of. My small plate has been spoiled by someone, the thread is nearly gone. I have made taps of those holes which will make them, and will take the liberty of sending out two of the smaller ones for the screw from your plate, and then I shall try & finish a plate which I have already forged. The small screws I need are those inside a lock, particularly that which goes through the pan. I have got the chief & a few of his principal men to try their hands at the anvil, and this although they believed they should die if they did. One of the hereditary smiths[22] came and taught us how to make Native axes. I did not know [how] to fold in & weld a thin bit before I saw him do it.

I took one of the antient smiths with us to Sechele's to shew me where his forefathers found the tsipi e cueu.[23] There are many mines, and the smoke of the fires is still adhering to the roofs, but they don't go in far. The veins reach the surface & are about 2 inches in diameter only. The man asserted, while in the first recess or mine, that the rock above contained the ore. It is nearly identical with the Kuruman trap.[24] I doubted, but as he repeated his assertions with great confidence I thought perhaps it was the ore of tin, as I have nearly forgotten its appearance. But when we came out I noticed a piece of the pretty green copper ore in a vein of about $\frac{1}{2}$ an inch diameter & pointed it out to him. He said, "Yes, it is so after it is subjected to

from Bechuanaland in Moffat, *Matabele Journals*, and *Journals of Elizabeth Price*, ed. Una Long (on p. 48 of which there are some interesting notes about his personal history).

[21] While he was visiting Griquatown in October 1823, Hamilton's house at Kuruman had been destroyed by fire (J. S. Moffat, *Lives*, p. 125). Thereafter he lived in a small cottage at the back of Moffat's house.

[22] "Though the Bakhatla have the reputation of being workers in iron, only a very few families in the tribe possess the knowledge of the art . . . There are not half a dozen families in the tribe who work in iron" (23.iii.1845 Tidman).

[23] *Tshipi e tshweu*, lit. "white iron". "What they call 'white iron' I have not seen and don't know what it is, but copper is used over the whole country as arm and leg rings" (22.xii.1841 Bennett). The context suggests that the name was applied to either copper or tin.

[24] "Dark-coloured eruptive rock of columnar structure" (*Concise Oxford Dictionary*).

the fire." These were copper mines. The tin I believe is found nearer to this place, but in the same direction Mr Evans[25] found a piece of the ore much richer than any I have seen, although I have been on the look out for it every time I have been in that country. The hill where I think it must be in is called Tsipcane, or as Batlapi would say Tsicane.[26]

Sechele, you will have heard, lately put a man to death for witchcraft. We of course had a great deal of conversation on the subject & on that of revenge. Before the former subject was introduced he asked me, if an individual acted justly, fairly avoided fighting, treated both his own people and strangers kindly, killed witches, & prayed to God, would he be saved? This question made me see he thought he had committed a meritorious action in killing the man.

The above affair became mixed up with another which you will perhaps also hear about. One of his people who formerly killed an uncle of Sechele fled on hearing that the witch had been killed, & came here, being afraid that he might be the next. When he arrived here he told the people that Sechele wished to kill him on account of his cattle &c. The man's father brought all his son's sheep &c to Sechele after the latter had fled, & divided them among the principal people. Sechele took one only & eat it, & told the others not to slaughter any of them untill he had tried to recover the man. The man was sent for & returned, and is now alive & well.

Mr Edwards, believing the man's testimony against Sechele, sends him "a severe reprimand", as he expressed it to Mr Greig, for a deed which he did not do. Mr E. does not like Sechele, because Sechele is rather friendly with me. When leaving in order to visit Sechele last time, the chief here said to me, "Yes, you can go to visit Sechele, you don't know him; Edwards knows him, & he says 'When I took the Doctor to the Bakwain country I let him

[25] An itinerant trader working for Hume. He subsequently established his own business in Natal. Cf. Moffat, *Matabele Journals*, vol. ii, pp. 26, 111, and *The Matabele Mission*, ed. Wallis, p. 185.

[26] The name seems to be a diminutive form of the word *tshipi*, iron. I cannot identify the hill mentioned.

see what Sechele was, but he does not see now.' "[27] If I liked I could get plenty of evidence of "going to Natives",[28] for expressions are let drop perpetually which convince me that the rogue was suspicious because he knew his own deeds. I believe he thinks I have mentioned to you all the nonsense he talked about you & everybody else at times, and that you have told me all he wrote about me. But in your case it was simply impossible, for it has all gone from my memory. If I shall be worried by the reiteration of his little childish tricks & talk, as Mr Hume was, it will be a great hindrance to me in my work.

I have written Mr Arundel[29] about my watch, but I believe I mentioned this last time. I am sorry the wood split up so. I spoiled a pair of shoes after the ash, but could not succeed. I was at the same time warned by Mr E., all the good ones have been cut down by the Bakhatla. I know however of good ones at a little distance. Could you spare another bottle of linseed oil for the . . . begging as . . .[30]

[*Signature cut out*]

Mary has been ill, but a small bleeding has relieved the most troublesome symptoms & she now does well. My arm is very much stronger, but the splint is still in the same state.

We wrote by Mr Edwards, & hope you recieved all safe. Will you purchase for me some pencils from Mr Greig? We shall be obliged by some cows from Mr Hume as soon as possible, young ones if possible. The last were rather old. We want milk for winter.

[27] On their first visit into the Interior (1841), D. L. and Edwards had visited Sechele at Shokwane. D. L. does not mention him in contemporary letters, but Edwards described him then as "a youth, a despotic character, and very selfish" (letter to Tidman, 8.xii.1841).

[28] Edwards had complained, *inter alia*, that D. L. had gone behind his back by seeking information from Natives about a dispute between Mrs Edwards and Mebalwe's wife; cf. below, Letter 22.

[29] Rev. John Arundel (1778–1848), Home Secretary of the LMS 1819–46.

[30] Paper cut, apparently for the autograph.

21: To MRS N. LIVINGSTON

14 May 1845

Address: (Care of Revd. Dr Phillip, Cape Town) Mr Livingston, Almada St., Hamilton, Lanarkshire, N.B. *Postmark:* Hamilton, NO 22, 1845. [Wilson Collection (Mrs G. R. Morgan, Edmonton, Alberta); published in part in Blaikie, *Personal Life*, pp. 74 f.]

Mabotsa
14 May 1845

My dear Mother,

It is now some time since I addressed you personally, but have addressed you so often conjointly I perhaps may be forgiven the omission. I hope you are well both in soul & body. We are now far enough apart, and we shall never be nearer on this side the grave. Yes, but there is a home where the friends of Jesus find eternal rest and all who trust in Him are everlastingly blest. May you enter into that rest is the earnest wish of your far distant son. I often think of you, and perhaps more frequently since I became married than before.[1] Only yesterday I said to my wife, when I thought of the nice clean bed I enjoy now, "You put me in mind of my mother, she was always particular about our beds & linen." I have had rough times of it since I saw you.[2] When with the Edwards' my bed was made about once a fortnight, fleas danced the reel of Tulochgorum[3] as soon as I drew the clothes over me, and when in the waggon I often tumbled in without taking off my clothes at all. If I came out again unmarried I would not again board in a missionary's house. Because I was in some small measure dependant on Edwards for domestic arrangements, he is now mightily offended with me because the Directors don't in the Magazine make him the great man of this mission.[4]

[1] D. L. had married Mary Moffat at Kuruman on 2 January.
[2] "rough times of it before" (Blaikie).
[3] Cf. the song "Tullochgorum", by John Skinner (1721–1807).
[4] "The fact is, I unfortunately lodged in his house, and being an old fogey gent he thought all I had done was in subjection to his superiority" (23.v.1845 Watt). An extract from a letter by D. L. about Mabotsa, dated 30.x.1843, was published

At present we have everything comfortable & clean, and I may without distraction devote myself to the great work for which I came into this country. My wife is amiable & good-tempered, and my new connections pious, which you know to be the best certificate of character. I cannot percieve that the attentions paid to my father-in-law at home have spoiled him. He is of course not the same man he formerly must have been, for he now knows the standing he has among the friends of Christ at home. But the plaudits he recieved have had a bad effect, and though not on his mind yet on that of his fellow-laborers. You perhaps cannot understand this, but so it is. If one man is praised, others think this is more than is deserved, and that they too (others, they say, while they mean themselves) ought to have a share. Perhaps you were gratified to see my letters quoted in the Chronicle.[5] In some minds they produced bitter envy, and if it were in my power I should prevent the publication of any in future. But all is in the Lord's hands. On him I cast my care. His testimony I recieve as it stands. He cares for us, yes He does, for He says it who is every way worthy of credit. He will give what is good for me, He will see to it that all things will work together for good. Do thou for me, O Lord God Almighty. May his blessing rest upon you, my dear Mother.

I have not recieved any letter from you for a long time. Your last was nearly a twelvemonth ago. I have written twice since. I recieved the box from Mr Drummond, but the barrels have not yet come. I shall write to him immediately to acknowledge his kindness. The clothes are all too wide by

in the *LMS Chronicle* for April 1844 (vol. 8, p. 50). "The fact that I did not in my letter . . . exhibit a connection between . . . our first journey and the establishment of the mission at Mabotsa constitutes the root of bitterness from which most of the other evils have sprung" (17.x.1845 Tidman); "He thinks that I took too much honour to myself in giving an account of the commencement of the mission" (23.v.1845 Watt). The extract is preceded by a short editorial note stating, *inter alia*, "Our intrepid Missionary, Mr. Livingston, . . . has made preparatory arrangements for the opening of a station among the tribe of the Bakhatla", but making no mention of Edwards. Hence Edwards's complaint that all the credit was being given to D. L., though he himself had suggested in a letter to Tidman (8.xii.1841) that a mission should be started either among the BaKgatla or at Mosega.

[5] In addition to that noted above, extracts from D. L.'s letters to the LMS had been published in the *Chronicle*, vols. 7 (1843), pp. 37–8, 57–9, and 8 (1844), p. 20.

four inches at least. Did he think that aldermen grew in Africa? Mr Naismith too fell into the same fault, but he will be pleased to know (I shall write him too) his boots will be worn by a much better man, Mr Moffat. I am not an atom thicker than when you saw me. My coat made in London fits me as it did the first day I put it on. However, the clothes are of most excellent quality. Is Mr Drummond grown so much stouter himself?

I hope to be able to send you a little assistance soon, or it may go to Charles if you prefer. I have not yet heard from him, nor from John, although he spontaneously promised to write me every month. Ya Mynheer, pork and potatoes are more agreable to him than pen & ink. I forget the names of people now whom I knew at home, & sometimes when individuals are mentioned in your letters whom you suppose I know I have not the smallest recollection of either name or feature, and this too although I have not been long out.

Please give my love to Janet and Agnes. I have written them both since recieving theirs.

Respecting the mission here we can say nothing, it is all beginning yet. The word seems to take but little if any hold of the minds of the people. "Yes, these are your customs, but we are Bechuanas", is conclusive clenching argument with them. They have not the smallest love to the gospel of Jesus, they hate & fear it as a revolutionary spirit is disliked by the old Tories. It appears to them as that which, if not carefully gaurded against, will reduce[6] them & overturn their much loved "domestic institutions". No pro-slavery man in the Southern States dreads more the abolition principles than do the Bakhatla the inovations of the word of God. Nothing but Power Divine can work the mighty change.

I lately visited Sechele and like him better than I did formerly. He is more acute by far than our chief, & more disposed to admit of improvements in everything. He would be a good hand to be located with, and perhaps I may go to him ere long.

Mary joins with me in kind salutations to all. May you

[6] "seduce" (Blaikie).

enjoy every needed blessing through him who loved &
gave himself for us.

D. L.

22: To ROBERT MOFFAT

6 June 1845

Address: Revd. R. Moffat, Kuruman. [Bruce Collection.]

Mabotsa
6 June 1845

My dear Father,

We recieved your several communications by Mr Cumming[1] on Saturday last, a bitter cold day having ice standing
on all the pools in the morning, and as Mr Greig was
preparing to leave on the same day as he (Tuesday) we had
not a moment's time to answer yours untill Monday night.
I sat up nearly the whole night in order to give you some
particulars anent Mr Edwards's charges &c. But another
opportunity being about to present itself in the person of
Mr Milligan, I sit down to talk a little more leisurely than
I could do on the former occasion. We are heartily glad at
the departure of Mr Greig, but as he is only three days
gone we cannot yet rejoice with very great confidence, as
the fellow may come stalking accross our path again. We
liked Mr Cumming very much. He is now fairly on his
way to the Bamangwato. He seems just the right sort of
person for exploring so far as courage goes, & I hope he
will come safely back.

Matters go on in much their usual way here. The meetings are not full. A certain number seem always to come, &
others only when greater efforts for their attendance are
made. They sit with much more sedateness than formerly,
but as yet I see not the least evidence of any change in their
habits. Last Sunday afternoon we had the smallest meeting
we have had since our return in March last. The reason
was the feast of harvest fell on that day, or rather the

[1] Roualeyn George Gordon Cumming (1820–66), the famous hunter, and author
of *Five Years of a Hunter's Life in the Far Interior of South Africa*, 2 vols., 1850.
He was at Mabotsa 31 May–3 June (*op. cit.*, vol. i, pp. 206–9).

preparations for it were made for its celebration next morning.[2]

A Divine power is certainly requisite for their conversion. I fear that influence will not be granted so long as the present state of feeling exists between Mr E[dwards] & myself. This consideration makes me more than willing to leave the station to himself, for from what I know of his quarrel with Hume ours will not soon terminate. If this were my only motive I should be deeply grieved, for then I could not expect the Divine blessing anywhere. But I know that I had a desire to be the means of carrying the gospel to another tribe before I knew anything of the state of feeling which had existed;[3] and when I asked myself the question whether I were not in any way influenced by a desire to get quit of a peculiar tempered colleague, it seemed to me then that his peculiarities only rendered it less desirable to remain than it otherwise might have been. There are other feelings in my mind now, but I hope & pray that if parted I may be able to forgive, as I hope to be forgiven. I however shall feel no respect for Mr E., aged though he is,[4] and feeling none, none will be expressed.

It is probable I shall adopt the same course I adopted (not soon enough) with respect to Mr Ross. I shall not speak about him. When we came to Kuruman I began it, & continued it for three months, but foolishly departed from it when informed that an opposite course had been adopted towards me. I have forgiven him & Mrs R. from my heart, and I fear to hear any of their statements now, lest all the bitter feelings I once had should return. Against the injurious speeches uttered again & again by Mr & Mrs Ross I have often spoken in bitter anger, but now feel sorry I had not more philosophy, or rather Christian meekness & forbearance.

[2] In years of good harvest, every household in a Tswana tribe gives a basketful of corn as tribute to the chief. Some of it is made into beer, which the people gather to drink in his council-place on an appointed day of rejoicing.

[3] As noted in the Introduction (p. 17), D. L. had written to Pyne on 28.i.1845 from Kuruman that he did not expect to remain long at Mabotsa but was intending to move to the BaKwena.

[4] Edwards was born in December 1795, and was thus 49 years old when D. L. wrote; D. L. himself was then aged 32.

For an investigation of the charges brought against me by Mr & Mrs Edwards I feel very desirous for an impartial investigation in the presence of the bretheren. If I could come I certainly would now write to you officially by this opportunity to demand a Committee meeting. But the probable circumstances in which my dear partner will then be placed[5] convince me that I need no revelation from heaven in order to pronounce that it is clearly not my duty to go out. I should be loath besides to leave the station without any one on it but Mebaloe. My leaving the station is, I am convinced, that which Mr E. desires; but that very desire, and the version he will afterwards give of my leaving, present the greatest obstacles to the following out of my own desire, viz. to go to another tribe. I will not leave, unless in the decision of the Committee there is something to shew that my leaving involves no acknowledgement of guilt. In my heart, & before Him who knows my heart, I am not conscious of having up to the time of our interview given him any just cause of offence. Now I will not, whatever others may think, do that which would imply that such consciousness did exist.

Ought the meeting of Committee not to be here? Certain statements could be better investigated here than anywhere else. For instance, Mebaloe's garden. It is not a hundred paces yet. And then the assertion that I went to Natives. Who are these? One Native deacon was the only individual to whom I mentioned it previous to speaking to Mr E., & to *his* wife (Mapoelan) afterwards, and to no other.[6] If Mr E. asserts I did anything else than what I have related to you, it is either by mistake or[7] malice utterly untrue.

It is entirely untrue that I accused him of feelings of revenge in excluding the woman. His own way of relating the story shews that it is so. When asked about the exclusion he denied it. I believed him, but urged that something should be done in it, as the woman had a wrong impression of what had been done, she evidently understood

---

[5] She was expecting the birth of a child at the end of the year (cf. below, Letter 30).

[6] "I . . . enquired of Mebaloe, who has always acted as deacon, the reason of his wife's absence [from communion]" (17.x.1845 Tidman).

[7] MS. has "of".

exclusion.[8] "Now as the object of discipline was the good of the offender, as well as the purity of the church, let us remove the wrong impression. Let her be subject to discipline so that she may not go on in sin." He replied that he would do right, & not care what impression was produced. I replied that we ought to be careful not to produce a wrong impression lest our good be evil spoken of—that in discipline especially we ought to be careful not to produce the impression that we acted out of private revenge, and that we ought even to have a good report from those who were without. He replied, "But she is within"; and then, as he had repeatedly done before, that he did not feel at liberty, because the affair had happened in his own house, &c.

It is utterly untrue that I ascribed feelings of revenge to him. He denied that he had excluded at all. I believed him, & every act of mine afterwards shewed that I did so. This case, as the case of the garden, was handed over to me, and I solemnly declare I thought that in both cases I had done the very things he wished me to do. I thought I had obliged him in the case of Mapoleane, up to the time of our interview, by taking a disagreable subject off his hands. And my thoughts were the very same about the garden up to the receipt of your letter on Saturday last. I nevertheless could in justice have ascribed feelings of revenge to him about the meat, or what feelings the expressed resolution that Mapoleane should get no more of his meat indicate. But I never did to my recollection ascribe anything improper to him on any occasion previous to our interview, nor did I ever say or do anything which I thought could offend him.

In the case of the garden, he came to me and said something like what he gave in version No. 2 ;[9] and that something to me implied that he had not given satisfaction to all parties, and he wished me to interfere and give a larger piece of ground, so as to effect a good understanding. To this I

[8] As mentioned in Letter 17, Mrs Edwards and Mapoleane had quarrelled about some meat. Edwards had reprimanded the latter, who apparently took this to mean that she was suspended from communion. D. L. tried to set matters right, which Edwards regarded as interference in a private affair.

[9] Presumably the second draft of Edwards's letter of complaint.

remember distinctly I was decidedly averse, & said that I
thought the amount he then stated was quite enough. I was
then walking about.[10] But a considerable time elapsed
before I did anything. A considerable time, I say, for an
interval elapsed sufficient to convince Mr E. that a great
number of Kurumanites would not come to live with him
as he expected. I think it was the return of Merupe[11] with
the waggon that made him first doubt the affections of the
Kurumanites. We had conversations on the subject, and we
both agreed that those who had come first ought to have
the largest share, & that ground ought not to be kept for
those whom he expected.

At least two months had elapsed after what he related
to you, and he had spoiled the lower part of the water ditch,
before I did anything in it. I had previously thought of
having my garden below his, but when I saw that the ditch
was useless in a portion or nearly all of his, and quite
impracticable all below it, I proposed that he should shift
up a little. I did not tell him the principal reason, but
shewed him that the ground was better as you ascend. He
said he had fixed, and I might do or go where I liked.
Mebaloe & Kobopure[12] were next to him above, so I
proposed to them to remove to oblige me. Both readily
consented. So when I took Mebaloe's garden I must of
necessity measure off a garden for both him & Kobopure.
Mine was & is equal to all Mebaloe's & part of Kobopure's.
I remember distinctly saying, "It seems none of our Kuruman friends are coming, untill they see whether we die or
not; we need not keep land for them till then." I measured
off 80 paces, and asked if he were satisfied. Kobopure complained of more trees in the new than his former. I said,
"Then take farther than the 80 paces if you can pick it, but
you will never pick it all." He then went forward about 20
paces more, and I asked if he were satisfied, & he replied in
the affirmative. Now it occurs to me, if Mr E. is such a

[10] After his recovery from the illness caused by his encounter with the lion.
[11] Medupe, a Kuruman Native who went on hunting and trading expeditions into
the Interior. He is mentioned in Moffat's *Matabele Journals*, vol. ii, pp. 59, 88, 92.
[12] Koboyapudi, a convert from Kuruman who had come to help establish the
mission at Mabotsa.

bold outspoken man, why did he never say one word to me implying dissatisfaction?

There are several questions I should like to put to Mr E. One of them is, On what occasions did he interfere between Natives & me? If he says he ever did, except in the one case of appeal which I related and to which I put a stop at once,[13] he tells what is decidedly untrue. When I was ill, he is quite right in saying that the men were sent to him. What had they to do with me then? They were more of men than trouble me with anything but sweet reed, beer, and their own kind sympathizing company, more than I liked too sometimes. There were only one batch of seven men employed while I was able to work. These were asked for by Mr E., and I now recollect he asked for them in my heinous way, "I want". By the by, there was a fine row with these same men's wages, in which had I been so disposed I could have interfered to advantage. But I defended him when they asserted he cheated them. Now these same men finished the ditch & the house. I had no more to do with these works after I was better. When I went out the first time to see Mary,[14] the walls of the school were built in my absence. So we never worked conjointly except for a very short time, & with that same one batch of seven men whom he asked for with the "ego". Now what he means by saying the men we asked were always sent to him? *Always*, what does the *always* mean? We never did on one occasion ask for men conjointly. If the men whom I employed on my own works were sent to him first, he may thank me for calling him "eo mogolu"[15] for that, but I don't believe they ever were. But now I am blamed for calling him an old man.

About the letters I think too he mistakes. They may have gone occasionally first to him. But this I know, I have

[13] While D. L. was working on the watercourse, one of the BaKgatla helping him refused to continue, and on being reprimanded appealed to Edwards. When Edwards sought to intervene, D. L. told him "that it was quite improper to allow a Native to appeal to him, as such conduct would make a nonentity of me, a fellow-laborer; this man had refused to work to me, and I must settle it". Edwards left the scene, and the man began to work again (17.x.1845 Tidman).

[14] In June–July 1844.

[15] *Yo mogolo*, "the old one, the senior"; usually considered a title of respect by the Tswana.

sometimes sent them when I saw his name & not mine,
which I believe happened at least once. After my return
from my first visit to Kuruman I am certain they always
came to me first. But it would have been all quite right had
the paltry circumstance not puffed up the poor old man's
self-importance. Don't mistake the tone of my voice when
I say, if grey hairs may catch at every straw to bolster up
its own importance, surely *I—I—I—I*—may do the same.
Indeed, if Mr E. really believed he was of $\frac{1}{20}$ part of the
importance he wishes you to understand he is, he would
not be in such a dreadful fright lest it should be annihilated.
I know however that if it is destroyed it will not be by anything that I have said or will say to his disadvantage.

I cannot accuse myself of having behaved in the way he
mentioned to you. Previous to our interview he had no just
cause of offence. And yet his first sentence, which I took
down in his presence, was: "Your conduct has been dishonest, dishonourable, & mischievous; there never has
occurred an instance of conduct so base between one missionary & another, I don't believe there is another instance
on record", &c. Now I should like to hear these words
poured out with the lamb-like meekness, tears & groans
he assumed before you. To all this and a great deal more in
the same strain I returned only a fair explanation of the
whole of my conduct, with my motives for acting as I did.
He then went on talking of his honesty &c, and accused
me of the opposite. To this I only replied, "O, don't talk
so much of your honesty, it puts one so much in mind of
Inglis." "I must have an apology", said he, "for certain
words you made use of; it is true you made a sort of apology,
but I have no right to be satisfied with that." He then
mentioned the words.

I then, & then only, made use of words which you may
find fault with; for all his hidden anger, of which I had in
the note been informed by Mrs E.,[16] came back to my
mind & ranged side by side with his boasts of honesty, and

[16] About five months after the incident with the workman (n. 13), "a note was
put in my way by Mrs Edwards, containing the information that ever since the
above circumstance her husband had entertained feelings towards us which would
prevent the Divine blessing on our labours, and that as these bitter feelings were
increasing she felt very uneasy, &c" (17.x.1845 Tidman).

I told him of it, but I used no epithet such as, "You are an old man". I said, "You informed me that you thought I wished to drive things all my own way. At that very time I was endeavouring to uphold your character in the eyes of the Natives, for when you were weak enough to endeavour to make yourself a source of appeal I was refusing to be one against you. These same seven men (one of whom refused to obey me & went to you) declared to me that they had been cheated, and asked why I had brought a man like you with me. I said, 'No, you are not cheated, you don't yet understand wages.' One said, 'But all the people who come from the Southward tell us that man is Satan.' Now I was defending your character, and telling them never to come again to me to say a word against Mr Edwards, at the very time you thought I was wishing to drive things all my own way. You insolently told me", I added, "to let the watercourse alone, & you would carry it on, for I was always contradicting you. Well, you got it all your own way, & from the point at which I was bitten by the lion it had all to be digged over again." I said all this but no more on that subject, & I shall repeat it.

I was then accused of having engaged Mebaloe privately. To this I replied (but not before he had accused me of holding the sentiment that no one should have authority over him but myself) that he knew of my requesting you to give Mebaloe a public charge to make no difference between him and me, and that my sentiments were that no one should have authority over a Native who had none over his own temper. "You, Mr E., are an example of what I mean, and the proof is you never speak out, notwithstanding all your boasts of honesty, unless your temper boils over & compels you." I then asked why he had not spoken to me, as an honest outspoken man would have done, before going to another to introduce for him a subject into the Committee. "I can't prove that you did, but it has always looked so to me." He denied it point blank. I then gave him another instance of his honesty. But I never said one word about his temper or his honesty untill the subject was introduced by himself. He charged me first with bad temper by saying my temper was my ruin, which from him tickled me not a little. Every statement I made was introduced by himself.

But why does he shift the ground of controversy from the case of Mapoleane & the nonentity sentence to what took place entirely at the interview? I assure you, I did not say one word calculated to exasperate untill after I had been informed that he had written to all the bretheren on the subjects before speaking to me. And had I not been quite confounded by the unexpected explosion, it is probable I should have given him a great deal more.

When coming away from the interview, he asked me if I objected to any statement in his epistle to the Directors. I said it had got a twist through the whole of it, & that my proceedings with respect to the Interior had had no reference to him, for as he might remember he did not know untill long after my resolution with respect to this station whether or not, to use his own phrase, he should still be Moffat's lackey.

Had he not delivered Mrs E.'s message concerning her writing to Mrs M.,[17] I should have been able to bear most of what he said. But that, with impeachment of my veracity in what he knows to be the truth, was rather beyond me.

In conclusion on this subject I may state that, whatever charges refer to a period antecedent to our interview, I protest that, except in the one case (of nonentity) about which I was informed by Mrs E., I was not conscious of ever having offended either in word or deed. And that I should be informed immediately if I ever did offend in either word or deed was my pointed request on that occasion. It is scarcely fair in Mr E. to jumble all together, viz. what passed at the interview & everything else he can think of.

I feel most anxious to have an unravelling before bretheren, but I must be guided by what you think best as to going or staying. I feel very unwilling to *go out* to a meeting, and yet I feel very anxious to be present at it. It cannot,

[17] "He likewise informed me that he had during my absence written what he thought of me to the other bretheren, [and] that Mrs Edwards had desired him to say that she had formerly written favourably of my character to Mrs Moffat, but that she too had (in my absence) thought it her duty to write what she thought to Mrs Moffat, &c" (17.x.1845 Tidman).

however, be at that time if called for my accommodation. December or January either would prevent my going quite.

I may say again that I am even more willing than I was at last Com. meeting to go to another tribe.[18] I should prefer Sechele to the Bahurutse, but should be content to go to the place where there is most hope of doing good. Bube has always professed great friendship, & when here last week asked me if I would not come & live with him. Sechele we met on the path leading up to his town, & after saluting Mary he said, "Have you come to teach us? I shall come to Mabotsa & take you away from Moseelele,[19] & make you my teacher." When we talked to him afterwards on many other subjects, we found that he always said just what a sensible man in his circumstances would be expected to say. He never said, like Bube & others, "O, I like the word of God", &c. But when he told us that he intended moving to a fountain called Kolobeñ as soon as he heard that the Matibele intended to come that way no more, or were defeated, in order to get a missionary, his reasons were, a missionary could help him in sickness, mend his gun, teach him to read, & 'nthuta botlale.[20] He seems very fond of improvements, and altogether a more likely subject than any I have seen. He & Moiloe[21] resemble each other in many respects. I did not like to propose anything lest it should seem like anxiety on my part to go to him. If you come, as you mention, before August, the proposal would come much better from you.

I long to be away from all khañ.[22] If I get in there, Mr E. will be clever if he can hook me into another scrape. The worst I fear here, in leaving without giving to them any sort of what they will consider a plausible explanation, is anger on account of appearing to leave in discontent. Or, if my residence were as near as Bube, I fear blame might be

[18] The second meeting of the District Committee was held at Kuruman on 10–11 February 1845. The minutes contain no reference to D. L.'s contemplated move from Mabotsa.

[19] Mosielele Kontle, chief (1842–73) of the BaKgatla at Mabotsa.

[20] *Nthuta botlhale*, "teach me wisdom".

[21] Moilwa II, chief (c. 1845–75) of the BaHurutshe-bagaGopane at Pôwê (near Mabotsa).

[22] *Kgang*, "strife, quarrel, argument, contention".

attached to me (if they removed nearer to that locality) as having used improper influences to induce them to that step. They will not come near Sechele. But it might be different with Bube or Moiloe. I think it would be right to make provision against the possibility of blame.

Certain remarks made by Natives, but to which I never return an answer, induce me to believe that some talk has taken place other than what a well-wisher to the cause should like to hear. For instance, repeated allusions to the gardens as mine, as having known me first, &c, without any connection; and one said, "Do you know what we said in the peecho?" [23] (I did not know there had been a pico.) "Mosielele said you were his father, and if you left this place so would he." I made no reply, but it has made me think since. What can induce them to speak of the gardens as mine, when I have invariably declared that they are not mine, but those of the teachers for the time being for ever?

But I leave this subject. You will percieve that Sechele would perhaps be the most eligible situation. It would be $2\frac{1}{2}$ days distant, and as there is enmity between the chiefs, & between Mr E. & one of them, we should not probably trouble each other.

The plough met with an accident, in getting the mould board broken off accross by the hinder bolt. An unseen root was the cause. Another $\frac{1}{3}$ of it has since been broken off by another hidden root. But it continued to plough very well untill this evening, when the foot board was broken accross by the first bolt. I have put a strong band from the iron which recieves the share round a portion of the wood, & it is now on its legs again. We employed men to root out the trees, & they don't seem to have acted conscientiously, for we have found stumps which held 8 oxen covered over with mould. Your band is a fail-me-never, the iron does for everything. Will you favour me with the measurement horizontally of the distance between the end of the foot board & the tail end of the mould board? I think I must have given the mould board too great a lateral set, for though well supported it broke off. Can I fall heir to the other mould board belonging to this plough? Mr E. made a

[23] *Pitsô*, a mass meeting of tribesmen for the discussion of public affairs.

"tutlua" plough[24] last year & he has it yet. I think I shall be able to make a good one next time, for Mr Milligan gave me an idea of the shape. We have got 5½ buckets of wheat sown. Manured the land by making a kraal & shifting it, Highland fashion. Have you any pease or beans to spare for seed? I never saw the "Cobbet's corn" you gave us. We have mangold wurzel & carrots growing well, but the potatoes were nipped off by frost. I thought of putting up a smithy. Do you think it would be proper in present circumstances?

I have bought of Mr Milligan sheep & goats &c to the amount of five pounds, and as Mr Cumming has proposed selling some things to us on his return, such as coffee &c, I prefer keeping the money I have here for that purpose. So I send an order on you which I hope you will be kind enough to honour, discount, or whatever ought to be done. If you ever send for tools will you order a large saw for me? That strong hand-saw you kindly gave is completely bent in sawing up trees for planks. I see nothing will do but the large pit saws for that purpose. I hope you did not forget the smith's bellows. If I leave this they will be indispensable for a new station.

I intended to have written the Directors by this opportunity on the subject of Mokoteri.[25] The burden of that affair you will find by what I say will [lie][26] with the Committee. I shall let you have it, and with it Mr Ashton's & your advice to me, "Get out of it the best way you can". I shall state my belief as an individual that it would be improper to employ Mokoteri in any way whatever in the Mission, that belief being founded on the testimony of M[ess]rs — — — —,[27] which I recieved as true in the

[24] *Thutlwa*, "giraffe", the name applied by the Tswana to the single-shafted ploughs used by the Boers. Cf. Letter 55: "From its length & only one handle with two wheels the Natives call them cameleopards".

[25] At its first meeting (January 1844), the District Committee had decided that, because of his "character and conduct", it could not recommend Mokotedi's employment in mission work (cf. 12.9). The Directors asked that the decision should be reviewed, suggesting that Mokotedi might possibly be of some use to D. L. The Committee at its third meeting (March 1846) adhered to its original opinion.

[26] Small tear in paper.

[27] Short dashes in MS. "Our unanimous opinion, founded on the united testimony of the bretheren who witnessed his conduct, was that he was then quite unfit to be employed in missionary labour" (17.x.1845 Tidman).

first Committee, and also on the consideration that it is in general improper for one missionary to give countenance to a Native when that countenance might be construed into opposition or condemnation of his bretheren. Witness the same case in the hands of Inglis at Bethelsdorp.[28] And then, as being a man of yesterday, I shall politely hand it over to the "collective wisdom" of which we all entertain a high opinion. I should have written now. Mr M[illigan] has come before I anticipated. I don't understand what you mean by being "in it". The Directors, Mr Ashton, Inglis, & you, are in it, & ought to get out of it. But I have not been in it yet except as part of a Committee. Perhaps I ought to be called a nothing or ne'er do weel or thing of yesterday, because the Directors in your & my own views are to [blame] for not recieving our unite[d testimo]ny.[29] We shall see what the Committee will say of *me*, whose testimony was set at nought just as well [as] yours. Unless you mean to address yourselves to me I don't understand the advice, "Get *out* of it". If I were a Director it would do.[30]

[*No signature*]

18th June. Please observe the bill I have given is eleven pounds sixteen shillings, not five pounds as stated within. The increase was for cows.

Please send a bit of old copper for soldering. See how attentive I am to rid you of your rubbish.

[28] After Mokotedi's conduct had disgusted the members of Moffat's party who were detained with him at Bethelsdorp (20.12), Inglis, on returning from a visit to Hankey, "took [him] by the hand and made him a confidant" (Moffat to Tidman, 3.xi.1845).

[29] Insertions in brackets owing to tear in paper.

[30] In reference to this, Moffat endorsed the letter: "The third sheet to be answered, as it contains a libel & makes me an enemy to one important department of Missionary labor. Mr L. wants light. R. M."

23: To ROBERT MOFFAT
18 July 1845[1]

Address: Revd. R. Moffat, Kuruman. [Bruce Collection.]

[First sheet missing]
... We hear that Inglis's visit to the Bahurutse has put a quietus upon their removal.[2] We suppose he will find out you are of more weight in effecting removals &c than either he or Andries[3] or both put together.

We received the cow bought by Mameri[4] and another I had at Motito, but what do you mean by "your cow"? If you refer to that which was at Obonyeñ,[5] you do very wrong (excuse my saying so), for I shall never accept it. It did not come, & I hope never will. If it lies on your conscience, give it to Ann as part of her dowry.

I thank you most heartily for the gun affairs, barley & everything else, but I shall do so more fully by Paul, who will go on Wedensday next.

We have enclosed our thoughts on Helen's affair. We think the young man did right in speaking to Helen first, but it is a pity she was not at the time of age.[6] I would not have come to you first for the world. It may be well for her future prosperity if she is directed past this match. But all

---

[1] The date of this letter is fixed by Moffat's endorsement: "Livingstone, Mabotsa, 18th July 1845. Of no importance."

[2] Inglis had decided to work among the BaHurutshe who were living as refugees along the Harts River in the south (cf. 20.9), but wanted them to return to their former home in the vicinity of Kaditshwene, since he considered the locality they were then occupying unsuitable for a mission station.

[3] Possibly Andries Waterboer (3.5), in whose settlement at Griquatown Inglis was then living.

[4] Mma-Mary, "mother of Mary", the name applied to Mrs Moffat in accordance with the Tswana custom of calling people by the name of their firstborn child with the addition of the appropriate prefix (*Rra*, father, or *Mma*, mother). D. L. and his wife similarly became known as Rra-Robert and Mma-Robert respectively.

[5] The Native catechist at Nokaneng (an outstation of Kuruman). The context suggests that he was looking after some of Moffat's cattle.

[6] Helen (b. 1829, and therefore now only sixteen years old) was the Moffats' third daughter, and had been left behind in England for schooling when they returned to Kuruman in 1843. She subsequently (before the end of 1847) married James Vavasseur, a merchant of Knockholt, Kent, but I cannot say if he was the "young man" mentioned by D. L.

we say is freely, & after we know your decision has been given.

My dear Mary is very well. In fact, improving on the subject, this journey is evidence; she could not have taken it three weeks ago.[7] We were much better without Mr Edwards's presence. The chief once asked me when Mr E. would come with his gun & cow. I told him I believed he would go to the Colony first. Perhaps this statement may be included in the charges. He told the chief on his arrival that he had come to ask the loan of his brother (a fine young man), to take him to the Colony go mo kopela khumo.[8]

This is not a letter, it is a tumerisho[9] only. You must never take any expression in my letters as implying dis-respect, or dis-anything bad, unless I tell you it is such in addition to the expression. Take this, to prevent any mis-apprehension, ka bosina bokhutlo yotle Amen.[10]

Our united love to Mameri & all others.

[No signature]

There is a letter of Mr Murray[11] to be forwarded.

24: To ROBERT MOFFAT
13 August 1845

[Bruce Collection]

Mabotsa
13 August 1845

My dear Father,

The bearer of this to Moiloe is a Mokwain sent by Khake[1] to announce the death of Bube, which took place a few days

---

[7] D. L. does not refer to "this journey" in other letters of the same period. It may have been a trip to Chonwane.

[8] *Go mo kopêla khumô*, "to seek wealth for him", i.e. by giving or finding him work.

[9] *Tumedisô*, a greeting or salutation.

[10] *Ka bosenabokhutlô jotlhe*, "for ever and ever" (lit., without any end at all).

[11] Mungo Murray, of Lintrose, Cupar Angus, Forfarshire. He and Oswell were on a hunting expedition, and had spent two days at Mabotsa towards the end of June, when they first met D. L. Cf. W. E. Oswell, *William Cotton Oswell*, 1900, vol. i, p. 108.

[1] Kgakgê, agnatic half-brother and successor of Bubi; rejoined Sechele's section of the tribe in 1853, and was killed in war (1880) by the BaKgatla-bagaKgafêla.

ago. As you may not hear a correct version of the circumstances which preceded that event, I may mention that it
was occasioned by an explosion of gunpowder. The people
had been out hunting elephants, and having killed none
thought the reason must have been in their ammunition not
being charmed. The principal men were therefore requested
to try the same medicines they employ in charming their
spears. All the powder in the town was collected on a karross, & the three principal men with medicine burning
(roots, I suppose) came close, and pointing the stuff to the
combustible material uttered a sort of whistling incantation.
The explosion burned Bube nearly all over. His body was
nama hela.[2] The others suffered chiefly in the limbs & face.
From their discription of the quantity of powder, it seems to
have been about 10 or 12 lbs in amount. They sent immediately to Mabotsa for medicine, but I was gone to Sechele's.
Having followed me thither I gave them a note to Mary,
and the poor fellows trudged all the way back again. But
Bube was no more before the medicine arrived. The people
don't wish it to be known in what way the fire was communicated to the powder. They say there was no fire near,
and as some of the powder was procured from Sechele they
may believe it to have been bewitched.[3] But the above
account I recieved from some Bamaleti[4] who were there at
the time the accident happened, and who can have no
motive for falsifying it.

In my last by Paulo I informed you of our determination
to leave Mabotsa as soon as possible. I took our trees &
planted them as the first step. Bought sufficient ground for
three large gardens for a gun, some ammunition, & beads.
Sechele said he never expected that we should buy it, but the
whole of the plot being cultivated I could not request him to
remove his people from their gardens without remuneration.

---

[2] "Flesh only", i.e. blown to bits.

[3] Cumming, who tells the story in more detail, says that he himself had given
Bubi the gunpowder in exchange for curios (*A Hunter's Life*, vol. i, pp. 234 f.).
Tribal tradition supports D. L.'s version that it was a gift from Sechele and conse-
quently suspected of having been bewitched (Schapera, *Ditirafalô*, p. 50).

[4] BagaMalete, nowadays generally considered a Tswana tribe, though originally
of Transvaal Ndebele (Nguni) stock. They were then living at Rabogadi (8.4),
but their main settlement is now at Ramoutsa, Bechuanaland Protectorate.

He was highly pleased with the price.[5] In the event of removal it is stipulated that the missionaries are to recieve an equal amount of garden ground for nothing. I intend to build a good large house, whether the station be permanent or not. We shall have the pleasure of it while there. Mary says this is not an inch too large for us. I go next week to begin, & if I am no longer with it than I was with this, it will be fit for residence in December or January.

I should have left this week, but did not like to leave my dear rib to encounter Mr E. alone. I left a note for Mr E. when I went last time. Mary had just delivered it when I arrived, & he had not troubled her.[6] The note was to the effect that he (Mr E.) was to set his mind completely at rest respecting my leaving Mabotsa; he might consider the whole establishment as entirely in his hands. And in order to prevent him concieving I did this now in order to impede his Colonial journey, I stated that I did it simply to relieve his mind from the great anxiety he seemed to feel for my departure. I shall not alter my plan of preaching or keeping school while here, though I have renounced connection with the station. I likewise requested him to furnish his letter to the Directors in its original form only.[7] I intend making use of my notes of it in that form & no other.

I greatly long to hear what you have thought of our correspondence. I did not wish to keep up the quarrel, but did not see the smallest probability of any amicable arrangement being come to by our meeting alone. I do not expect it by our meeting at all, but the gross perversions he has penned of what I said made me afraid again to come into interview with him. The very first "charge" is false. I never charged him with putting out a member from revenge. And all the others are culled out of the "interview". Now when I saw by

[5] "About 5 *l.* worth of goods were given for a piece of land. . . . The particulars of the sale sounded strangely in the ears of the tribe, but were nevertheless readily agreed to" (*Travels,* p. 19).

[6] Edwards, after moving to Motito in April, "made one visit of a few days to Mabotsa about two months ago for the purpose of preparation for a journey to the Colony in which he is now engaged" (17.x.1845 Tidman).

[7] The letter, if ever sent, did not reach its destination: "we should feel it unjust to pass any positive opinion on the proceedings of Mr. Edwards, from whom *no communication on the subject* has been received" (Tidman to D. L., 29.x.1846; underlined in original).

the written charges that he had shifted the ground of his attack entirely, I believed unless I had a witness to attest what might pass he might get something more against me. Mr Edwards has not put a single point against me exactly as it happened. Now I had no witness here. I should have been very glad of an interview had I only had one witness. In what I wrote I tried to be frank & plain. I believe, as I told you before, when he got the assurance that I should leave he had gained the point he wished from the first. Had Ashton not been as he has been, the second conjecture I made would I have no doubt before this [have] been verified. My going to Sechele is however against the realization of their hopes. You will have seen by his note, which I sent by Boe,[8] that had he known of my intention to have another station he would have waived all this "row". He would not have cried & groaned before you. Not he, had he only known that the "nonentity" would probably withdraw himself from the immediate vicinity of his supreme importance.

Pilanie seems to think him as much a nonentity as I am, for in his recent visit Pilanie went out of his way, but let it be known that he thinks him "a child of Mosielele". Pilanie said in his last visit to Mosilele, "Edwards o 'mpehile" (from beha), "ñuana oa Mosielele hela eo".[9] Mr E. gave him a present when here. I gave him nothing. If he of importance is so much esteemed, what must I be?

I think I did not tell you of the grand conference of kings once projected to take place at Motito. Sebegoe, Moiloe, Mokhatla,[10] Mahura, Andries,[11] &c &c &c were all to be there. Sebegoe was sent for here and urged to go. He thought Edwards wanted to betray him. I was sent for, & found the poor man did not know what to make of Mr E.'s earnest entreaties. Mr E. thought I would assist him. I unfortunately expressed a doubt about the safety of Sebegoe

[8] "Boy" or "Booi" (Afrikaans), a Griqua who used to go on hunting expeditions into the Interior. He is mentioned in Moffat's *Matabele Journals*, vol. ii, p. 14 (August 1857).

[9] *Edwards o mpehile, ngwana wa Mosielele hěla yo*, "Edwards disappointed me, he is merely a child of Mosielele". *Mpehile*, as D. L. mentions, is derived from the verb *beha*.

[10] Mokgatlha, regent (c. 1824–45) of the BaHurutshe-bagaGôpane.

[11] Andries Waterboer, the Griqua chief (3.5).

putting himself into some of their hands, and the famous congress was knocked on the head. Sebegoe said he would go if I would take him, but I did not feel inclined to interfere in kingly affairs. I don't remember that you were to be one of the party, but Ross, Helmore[12] &c certainly were. I think of it now as if it would have been very fine.

I now hear the car passing the window, but we don't send letters by him.

I have taken out two door frames, & two of the window frames I intend to take also. If this house is made a meeting house of it will not need the door frames, and if he makes it a dwelling house he (Mr E.) can make others more easily than I. I don't think spite will allow him to do anything with it. If the inside walls were removed it would make a much better church than that at Motito.

Mebaloe goes with us. I said not a word to him, but when digging up the trees he came & asked if I should help him by taking his. I replied that though I contemplated removal I had not thought of requesting him to move, I had wished to get another to go forward with me. To this he requested, if I had any fault to find with him not to hide it; and on my saying I had no fault, but supposed as he had at great expense cleared out all the roots out of a fine garden, built a good house, &c, I thought he would prefer to remain and another could go with me as assistant, he then entreated me to allow him to go forward & let the other of whom I spoke remain here & take his place. To even this I would have objected, had Mr E. not in his letter to the Directors quite discarded him.

The chief made many objections, and it was with great difficulty I could remove the impression that I had some cause of dissatisfaction either in him or people. Had any one stolen anything? He would give orders immediately that no one should from that day forward beg. If any one had vexed us, "Tell who it is, & I shall punish him". Were we tired

[12] Holloway Helmore (1815–60), born at Kidderminster, came to S. Africa as an LMS missionary in 1839, and at the time to which D. L. refers (1844) was working at Dikgatlhong. He subsequently led the ill-fated expedition to found a mission among the MaKololo (1859–60), in the course of which he and several others, including his wife and two of his children, died of fever at Dinyanti (*Register*, p. 45).

because the hearts of the Bakhatla were hard? He explained that the hearts of all Bechuanas were so, & he could observe they were just about to begin to give way to the preaching of the Word. If any one wished to believe, he was at liberty to change his customs, &c. I tried to persuade him that I was not in the least dissatisfied with either him or his people. I promised to mend his gun for him where I was in future as if I were living with him, &c. But they all say, "Loa re latla".[13] I did not expect they would have shewn anything like the concern for our leaving which they do. It made me sorry, for there are many of the younger men who seem to have affection for us, and I suppose that affection might have been the means of leading them to the Saviour. I hope they may be converted, although not by our instrumentality.

We have sown a great many garden seeds presented to us by Mr Methuen.[14] The endive, spin[a]ch, turnip, mangold wurzel & Knight's early cabbage have come through the ground, also some lettuces & carrots, so we shall have vegetables. I have got three large Swedish turnips, intend them for seed. None of our onions have come up, the seed seems bad. I am very sorry the olive is dead, but there is hope in the roots. There are wild olives at the bottom of our garden at Chonuane. The soil is black deposit, with at some parts small portions of limestone intermixed. The banks of the stream are clayey. The water is small, but it will serve.

The prospect of success in the great object of our mission is greater there than here. The Bakwains are not so degraded as we found the Bakhatla. The people there all profess to be highly pleased with the prospect of our residence among them. Sechele is building a wall round his town, it contains loopholes for shooting. The shape of the whole is a sort of triangle, and the base line is longer than the wall in front of both gardens at Kuruman.

From what I have said of our plans you will understand that we cannot come to a Committee till February. I suppose

---

[13] *Loa re latlha,* "you (pl.) are abandoning us (casting us away)".
[14] Henry H. Methuen, naturalist and traveller, author of *Life in the Wilderness: or, Wanderings in South Africa* (1846; 2nd ed., 1848). He and three European companions had been at Mabotsa and in the vicinity in August–October 1844.

the bretheren will make some allowances for our convenience as well as for Mr E.'s.

[*No signature*]

25: To ROBERT MOFFAT

5 September 1845

[Bruce Collection.]

Mabotsa
5 Sept. 1845

My dear Father,

The present note must be as hurried as any of yours. Mebaloe goes out on Monday in order to bring home his wife before he is required for thatching, and as I have returned here on horseback and go again tomorrow there is no time for corresponding. Everything you sent, so far as we have been able to ascertain, has come safely, and we thank you heartily for the whole. I heard at Chonuane that Mary had headache, & when the Griqua messenger came I did not require any pressing to accept the invitation. She was better before I came, but I mean to purchase a horse so as to come here oftener. The walls are three feet high. This is to be the level of the floor, the outside to be raised for some distance round the house in order to avoid damp. We are 19 in all, & hope soon to get up our tabernacle. The heifer which came from Obonyeñ, & any others you can conveniently procure, I shall be glad of by Mebaloe. Mr Milligan promised to bring me a dozen.

The children here come to be taught by Mary at the house.[1] Sechele acquired a perfect knowledge of the alphabet, large small & mixed, in two days. I try to get breakfast before sunrise, & keep school in the kotla[2] as soon after as possible, so as to have all set agoing in good time in the morning.

[1] Before her marriage, Mrs Livingstone had been in charge of the infant school at Kuruman (Moffat to Tidman, 12.x.1844).

[2] *Kgotla*, council-place, a large circular enclosure found in every Tswana village, where meetings are held and other public business conducted, such as the trial of cases.

I am extremely sorry at having involved you in the unpleasant affair with Edwards. It was entirely by a mistake on
my part. The appearance of the man, & his communication,
produced a sort of bewilderment; and as we were on the
point of starting for Sechele's I was willing to give him a
frank statement before we did so, & in doing so wrote with
more hurry than[3] such a matter required. I read over yours
hurriedly & thought that the paper was official, and it was
not till a reperusal of yours convinced me I was wrong that I
knew the error I had made. He however takes it for granted
that you have informed me of everything, for he begins his
note by, "You have been informed that I applied", &c. But
he has not the engenuity to allow anything if he can make a
peg of it on which to hang an accusation.

And, by the way, I may mention that I have nothing to
do with his application for advice [on] the form in which he
now puts his absence from the ordinances & station. He left
this, as he informed me in his note, in order to submit the
affair to a Committee of the bretheren. I do not feel[4] willing
to allow him to make turn-rounds as he has done in the
affair. The charges as he now puts them are *false*. Not one
of them has he put in a plain straightforward way. So I don't
see what I can do, except give a fair straightforward narration
of all that I know on the subject. It will be prolix, but these
"charges" don't contain a tithe of the differences. There is
not a word about the "dishonest, dishonourable, mischievous conduct", the "going to Natives", the garden, the
employing Mebaloe privately, &c &c.

And, by the way, you need not suspect the Directors will
imagine my declining to have Mokoteri is on your account.
My declining to employ not only one, but every one, I shall
attribute to one of the proper causes, viz. that there is not the
least probability of my recieving that cooperation without
which my single efforts would be futile. Send Paul to Poe,[5]
and, whatever your motives may be in reality, before twelve

---

[3] MS. has "that".   [4] MS. has "feeling".
[5] Pôwê (20.9), a hill immediately north of the village of Dinokana, 18 miles north-
west of Zeerust; the village itself was sometimes called by the name of the hill. It was
inhabited by BaHurutshe, and is still one of their main settlements. In 1847 Inglis
established a mission station there, referred to in contemporary literature as "Matebe"
(Mathebe, after an adjacent stream).

months pass over you may have, as I have had from my beloved coadjutor, all manner of motives kindly laid at your door. Unfortunately my letters for England are at Sechele's. I shall leave that for the Directors open. Please peruse it & tell me what you think of it. I thought at one time that I ought not to say a word about Mr E. untill the Committee had decided, and that has made me delay Mokoteri's affair longer than I intended or wished. The subject of my leaving, & of Mebaloe & of others, are so connected dove-tailed I found I could not write without taking them in. I hope your promise to prevent my former letter does not apply to this. If it does, you may stop this till you think proper.

Mr Lemue seems rather sulky in his answer to what I wrote—does not wish to say anything more on the subject. I did not wish him to begin. "Mr Lauga thinks the ideas of Mr & Mrs E. very much exaggerated, & that they don't seem to percieve to what their conduct will lead." [6]

We are very happy to hear that Robert[7] tries to improve. What he does is very commendable, but he seems to want a guide in his studies. His letter indicates considerable mental activity. We thank you for the perusal. Many of his thoughts would vanish, as many of ours have, as soon as he breathed this pure atmosphere. The lack of material for mechanical operation he does not know. But nothing is like the preaching of the Word. Dogged perseverance at this is infinitely preferable to doctoring, tinkering, or anything else. You have but a small quantity of iron in the Kuruman district, none at all I imagine in Griqualand. Copper has been worked very extensively at Chonuane; enormous must the labour of extraction have been. There is abundance of iron ore here, but would Robert like to be Mr E.'s mechanic if he came out as an artizan? I for one should bitterly regret it. And then who is to support him in his journies? And his *wife* too! But it is unfair to criticise. They are the dreams, amiable speculations, of one who seems quite on the right side. Let us pray that he may be guided into the right path for the Redeemer's glory, and that he may yet become

[6] Lemue and Lauga were the French missionaries at Motito, where Edwards had gone to live in April.

[7] Moffat's son (cf. 19.5).

instrumental in more good to Africa than his young heart has ever concieved.

Poor little Helen. We don't think your decision wrong in her affair, but we can't help wishing, what was beyond all our powers to effect, that she had fallen into other connections.

We thank you for all you have sent, and that most heartily. Thank you for the consolation in the barren cow case. Don't forget the noting down the gun locks & every thing else requiring payment. If you do, I shall give you a return of as strong consolation, for I don't keep note. If there are any things in the barrels which you, Mr Ashton or Hamilton need, don't spare them, take what you want. I have not a moment's leisure to answer theirs which I re- cieved and for which I thank them through you. In regard to the bead chest at Philipolis[8] you have said & done enough. We must now leave it to time, which effects such mighty changes in our world.

Inglis may chuckle, but to me it is no mystery how he got information. When we were sitting in Committee, a report was made to Hume regularly of our proceedings. Could that tongue keep a secret? We have our justification. We are all willing that proper subjects be engaged. He (Mokoteri) was not a proper subject at that time. Can we be blamed for taking time to ascertain the latter fact more fully, by our bretheren taking silent observations of him without his knowing it?

We shall feel obliged if you furnish our accounts at your convenience. We wish it lest we run too deep into the mud ere we are aware. We must exercise the bump of caution in order that it may grow bigger.

Mary says if you come do so in December. I put it down from her mouth, I don't know her reasons.[9]

The vine cuttings &c are very acceptable. Our peaches are in blossom, but the figs, it was too much for their con- stitutions, many have died. I mean to plant (how did the

[8] Philippolis (9.4), an LMS station, founded 1823, about 18 miles north of the Orange River in the south-west of the present Orange Free State. It lay on the main road from Colesberg to Kuruman.

[9] Presumably she was expecting her child to be born in that month.

dried figs in the jar do?) a hedge of hackey dorn,[10] but don't need the shears. O, I mean to do many things, but time, so difficult to be killed by some, expires always sooner than I want it. Mr Oswal[11] says all the features of the Bamangwato country are Indian. The bushes, trees, &c are exactly similar. Mahatla,[12] hackeydorn, rose (or as he calls it black) wood, & wood apple, that which I brought out, are plentiful in India. (Mr E. has taken a specimen of rose wood to Grahm's Town.) They saw & measured Hume's big tree, 51 feet in circumference.[13]

Cumming is gone to the range of hills E.E.N. of the Bakaa. I did not hear of the "long white man".[14]

We have heard that Charles recieved the ten pounds safely. The previous five I sent by another route are not mentioned. My father's family are all in a state of poor health. My sister's constitution seems broken up by typhus fever. Not the one you saw,[15] but she too has suffered from the same cause & has palpitation of the heart. Charles's college term expired last month. Divinity or something else comes next.

[No signature]

[10] Afrikaans *haakdoring*, "hook-thorn" (*Acacia detinens*).

[11] William Cotton Oswell (1818–93), who with Mungo Murray (23.11) had recently visited Mabotsa. He was then in the Madras civil service (from which he resigned in 1851), and had come to S. Africa to recuperate after a severe illness. He became one of D. L.'s closest friends and benefactors, went with him to L. Ngami in 1849 and to the MaKololo in 1851, and was a pall-bearer at his funeral.

[12] Pl. of *mohatla*, the Tswana name for the tree *Tarchonanthus camphoratus*.

[13] The tree was evidently a baobab (*Adansonia digitata*), which does not grow as far south as Mabotsa. Hume had presumably come across it on his journey to the BaNgwato in 1833.

[14] Not mentioned elsewhere by D. L.

[15] Probably when in Glasgow in October 1842 (cf. 14.19).

26: To ROBERT MOFFAT

22 September 1845

[Bruce Collection.]

Mabotsa
Septr 22, 1845

My dear Father,

As Apie[1] leaves tomorrow I begin another hurried scrawl. For the first time in my life I feel that my hands are really full. Too many irons in the fire, over head & ears, and the rain will come, I have no doubt. I came here last Friday week,[2] & after a fortnight's sojourn intend to leave on Thursday or Friday next. My window frames must be done then. I am now busy at them. When the first row of thatch is on "I shall sleep a month". The letter to the Directors[3] is not finished & lies like an incubus on my mind. I can't make it to please myself. Tired out every night, I fancy I feel like you in your perpetual bustle. I have been in bustles frequently, but never felt as now. But I don't by the above ask help either sideways or any-ways. I just speak as I feel. The more we toil here, the sweeter rest will be. Let us look to the Heavenly rest & peace with more intense desires.

Mary I suppose will give all the news. I have none. I mentioned your waggon. As it was principally for the beads you will not of course send it now. Fear we do not thank you sufficiently for all the things sent. It is not want of gratitude but want of thought prevents us enumerating all the things & thanking for each. Maybe the gratitude is not quite the thing either. Thank you for the barren cow consolation. It equals what one might have given the gravedigger's wife who complained of the hardness of the times, "Naething

---

[1] The nickname of a Griqua who used to go on hunting and trading expeditions into the Interior, and who, like others calling at Mabotsa, carried letters between that station and Kuruman. His true name was Adam Januarie (Moffat, *Matabele Journals*, vol. i, p. 363, where the editor renders it "Janewain[?]").

[2] From Chonwane, where he was then building a house.

[3] In which D. L. replied to the charges made against him by Edwards; the version ultimately sent to Tidman is dated 17.x.1845.

doing at a' noo, Jamie has na had a job for three weeks, I dinna ken hoe we can fen ava".[4]

Have got seeds of the gigantic tree 51 feet in diameter. Very good food, Native testimony. The one I broke has a good flavour, you will taste. These are small. I have seen them as large as ostrich eggs. Oswal & Murray may take them down. They were extremely kind to us. The former promises to send seeds from India, & the latter offered to do anything in his power in Scotland. If I had had the money I should have entrusted him with an order for a magic lantern. It would be cheaper in Edinburgh than London, & he being acquainted with many ship captains says he can send anything safely. Surgical instruments are $\frac{2}{3}$ds cheaper in Edinburgh than London.

Did you talk about Rome? Masepa hela.[5] The account reconciled me to the ——[6] of the Bechuanas. They talked frequently about Edwards. We could with difficulty answer their questions, they were so pointed. But we avoided saying anything to shew we were obnoxious. He (Mr E.) has not however observed the same rule respecting us. Mr Murray said, "Mr E. is the coarsest & most uncouth man I ever saw, I was ashamed to be seen in his company." Mr Oswal said, "What is that tall queer-looking man we saw at Motito? He seems to speak as if he were always in a rage." Many questions were put to Mary when I was absent,[7] which shewed Mr E. had been going on at a fine rate to them. She felt very much at a loss what to answer. He told them he intended to go along the East Coast before he returned. He likewise told Mr Greig that he intended doing wonders in the travelling line Northwards. How daring I was to make such a one an appendix.[8] Whether he has done anything or not when last here, or whether it is merely the effect of

---

[4] "I do not know how we can manage to subsist at all."

[5] "Mere rubbish". (*Masepa* is the Tswana term for human excrement.)

[6] The MS. has a small squiggle, which may possibly be *in*, D. L.'s rendering of the Tswana interrogative *eng*, "what?".

[7] This must have been when Oswell and Murray called at Mabotsa on their way back to the south.

[8] In his draft letter to the Directors (portions of which D. L. quotes in his own letter to Tidman, 17.x.1845), Edwards had written "that he is not the mere appendix Mr. Livingston wishes him to be".

knowing that we shall leave, the people now don't turn out to the meetings. We have not a quarter of the former number, so I don't feel bound to remain here longer than I can help. Before his visit the house was generally quite full, since then we have scarcely ever $\frac{1}{3}$ of the former number.

The only relaxation we have is half an hour in the garden before sunset transplanting. Mary is a real gardener, & enjoys this much when not too tired. She is wonderfully well. We have had some dishes of Scotch kale, spinach, leaves of mangold wurzil, carrots an inch in diameter. Lettuces we shall have in abundance, & broccoli & cabbages & turnips ad nauseam, endive in abundance. But we don't know how to eat all our good things. Perhaps I shall turn out a half gardener at my ain hand, like the boy's brither Jock & the diel[9] at sinning. I like it very much. Many thanks for the vine cuttings. When you come you must give me some instructions. I send out some oats & barley from England. The latter is perhaps superior, the former may go to comfort the stomachs of Ann's winged friends if you don't like to sow it.

Thank you for the music book. I am precentor now, & such a precentor! I am in agonies before I can screw out anything like a tune, & then Rira[10] drowns me. I have to watch for a chink here & there in his voice & stick in a note just to let them hear the leader is not asleep.

[*No signature*]

27: To MR AND MRS N. LIVINGSTON

1 October 1845

Address: (Care of Revd. Dr Phillip, Cape Town) Mr Livingston, Almada St., Hamilton, N.B. *Postmark:* Hamilton, AP 10, 1846. [Wilson Collection.]

[9] Devil. I cannot explain the allusion.

[10] One of the converts who had come from Kuruman. Moffat, who found him among the BaNgwaketse in 1856, wrote of him: "Rirá and his wife are there, the same old sinners" (*Matabele Journals*, vol. ii, p. 27).

Mabotsa
1st Octr. 1845

Dear Parents,

We lately recieved your letters and other things you have kindly furnished. We return you hearty thanks for all. The seeds I planted today. The beads I may remark are nearly useless, because they are not in fashion. The real fashionable sort are about this size ● . Large as ⬤ are not a third part of the value of the small, and oblong ⬭ are of no manner of use. The proper sort too ● are I believe much cheaper than the others when bought where exported for foreign use; not transparent, but bright red, blue, or white. But you must not send anything else.

Mary & I have resolved to send you a bill for £20 next April. We hope it may enable you to accomplish your wishes as to emigration. It is more than is convenient, but we try to promote your desires by an extra effort. April is the soonest or nearest period at which I can draw. I shall send to Cape Town so that the bill may reach you in that month. You have then to count its sea voyage & the time Mr Pyne may be occupied in doing the needful. And I give you thus early notice of our intentions, in order that if it comport with your notions of propriety you may ask John to come down to Quebec, or perhaps, what will be more pleasant, give you the needful which, may be, will be better company. Now don't set Janet a-begging. Tie up the old Highland pride in your kilt for once & tell him plainly to table the dust. Tell him plainly if he does not now he is worse than Mungo Menzies.[1] You need not or you must not suppose that silence will be praiseworthy. You need it, & it is virtuous to tell him so. It will be absolutely impossible for us to add to it for at least two years after that time, so you must make an effort now. If we can plan for you, could you not by that time save what with the sale of your effects would furnish provisions? Strong dove-tailed chests, not very large, with iron handles, are most convenient on board ship, those containing clothing to have a few screw nails in

[1] Not identified.

151

the lid to hold down as well as the lock (serves instead of ropes). These are all the furniture you need. The half sovereigns will do yourselves more good than Charles. A few medicines in your stock must not be forgotten, & flannels in changes of weather. If well, you may calculate on the bill reaching you about four months after the first of April. Will August be too late for sailing? It may come a month sooner, as a good deal depends on the ship by which it is sent.

Very sorry to hear of the poor health of Agnes. Her constitution seems to have been spoiled by the fever.[2] Try & procure for her the Iodide of Iron, I o d i d e o f I r o n, in Glasgow. Go to Apothecaries Hall & ask for the solution of it, of the strength recommended in the London Dispensatory. A bit of wire must be kept in it to prevent decomposition. They will tell you the dose, & you must increase by degrees. This will strengthen & improve her constitution. Or you might request Dr Thomson[3] to furnish it. Give the latter my very kind regards. It is the solution recommended by his namesake[4] I speak of. I daresay he uses it too. The state of the bowels must be attended to also, & constipation avoided. Sorry to hear Janet too is poorly. But you are in the hands of Him who knows what is best for you.

I leave Mabotsa in a month or two in order to commence another station at Sechele's, the chief of the Bakwains. The spot is about forty miles north of Mabotsa. The climate is Indian, and most of the trees are identical with those of that country. I have a "kail stock" growing in water. We got several dishes off our old acquaintance.

My colleague Mr Edwards was sent out as mechanic, & is only now recognized as a missionary.[5] He has been exceedingly jealous lest he does not get sufficient honour. In the account I gave of the formation of the Mabotsa mission

[2] Cf. Letter 25.

[3] John Thomson, M.D., of 32 Cadzow Street, Hamilton; he was also a deacon of the Independent Church.

[4] Possibly John Thomson (1765-1846), "reputed the most learned physician in Scotland" (*D.N.B.*).

[5] D. L. may have forgotten that on 14.vii.1842 he himself had written to Mrs Sewell asking her to suggest tactfully to Dr Tidman, Foreign Secretary of the LMS, that Edwards, "a most worthy man and more useful among the Bechuanas than any one I know", might be recognized as "a full missionary".

he thinks he was overlooked, & took great offence.[6] Rather than continue on disagreable terms at Mabotsa I gave him the whole station to himself. He has a most unfortunate temper, and it will be much more pleasant for us to be at a distance than within the sphere of its influence. I have borne with it as well as I could, but now leave it to take its course. It was my previous conviction that I ought to endeavour to introduce the gospel to another tribe & leave Mebaloe & Mr E. to take care of this. The jealousy[7] & bitter feelings above alluded to render it easy to part.

Mr Inglis is doing very little. Took a side in the political affairs of the country & got himself excluded from a very interesting tribe & locality. To the latter they were just on the point of starting, having sent repeated messages to Mr Moffat to come & take them to it. He was ready to go to them in order to use his influence with the neighbouring tribes to allow the one alluded to [to] move in peace, but when he heard that Mr I. had gone to them he wisely left it in his hands. Any interference would have been considered "lording it". The tribe asked Mr I. whence he came, & being informed that he came from the party opposed to their interests in politics, they sat still in the locality they have for some time occupied & in which they know no European can live. He is now living at an adjoining station, waiting I suppose to see what will take place.[8] But that tribe will never recieve him.

Sechele is much more agreable now than he was when I first saw him. He learned the large & small alphabet perfectly in two days. May the Lord bless them all with his light & salvation.

Heard from Mrs Todd & will write. Love to Mother & all.

D. L.

. . . Mary sends you her kindest love.[9] We are happy & contented in each other.

[6] Cf. 21.4.　　　　　　　　　　　　[7] MS. had "jealously".

[8] Inglis was then at Taung, about 25 miles south of the BaHurutshe about whom D. L. is writing.

[9] The passage omitted (about 110 words) refers again to the person in Scotland who had sent D. L. the straw hat (12.4).

28: To ROBERT MOFFAT

1 November (?) 1845[1]

[Bruce Collection.]

[First portion missing]

... The house is 64 feet by 20, the kitchen 8 feet, a lean-to at one end. As the wall will be much lower than that of the house, it will be little more trouble than the verandah would. Nasty water, but I shall make a well. There is one already made by some animal, but it needs deepening. The water in it is excellent. I have remedies for everything in my head, but alas, they all need time. Hope however is a blessed thing. We enjoy the future in the present. But I need not preach about it. Excuse me to Mr Ashton & Hamilton. I would write if I could. Don't be displeased with the apparent slovenliness of this.

If you hear of Mr Milligan coming again, please let us know. He is to bring my hiefers for the house. If he does not, I shall be obliged to give most of our cows.[2] I thank you for the beads most heartily. Tools, every one of them. I made the rod iron into spikes 6 inches long. I would have made the other piece you gave into these also, but it was manufactured into a sort of travelling tripod, & I did not like to spoil my in my own eyes beautiful workmanship. What I have will suffice. A large quantity of reed is cut, beams & litlomesho[3] in plenty. The Bakwains I have work famously. The fellows deserve cows. From sunrise to sunset they pull away manfully, & their wives come & assist them while they eat. And as they have plenty of corn, the potfulls of bogobe[4] devoured are truly astonishing. The Bakhatla did not believe we were going to leave them untill they saw our oxen going off a short time ago. This event excited universal attention.

Isaac, it seems, has left Mr Cumming. His heart seemed ready to die within him here. Mebaloe encouraged him to

[1] The context suggests that this letter was written from Chonwane, but the date cannot be fixed precisely.

[2] As payment for the men helping to build the house.

[3] *Ditlhomeʃó*, rafters. [4] *Bogóbé*, Kafir corn porridge.

154

proceed, but when **Mr C.** proposed to return again to a part of the Bamangwato country where he had been hunting elephants, after having his face homewards he could not endure turning round again. . . .⁵

[*Rest of letter missing*]

29: To AGNES LIVINGSTON

11 November 1845

Address: (Care of Revd. Dr Phillip, Cape Town) Miss Agnes Livingston, Almada St., Hamilton, Lanarkshire, N.B. *Postmark:* Hamilton, AP 10, 1846. [Wilson Collection.]

Chonuane
11 Nov. 1845

My dear Agnes,

I was very sorry to hear a short time ago that your health is in such a poor state. I often think of you all, more so now than I did before marriage. You are all very dear to me, and if I have not shewn it in writing you more frequently my circumstance[s] may have been some excuse. I hope you are leaning on His bosom whose friendship & love never fail. They who once His kindness prove find it everlasting love. Never lose sight of the great atonement, the confirmation & manifestation of infinite love & wonderful condescenscion. To His care & mercy my heart commends you.

I have mentioned in another letter, still by me for want of opportunity, that Mrs L. and I intend to send £20 by next April. We cannot send it sooner. The object is to enable you all if possible to embark for America. It is not at all convenient, but we make an effort, in hope that our garden will yield well & furnish the needful for our necessities. I am greatly in need of books, & will be of clothes before another year, so you need not expect that by waiting a while this sum

⁵ Isaac, a son of Paul (20.20), had been employed by Cumming as an interpreter, but proved unsatisfactory: "instead of forwarding my interests, he actively employed his energies in sowing dissension between me and the natives, and disseminating mutiny among my Hottentots." On 1 August he was therefore dismissed, and ordered to "make himself scarce as quickly as possible" (Cumming, *A Hunter's Life*, vol. i, pp. 309, 320).

may be augmented. Make a grand effort now. Keep all your half sovreigns to yourselves. Charles won't starve. He no doubt feeds on clover compared to you. I entreat you all to be determined this time. Don't dillydally.

I had better give a word to Father, for my remarks seem to afford, to my great amusement, matter for a good piece of his answer. Well, Father, you tell me, do you, that there are people bold enough in Scotland to ascribe all the affairs of Tahiti to the missionaries, for had they understood the nature of religious liberty & taught the Natives the French would have had no pretext for taking possession of these Islands.[1] Now when you meet these bold people, did it never occur to you to pose them with their assumption that the Natives were so much better than themselves? Do they obey all the instructions of their ministers? If they don't, and the Natives do, how much superior the latter are? But unfortunately both the bold Scotchmen and the Natives are alike. There is a mighty gap between our teaching & their obeying. When I left Scotland the majority of the people did not understand religious liberty so well as the Natives. Would it be fair to lay all the blame to the Independant ministers' door, seeing there were so much teaching & inclination of an opposite character to theirs? This is the case at Tahiti. The missionaries understand religious liberty as well as canny Scotchmen. McKean,[2] for instance, came out of the midst of the discussion which only recently opened your bold friends' eyes. The French would not have had a pretext, forsooth. Did the missionaries aid them with a pretext in Marquesas, or do wicked men often stand still for want of a pretext? Do your Scotch friends often fail of a pretext for keeping their bawbees in their pockets, although the salvation of the heathen demands both their lives and substance? And yet Sandy with his hands in his pockets can heartlessly blame those who have given their all. I am ashamed of your heartless Scotchmen.

[1] Tahiti, where LMS missionaries had been working since 1796, became a French protectorate in 1842, following upon the forcible introduction of French Roman Catholic missionaries in 1838.

[2] Thomas Smith McKean (1807–44), missionary at Tahiti from February 1842 until he was killed during a French attack on his station (*Register*, p. 53; cf. *LMS Chronicle*, vol. 9, 1845, pp. 38 f., which D. L. had no doubt seen).

But as my object is to give you something for filling up your next, I may in conclusion ask you if, as the father of a family of both young & old, you would permit the disseminator of Socinian tracts to enter your circle? Would you allow him to rent a room in your house for the express purpose of greater facility in destroying by his heresy the souls of your family?[3] Now the paternal is the form of government in almost all tribes. Here a man cannot sell or do anything else without the permission of his chief. He is in almost every respect the father and guide of his people. Would a father enlightened as to the consequences of heresy sit with cool Scotchism, at its approach into a circle of which he was sovreign, & say, "O, oppose truth to error, truth is the only legitimate weapon", &c? Never repeat the words of apologists for French wickedness. All that is evil in the affair belongs to them, and all that is good under God belongs to the missionaries.

I am at present engaged at Chonuane. It is sounded as if spelled C h o n w a n e y, "a" as in "wan". We have far greater prospects of usefulness here than at Mabotsa. The chief learned the large, small & mixed alphabets in 2 days. This although I could only go to him before sunrise in the morning & after sunset in the evening. The building occupied my time. He is now reading or rather spelling words of two syllables. A clever man. Would much like to see my country & friends. Often asks if you are rich, & when I say no he disbelieves me. Wonders why I should persist, as he says, with tears in my eyes, to entreat his people to believe, seeing they don't want to hear about futurity. I point to my works and ask if I am a fool. As he has a great idea of my works, & I am now a jack of all trades, he believes there must be wisdom in my course of teaching. He seems much attached [to] me, and has named his firstborn son Libistune, oth[e]rs Mositane.[4] The name is difficult for their tongues. Praise the Lord for his kindness. It is through his condescension alone we have any influence or friendship. It was

[3] The Socinians, named after two Italian theologians of the 16th century, were a sect denying the divinity of Christ (*Shorter Oxford English Dictionary*).

[4] "Libistune" is evidently meant to represent the Tswana rendering of the name "Livingstone"; "Mositane" I cannot explain. Sechele's firstborn son was Sebele; there is no Native tradition of his ever having been called by D. L.'s name.

given me lately to prevent bloodshed. Sechele told the murderers of his father that he spared them only because he had promised so to me. He often entreats me to allow him to go & drive them out of his country. I entreat him to refrain from shedding blood.[5] May God be gracious to him.

Father's wallflowers, Indian cress, & turnip came up nicely. No dandelion, hip,[6] nor haws follow. The rest all failed. I am making a roof of rose wood. Sandal wood is plentiful, & many trees are common to India.

Pray for the inhabitants here, & never forget the heathen around you. May the Lord be very gracious to you. I have mentioned a medicine which will do you good, Iodide of Iron; get it by all means. The money will be sent in April. I cannot draw it sooner. Whatever others may have done, my efforts, little though they may seem, leave not out of debt. Much love to you all, Father, Mother, Janet. God be gracious to you, dwell in your hearts, & prepare you for his glorious kingdom, where I hope through undeserved mercy to meet you. My wife would, were she here, join in salutations & love, but she is 40 miles distant assisting in school at Mabotsa.

Much obliged by the "Visitors"[7] & everything else. Please send no more till you are rich. I shall write Janet next.

[No signature]

---

[5] After Bubi's death (cf. Letter 24), Sechele had asked Kgakgê's people to rejoin the main body of the tribe. They refused, but he refrained from trying to force them into submission "simply because of his promise to his missionary" that he would not shed blood (10.iv.1846 Tidman; cf. *Travels*, p. 35). He did in fact subsequently attack Kgakgê, without letting D. L. know of his intention. Kgakgê's elder brother, Moruakgomo, had been chiefly responsible for the assassination of Sechele's father in 1822.

[6] The fruit of the wild rose.

[7] "The Weekly Visitor" (cf. 11.26).

1846

30: To Mr N. LIVINGSTON

17 January 1846

Address: (Care of Revd. Dr Phillip, Cape Town) Mr Livingston, Almada St., Hamilton, Lanarkshire, N.B. *Postmark:* Hamilton, JN 10, 1846. [Wilson Collection.]

Chonuane
17 Jany. *46*

My dear Father,

It is now some considerable time since we have heard anything from home, and truly news from home are pleasant. You don't know how wearisome it is to hear the endless round of news, maka hela,[1] of this country. Lies are so common the Natives always begin to tell news by saying, "I have no news", or, "I have only lies to tell". Rumours of wars, contentions between tribes, &c, constitute the whole information we can get. Why don't you write us then? But I need not ask. You have some good reason. I wish you would tell Charles to write or send what he feels inclined to send always to the Mission House, Blomfield St., then it would come safe. As for John, pooh. When will he who promised to write every month write? When he sees my death mentioned in some newspaper he may then think about [it].

I have written you all by name since I recieved any from you. I have given Mrs McRobert an order to spend £4 in instruments for me, Mr Drummond other £4, & Mr MacLehose other £4, this being the Native teacher's salary.[2] I have written Mr D. I want a cloak for our new

[1] *Maaka hêla*, "lies only".
[2] Mrs M'Robert was providing D. L. with £12 annually for the payment of Mebalwe's salary (cf. 8.20).

chief Sechele, and dark printed gowns for my wife, from him. But lest you think this letter contains the advice of the bill I mentioned, I must tell you I cannot yet send that information. Next month this time however I shall, and write to you at same time, so you will know when you recieve my next that the needful is not far off. The bill must not reach Cape Town before April, that is the reason. I informed you what I concieved would do Agnes good, the Iodide of Iron in sufficient doses. Of these any competent apothecary will inform you. But it is no slight complaint, and I feel anxious to hear how she is.

Present love to Mother, Janet, & Agnes, from us both. We have lately had a little boy added to our number. I would call him Neil, if it were not such an ugly name, and I should be called Raneeley for ever. They always give the name of the child to the father.[3] You would be called RaJohnee, "Father of John". You must not be affronted if I call him something else.[4] Will Lucifer do, Janet? It means Son of the Morning, or Producer of Light.

We are happy to say that through the kindness of our Heavenly Protector our garden yielded abundantly, so we will not feel the want of the bill so much. We sowed $5\frac{1}{2}$ buckets wheat and got 168 in return. Formerly we got all from Kuruman, 8 buckets for 18 shillings, but now we have abundance. May the Lord make us grateful. I made a cattle pen & shifted it over the whole so as to manure it like the antient Highlanders, so it yielded abundantly. Your turnips, parsley and Indian cress, wallflower, all vegetated. None of the others came up. We thank you for them. I have applied to Mr Whish[5] for some.

I think I gave you information in my last concerning Sechele. He seems a much more likely subject than Mosilele. My heart yearns over them both. I have lately been much at Mabotsa in consequence of my dear partner's circumstances. I preach again and again in the plainest language, entreating them by every mode of putting it I can think of

---

[3] See above, 23.4.

[4] The boy was in fact named Robert Moffat, after his maternal grandfather.

[5] Charles Whish, of 144 New City Road, Glasgow. In Slater's *Directory of Scotland*, 1852, p. 662, he is listed as having a millinery warehouse at 103 St Vincent Street.

to believe on Jesus. But O, they seem dry bones indeed. They rise up & go away, and seem not the least impressed with all I can say. I seem to pray for them too little. How the Jesuits prayed, and what missionaries they were! I am not a missionary compared to them.

I go off to Chonuane next week[6] in order to finish the roof of our new house. Most of the climbing is done by me; the Natives literally tremble when they get up to the top of a wall. A tall gaunt fellow helped me much by climbing with me. His name implies the idea of a regular scold.[7] He was employed to collect the people for service once. Up he jumped on a sort of platform and shouted out at the top of his voice, "Knock that woman down over there, strike her, she is putting on her pot.[8] Do you see that one hiding herself? Give her a good blow; there she is, see, see, knock her down." All the women ran to the place of meeting in no time, for each thought herself meant. But although a most efficient bellman we did not like to employ him.

A short time ago a village about 14 miles off[9] was attacked by a party of Korrannas from the Vaal River, and besides a few people killed all the go[ats][10] cattle &c of the survivors were swept off. When [the] marauders arrived at their residence,[11] Mosheu, of whom you may have read in Mr Moffat's work,[12] ordered them to restore the whole. As he is a man of authority among them, they had to deliver up all, and Mosheu calling on the proper owners gave them all the spoil. The marauders got the trouble of committing

---

[6] Since the letter is unmistakably headed "Chonuane", this suggests that D. L. wrote part of it while visiting Mabotsa, where his wife had remained for her confinement.

[7] This identifies him as the man whose name is given below (Letter 40) as "Khalimele". The Tswana verb *kgaleméla* means "to rebuke, reprove, scold".

[8] Tswana women carry on their heads such burdens as pots and baskets, whether empty or full.

[9] "A village about 12 or 14 miles from Mabotsa" (18.i.1846 Mrs M'Robert). Its inhabitants were BaHurutshe.

[10] Small tear in paper at seal.

[11] "When the marauders reached their residence next to that of Mosheu, their horses & selves being all tired by the long journey (nearly 200 miles) . . ." (18.i.1846 Mrs M'Robert).

[12] Mosheu (more correctly Massau or "Massouw"), mentioned in Moffat's *Missionary Labours*, pp. 592–605 *passim*, was chief of the Taaibosch tribe of Korana, then living at Mamusa (Schweizer Reneke). He was a convert to Christianity.

wickedness as their only reward. Sekhomi, chief of the Bamangwato, is a contrast to him. Last year[13] a party of Matibele came to him, being sent by Mosilikatze to ask tribute. Sekhomi allowed them to depart and then, having an ambush before them, came upon them from behind & cut every one of the 23 men off. Not one escaped to tell the tale. A party of Matibele of another tribe came afterwards and asked permission to live under Sekhomi. But being dissatisfied with his government they began to flee from it to that of Shue, chief of the Bakaa.[14] Sk. in order to prevent this put every one to death a week or two ago. When will he feel the influence of the gospel? I reproved him once for killing his brother. He said, "But he killed me first";[15] and then afterwards he asked me if it was true that I said our forefathers were still in being, and when I replied, "Yes, and you will see your brother", he said, Maka hela, lies only.

Is Charles an A.M. or a dunce? I should like to hear whether he is able to give any more satisfaction than a temperance lecture implies. If I knew his sentiments I might recommend him to our Directors for China, where I long wished to go. But his not writing is a great drawback. The Board would deem a communication from me more satisfactory than any he could have from America except a diploma for A.M., and should he come to Scotland or England with a desire to devote himself to missionary work, without any gaurantee like what I could supply them in an account of his efforts &c, he would labour under a great disadvantage. He would be put through the same course as I was. Mr McKellar[16] did. He would be obliged to spend a considerable time in order that they might gain a know-

[13] In 1844, not 1845 (cf. Letter 20).

[14] Suwe ruled the BaKaa c. 1835–54. They were then living in the Shoshong Hills about 20 miles east of the BaNgwato.

[15] "When I reproved Sekhomi for having murdered his brother, he replied, 'but he killed me first', referring to the fact of his brother having broken allegiance" (18.i.1846 Mrs M'Robert). Sekgoma's half-brothers Phethu and Bathoeng had seceded from him, intending to establish a tribe of their own; he pursued and killed them, and brought their followers back under his rule (Schapera, *Ditirafalô*, p. 78).

[16] Alexander McKellar (1811–45), who, after studying at Ongar, went to the West Indies as a missionary at the end of 1842 (*Register*, p. 56). On 5.xi.1847 D. L.'s father, writing to Henry Drummond, referred to McKellar as "our late excellent friend".

ledge of his character and abilities. If recommended by Mr Kirk it would be a hindrance giving rise to suspicion of heresy in him,[17] and he might be more heretical than Mr Kirk without inconvenience if no suspicion were excited. Altogether it is a pity he does not write, for if he really wishes to be a missionary I could be of some use to him. Does he speak of China? Would he go there? Ask him.

[*No signature*]

31: To ROBERT MOFFAT
11 February 1846

[Bruce Collection; extract in Gelfand, *Livingstone*, pp. 40 f.]

Chonuane
11 Feby 1846

My dear Father,

We were very sorry to hear of the toss your system re-cieved from the mill.[1] The pain must have been intense, for an extensive laceration is of all others the most irritating. Mr Ashton seems to have done his duty in the surgical line. The only difference I should have suggested in the treatment might not have pleased you, as it would have been a sim-plification,[2] and might have appeared as doing less than duty.

[17] In 1842 Kirk had published a series of addresses entitled *The Way of Life made plain*, in which he maintained that "not only did Jesus die for every man, but that God's Spirit strives with every man, and that they who yield are the saved, and that they who resist are the unsaved". "The promulgation of the 'new views', as they were called, concerning the universality of the Spirit's work called forth much opposition on the part of Congregationalists, and many pamphlets and tracts were written at the time in condemnation of the doctrines taught by Mr. Kirk and others" (Ross, *Congregational Independency in Scotland*, p. 127).

[1] Moffat "had just set up a new corn-mill, and whilst seeing to its being properly started unwarily stretched his arm over two cog-wheels. In a moment the shirt-sleeve, and with it the arm, was drawn in. Happily the mill was stopped in time, but an immense gaping wound, six inches in length, with torn edges, was the result; and for many weeks the strong man was laid aside" (J. S. Moffat, *Lives*, p. 253). Gelfand, apparently misled by the absence of an address and by the salutation, says that the letter was written to D. L.'s father, "criticizing the treatment accorded the latter in Scotland when his hand was injured in the mill" (*Livingstone the Doctor*, p. 40).

[2] "the only difference I shall have suggested in the treatment which might not have pleased you is [*sic*] it would have been a simplification . . ." (Gelfand).

You ought to have had a strong opiate as soon as possible, in order to allay or prevent[3] the effects of the shock on the system, morphia perhaps repeated for a day or two and afterwards if pain prevented sleep, the wound dressed with lint dipped in water after the bleeding ceased or suppuration fairly begun. Till then nothing but dry lint is necessary. If there is too much inflammation set up in the wound and it looks red & angry (like Mrs R[oss]), warm water frequently poured over the lint and evaporation prevented by the whole being covered over with oil silk or oil cloth and a little cooling medicine will soon relieve it, and is far better than poultices. The wound should never be washed. Pus is the best salve. In dressing, the skin around alone needs cleaning; the sponge ought not to touch the red flesh.[4] If the new parts springing up rise above the surrounding skin, or are too large & flabby, a little of what salves are usually composed (zinc alum, lunar caustic, &c) may be dissolved in the water and applied. Nature does all. The water dressing is now used more than any other where people are willing to pay without a farrago of doctoring, and is asserted by those who have the best means of judging as better than any other. Hope you will never need to apply it on your own person.

Shall not be surprised if you feel numbness &c in your little & next finger for some time to come. It was a mercy the arm was not lost. You will be obliged to spend your time in better work than roofing & other manual labours, the which although all very necessary are not to be compared to the effects of translations,[5] for these will be known when our stations [are] swept away & we all dead & rotten. I am glad to think as it is the left arm you may be just as useful as ever.

I have got up the roof, and Mebala is now at the third row in thatching. I felt very nervous in roofing this time, in consequence of a piece of lath breaking & setting me a-swinging in the air like a pendulum. All my operations aloft were conducted after that in the crawling order and in perpetual fear of coming down by the run. The walls in con-

[3] "in order to allay shock or prevent . . ." (Gelfand).
[4] "ought not to touch on the flesh" (Gelfand).
[5] Moffat was then busy on his translation of the Old Testament into SeTswana.

sequence of long detention at Mabotsa were sadly dilapi-
dated on my return, and had we enjoyed the usual supply of
rain we should have found them prostrate. Is it the prince
of the power of the air[6] who arranges drought at Chonuane
this year as was last season at Mabotsa? If he has the power,
I suppose we may say he has the will, & no mistake. The
corn is short, burned, & shooting into ear at about 2 feet
from the ground, and I suppose many think we are the cause.

We have so many clouds around us I believe we are to be
favoured with success soon, and I feel the more inclined to
stick to and persevere in the great work. I would not go
back to live at Mabotsa with Mr E. for the good word
of seven or even seventeen ladies, for though I liked & do
still love the Bakhatla the prospects are so much more
encouraging here there is no comparison. This although in
addition [to] contentions between the tribes, Edwards's dirt,
&c, I have got the Boers about my ears. I send a note we got
last week,[7] almost if I understand it right prohibiting farther
operations without their sanction. As they seem to know
perfectly of this station, and are only five days distant, we
thought it would be imprudent to take no notice of their
mandate; so I answered shortly in English by informing
them of my object, an object which they as professing
Christians approve (?) and which they, I hoped, would
endeavour to promote. To this I added I was a Scotchman
& M.D., and without promising any obedience to their
order I hoped to visit them at some future time and might
be of some service to the afflicted. We thought civility the
best mode of dealing in the affair.

A chief named Mokhatla[8] lives in their direction, and
although he would be glad of Paul to come and live with

---

[6] A favourite expression of D. L.'s for Satan.

[7] The note does not seem to have been preserved, but on 17.iii.1847 D. L. wrote
to Tidman: "While still engaged in the erection of our dwelling at Chonuane, we
recieved notes from the Commandant & Council of these emigrants [the Boers],
requesting an explanation of our intentions &c, as also an intimation that they had
resolved to come and deprive Sechele of his firearms."

[8] Mokgatle, chief (c. 1835–89) of the BaFokeng, an Eastern Tswana tribe living
"about four days Eastward" of Chonwane (17.iii.1847 Tidman), close to the
present town of Rustenburg in the Western Transvaal; not to be confused with the
Hurutshe regent Mokgatlha (24.10). D. L. (lit. cit.) mistakenly called him "chief
of a large section of the Bakhatla".

him he says the Boers would not allow it. As it seems a favourable opening, he being a sensible agreable man, perhaps some friendly intercourse with the Boers may smooth the path for Paul. They will be sure to visit us, as they come to the Marikoe[9] to hunt every winter for sea kows.[10] They may come sooner, but we feel at perfect ease whether they come or not. I should not like them to come in my absence. If here I have no apprehensions of any unpleasantness, but don't know what they might do if they found the house standing unoccupied.

Mamary mentions Mrs Lemue's fears about Saul[11] coming here. He will not be so well as he is at Motito, and those who invited him must have told him so. Mebala has far fewer cattle now than he had on leaving Kuruman. Every one of his goats and sheep died. The ground he could irrigate is about 100 yds in length, and in my garden, which is situated in every respect as his is, if drought continues a week, although I turn the whole of the water in, a piece of ground four yards in breadth & one hundred paces in length will not be irrigated in half a day. Saul knows all, both losses in cattle at Mabotsa and that Chonuane is worse than Mabotsa, so if he comes it must be for other reasons than those Mrs L. might ascribe. And, indeed, ascribe what she likes her words are wind to me. When Saul came to nurse Mebala after the bite of the lion, he said to me, "Marry, & I shall come & live with you". To this I only replied by the joke of offering to employ him to go & seek a wife for me, as I had then no time myself. I should be sorry to invite him as a member of another Society, and equally so to say a word against him coming.

I put Mrs L. in nearly the same category with Mrs Ross. She must side with Mrs E[dwards], or woe betide her. It is not now convenient to indulge in the style of invective against your egotism & ingratitude for the immense assistance Mr Lemue afforded you in criticism[12] (of which criti-

[9] The Marico (Madikwe) River, about 30 miles east of Chonwane.

[10] Afrikaans *seekoei* ("sea-cow"), hippopotamus.

[11] A Native convert from Kuruman who was employed as an assistant by the French missionaries at Motito (Moffat, *Matabele Journals*, vol. i, p. 41).

[12] Lemue was also engaged in Biblical translation, and had presumably been invited to comment on Moffat's draft.

cism, by the bye, they confessed you had not availed yourself
in actual printing), and which was the burden of their song
on every occasion your speeches or letters came. Mrs L.
knows Mrs E. would make disclosures if she did not keep
friendly. Having heard so much of your egotism before I
ever saw you in this country, I remember having considerable dislike to you, and as your faults were always mentioned in the deploring crocodile strain I thought the men
really mourning & praying over your frailties. As however
I am now favoured with the same lugubrious prayers and
dolorous wailings, I know their value & wonder at my own
utter ignorance of mankind.

As for Mr & Mrs Ross, I feel strongly inclined to expose
their conduct towards me. I believed he treated me most
ungentlemanly in the way, and when I looked back after our
arrival at Kuruman I felt humbled that I had not been more
patient of insult &c than I had been. I thought I should
have borne more, and have uniformly taken the blame in
part upon myself. After accusing me of an intention "to
impose on his wife", calling me "a liar" when I denied it, &
repeating the insult in several ways, I could *not* esteem him.
My heart burned with indignation, for I was conscious of
just as little inclination towards his wife as I now have
towards my grandmother's cat.[13] Yet I felt distressed that
being a missionary I had these feelings. Many a sleepless
night I spent & wished I were not a missionary. Well, when
I came to Kuruman I tried to subdue my feelings, & never
mentioned anything to any one. Mrs Edwards has repeatedly told that Mrs Ross did not allow three days to pass
over before she began and made statements respecting me
which, to use Mrs E.'s own words, "made us afraid of you".
And that I never said one word about the Rosses for more

[13] During the voyage from England, the Rosses both "suffered much from sea-
sickness. Being entirely free from it, I was enabled to attend to them, and did a good
deal to make them comfortable. I suppose I did pay more attention to her than to
him, but in the simplicity of my heart I never dreamed that this could be a possibility of offence. Imagine, if you can, my surprise when, some time after that, I was
charged by him in a great rage with a design to impose on his wife, for I spoke to
her and paid more attention to her than to him . . . He afterwards explained that he
meant impose by making her work for me. This when he knew I would not permit
her even to spread down my bed (although she kindly offered to do it)" (13.v.1841
Cecil).

than three months. Why did I then begin? Because Mr & Mrs E. then began to tell me all they had heard from the Rosses about me. Their statements being gross misrepresentations, I was compelled to tell my way of viewing the subject. The Rosses went on month after month retailing scandal against me, & that was just as regularly re-retailed to me at table untill I was sick of it. I would have spoken to the Rosses about it, but was so disgusted with them I could not. This continuous scandalizing, which I bore as a nail in my shoe for two years, determined on no account to quarrel again, I called to my friends, and to Inglis amongst the number, most abominable mule-headed wickedness; and I shall repeat it as long as I live if Ross does not acknowledge it.

As a specimen of the details with which I was furnished, her first child was on the point of strangulation in birth, as Rachel did not know how to deliver the head.[14] I assisted the child immediately by doing what you know. But as it is very simple I never thought of mentioning it, untill told by Mrs E. that Mrs R. told both Mrs Helmore & Lemue that I had done nothing at all but pretend that the child was in danger, in order to take credit to myself. I was also told that Mr Ross said that when previously consulted by Mrs R. (having explained the nature of the pains) I had tried to make her afraid, and other things of a like nature.

Now in reference to this I have felt if they did not choose to feel gratitude, & Ross never once thanked me, they need not have told a lie in order to detract from my character. I never boasted of what I had done. Why shew hatred towards me? Why pursue me with such inveterate enmity, when during my whole intercourse with them after coming to Kuruman I never said an uncivil word or did one uncivil thing? Why begin detraction and lie to Mary Moffat about me as soon as she came to Kuruman? If I did not feel that I should degrade myself by giving her[15] an opportunity of familiar intercourse, I should speak to her frankly. But after being told by Mr R. that he looked to me "with infinite

[14] Cf. Letter 6. Rachel was a Cape Coloured woman, the wife of a runaway slave named Arend; they were both among Moffat's earliest converts at Kuruman (cf. *Missionary Labours*, pp. 497, 499; J. S. Moffat, *Lives*, p. 158).

[15] Mrs Ross.

168

contempt"—"Never mind", said he to Mrs R., "we are far above him"—I never come near them but feel I have no more esteem for them than I have for Punch the London Charivari. I give these few particulars that you may know whether I have had reason to speak against them. I have spoken against them, and can repeat every word again. I should like to bring a few things like the above to their remembrance, and if I met him should probably do so.

We thank you heartily for the bellows & beads. I was getting quite low spirited & gloomy, but their[16] arrival put fresh steam into our boilers. I was foolishly beginning to feel as if we were forgotten, pictured Hume as not come, you as no longer wishing to be bothered perpetually sending, my walls lying like droppings from a cow's tail. Perhaps you see it in my late letters, for I cannot write cheerfully if dull within. I hasten now with inside walls. Perhaps we may finish one room in order to remove speedily. Glad to hear of coffee seed, & will be thankful for a little, also rhubarb.

I see Dr Wallich[17] mentions my answer to his. Did you write by the box? I have not written again, and the lot sent was but a poor assortment. I expected you to tell this, but suppose you were busy. Ought we not in sending off another to beg some Indian fruits?

I expect the Committee will decide that Mr E. furnish me with something like what most of them know to have been his charges against me. I have no doubt but he has written to the Directors long ago.[18] "Minds of own" are so "honest", breaches of honour make scratches no deeper than cobwebs on long noses. The letters sent by the Bakwains to the Bahurutse were delivered into Mr Inglis's hands. We spoke in them of Mr Murray & Oswal's opinion of Edwards, given unsolicited by us, "the coarsest, most uncouth man

16 MS. has "these".

17 Nathaniel Wallich (1786–1854), botanist, superintendent of Calcutta botanic gardens 1815–50 (D.N.B.). "I have lately had a channel opened up for my transmitting parcels to the Cape. Dr Wallich, the East Indian Company's superintendant of Botanical Gardens at Calcutta, authorizes me to put any expenses I choose to his charge. This, for sending him the edible roots & fruits of the poor Bakalihari of the desert" (28.i.1845 Pyne).

18 D. L. was mistaken; cf. 24.7. It was not until 20.ix.1846 that Edwards wrote to the Directors, emphasizing his own contribution towards the foundation of the mission at Mabotsa, but making no direct charge of any kind against D. L.

they ever saw", "he will never make conversions", &c. I send a note by these open, requesting Mr Inglis on the back of it the name of the person to whom he sent. The present messengers will take on the note to you. If he refuses to write we shall have a guess.

Sechele was very much pleased with your message, but complains that he is plagued by Khake's people robbing his Bakalihari as the[y] come to him with skins. If another people he would bear all, but they are his own subjects, and he thinks he ought to remove them from that part of the country. He says he will do so, but will tell me before he does it. He sends a karros to Mamary, partly as an acknowledgement for the little red cap sent, and partly to buy clothing. Shirts & handkerchiefs would be very acceptable to him. She will know the value to be sent. He dresses in haartebeest skin on weekdays and in a red coat on Sundays. Can spell all through the spelling book fluently and reads with a little help. He lost his spelling book when out hunting during our absence, the second, which rather retarded him, for he had to revert to the first. He is greatly in love with your rifles, and wishes to know if he could buy one with either ivory or karrosses, and requests me to ask if you. . . .

[Rest of letter missing]

32: To ROBERT MOFFAT

11 March 1846

Address: Revd. R. Moffat, Kuruman. No. 2. [Bruce Collection.]

Chonuane
11 March /46

My dear Father,

Having written so fully by Boy I have nothing more to trouble you with now that it is appointed for Hendrick[1] to accompany him. Paul expected the conveyance of my waggon for Isaac, but the intention of sending it having been

[1] Son of the Native evangelist Paul. "Boy" is presumably the man previously called "Boe" (24.8).

relinquished he now sends his own. They have some hanker-
ings after Francina,[2] but having dissuaded the father from
sending for her I hope he will refrain.

The house has at length got a coat of clay on its top. This
was accomplished today. The kitchen and bedroom with the
vorhuis[3] are finished. Two inside walls alone remain to be
raised a few feet. We go to Mabotsa on Friday (this is
Wednesday evening) to remove our duds &c. The white
ants are already in possession here, a theme on which to try
our inventive powers for extermination.

Mr Cumming left a good deal of powder under my care,
with liberty to assist any of the people with it for karosses
whom I thought fit. Fortunately my engagements prevented
my using that power, with one exception. Sechele is now
apprehensive of an attack, and looked very queer when told
that I should place Mr Cumming's powder back again into
the hands of its owner, and never mend a gun, while there
was any probability of its being used in shedding blood.
Strange to say he goes on reading and listens to preaching
with as much attention as ever. He quotes Mahura's advice
in justification of his late deed,[4] & declares he will stand
everything but a direct attack on his town if from a nation
not his subjects. Says his reason for not telling me was, I
would have gone before or with them and spoiled all, for
they persevere in plaguing him, because they know he has a
teacher to hinder him from attacking them. The fellow does
not want arguments. He would beat many who look with
contempt on savages as void of sophistry. "Unsophisticated
children of nature", say they. A funny mother and stranger
children verily. Had Mr Ross been the first who got Mahura
to consent to hear the gospel he would not have found it so
easy as entering on other men's labours. Had I been to the
Committee meeting I suspect this pill might have been given

[2] Daughter of Paul; she is referred to more fully at the end of the letter.

[3] Afrikaans *voorhuis*, front room, hall, dining-room.

[4] Sechele had very recently raided Kgakgê's village. "Keeping the object of his
expedition a profound secret from us, [he] attacked & killed about a dozen of what
were the people of Bube. The remainder fled to Mabotsa" (28.v.1846 Pyne). The
incident is described more fully by D. L. in a letter to Tidman, 10.iv.1846 (published
in part in the *LMS Chronicle*, vol. 11, 1847, p. 26, and by Chamberlin, pp. 87–90);
cf. also *Travels*, p. 35.

to the translator of "The Flower Gathered".[5] This last was denounced by Edwards in no measured terms at the time.

Did a building line find its way out among the sticks of the tent? This brings to my recollection the other tent. Paul brought it and said it was to be left with us, we supposed till an opportunity of returning it occurred. A short time afterwards he required it again as a shelter for his family till their house was finished. Knowing you would have no objection to this I let him have it, and he has used it ever since. I have just been out to enquire if he could not send it with Hendrick, but he says he does not understand how it is, whether he is to buy it or give it to me to be sent back. I think it better to let it remain till you inform him. He seems to like it.

I am very glad of the "Lancets",[6] & thank you heartily for ordering them. I shall pay $\frac{2}{3}^{ds}$ price or the whole if you allow me to keep them. Hope this is not covetousness.

I am very thankful for the promise of old iron. My smithifying has been at a stand for some time, partly because of the house & partly because I was afraid of running through my stock. I often thrashed at it till I was fairly done up. You did not tell me how to temper cold chisels. I shall need mine tempered soon, for I must cut through a band of one fore wheel. A piece of diseased wood as large as that you cured exists which I must rectify. *Please remember the tempering in your next.*

The Captain at Philipolis[7] sent a note informing me of an addition to my stud in the shape of a filley, and asking if I wished means to be used for what George Buchanan calls in

<hr/>

[5] "I have translated into Sichuana, a part of the 'Flower Gathered, or History of Henry Packman Smith' [published by the Religious Tract Society in 1840], and read it to the young people on the station: they received it with very great interest, as being the first tract particularly directed to the young. The remaining part I intend as soon as possible to translate and publish" (Ross to Tidman, 20.i.1842, in *LMS Chronicle*, vol. 6, 1842, p. 170). The "meeting" referred to was the third of the District Committee, held at Taung on 9 March 1846.

[6] The well-known medical periodical (described at that time in its sub-title as "a journal of British and Foreign Medical and chemical science, criticism, literature and news"); published weekly in London since 1823.

[7] Adam Kok III (1811–75), chief since 1837; in 1862 he and his people migrated to the region now known as Griqualand East, whose capital, Kokstad, is named after him.

the Psalms[8] "another of the same". I had not time nor Dutch enough to tell him that the proposition was agreable. If you send for your horses, will you be kind enough to thank the Captain for me & request him to do the proper sort of thing? If not convenient, never mind. My not sending for the animal will be understood as wishing it to remain.

A horse of Mr Oswal strayed, and he having given it to me provided it was not found till after Mr Cumming had passed, I find it has been found by the Barolongs of Taoane.[9] Mahura laid a claim to it, but the saddle was too good for them to believe it his. I have apprised Taoane of its being my property, but have seen no one from his place since. I don't know how to come by it, but as it was the best Mr O. had, if there were any way of communication I would make an effort. Is there any intercourse between Kuruman & Taoane? [10]

We each enjoy by the kind favour of our Heavenly Father a fair measure of health & strength. Mary sends her love to Mother, sisters, John,[11] Mr Hamilton, & yourself.

Paul has just now entered to inform me that he had spoken to his wife on the subject of today's conversation concerning Francina. He mentioned the reasons we have against her coming. But these the mother overules by saying the people here will not take her unless she is boyalified.[12] Paul believes this, and wishes me to inform Mr Ashton that should she be exceedingly a[n]xious to come, so anxious as that in the event of becoming ill the disease might be aggravated, he might let her go in peace. Hendrick is instructed to say nothing about it to her. We hope she will be induced to stop where she is. We don't concieve the

[8] George Buchanan (1506–82) was author of *Paraphrasis Psalmorum Davidis Poetica* (1590), of which a translation into English verse by J. Eadie was published in 1836.

[9] Tawana, chief (1815–49) of the BaRolong-booraTshidi, a Tswana tribe then living in the vicinity of Lotlhakane (Rietfontein), 12 miles south of the modern town of Mafeking.

[10] In the margin Moffat wrote in pencil, "None".

[11] John Smith Moffat (1835–1918), who was then living at Kuruman with his parents, as were his sisters Ann and Elizabeth Lees (1839–1919, married Roger Price 1861).

[12] *Bojale*-fied, i.e. initiated into womanhood by going through the *bojale* ceremonies (4.11).

Bakwains such sticklers for boyalism. I should have given Paul's message to Mr A. if time permitted. He is to be judge whether it will be against Francina's future fatness to see Hendrick coming away alone without her.

[No signature]

33: To ROBERT MOFFAT

1 July 1846

Address: No. 2. The Revd. R. Moffat D.D. & L.L.D., of Maddison University, Alleghanie Mountains, via Kuruman.[1] [Bruce Collection.]

Chonuane
1st July 1846

My dear Father,

Having been disappointed in the time the people should leave, I have time to add a few remarks to my already lengthy epistles.

The most prominent topic on my mind is an attack of Mr Edwards. He, poor fellow, thinks that I have wickedly & wantonly attacked him. He does not know that I would just as soon have tried to perform the trick of St Dunstan[2] as do any such thing. In August of /45 he told me, when I requested my account from him, that he had sent Rogers[3] with it. But it never having come he said he thought it amounted to about £30, exclusive of the food of some Bakhatla (once a day a meal of Native corn). As he thought this might amount to about £5, I gave a bill of £35 & thought it was all over.

A short time ago he sent an account made up to £45. 15. 0. As I had not recieved the former I could not compare it. But as there were a bill of £2. 5. 6, of which I

---

[1] I do not know what occasioned this facetious address. Moffat was made an honorary D.D. of Edinburgh University in 1872, but received no other academic distinctions. D. L. endorsed the letter: "Main [contents]: Fine powder, geological specimens, a sight of your diploma".

[2] Possibly a reference to the legend "that on one occasion at Glastonbury (his birthplace)", St Dunstan (*c*. 909–88) "seized the devil by the nose with a pair of red-hot tongs and refused to release him till he promised never to tempt him again" (*Brewer's Dictionary of Phrase & Fable*, revised ed. 1952, p. 313).

[3] Edwards's son and namesake.

had his own reciept as having been paid to him once, and
two months' boarding which for both himself & me were
charged to the Society, I thought it right to ask some questions before giving away an additional £10. The two months'
boarding he stated positively to me he had charged to the
Society on two occasions. I requested to know on what
principle payment was demanded twice.

He once pressed 20 lbs of very bad beads on my acceptance & said, "O, you will give me an equal number when
our box comes". The box was weighed at Kuruman & a
note taken of the weight on the spot, 200 lbs & upwards.
The beads were divided, & a note of the division put with
my half into the box. This note shewed 88¾ as my half of
200 lbs. I imagined the 11¼ lbs of difference had been taken
for the 20 lbs of very inferior beads, & was satisfied. But
finding the 20 lbs charged in this account, as I had furnished
the half of the money I requested a sight of the invoice.

A tar bucket was presented to me by Mr E. The ear of it
was patched so poorly by himself, before one journey was
over it broke off. As it seemed an old one, & a new one I
had formerly got from him was only charged 4/6, I
demurred to paying 9/- now for what I concieved an old one.
I did not know that teak never became old. As he was putting down his gifts as debts, I thought I might as well
remind him of 10 lbs of tea which Mrs E. distinctly borrowed from me. A cap which cost me 9/- was put down as
7/6. An American axe he borrowed & never returned I put
down cost price, & then requested the production of the bill
mentioned in another sheet.

I recieved the enclosed meek communication lately, &
returned the answer I likewise send for your perusal.[4] I am
quite positive as to the Society being charged for every iota
of the expenses, but as it (statement) was made on his own
authority, on the same authority I have to retract it & beg
his pardon, the which I do very willingly, as you will see.
Look at the last page, & you will wonder still more at my
folly in being decieved by such a character. Ross's conduct
was so galling to me that I was glad to have any one to sympathize with me, & I allowed them to go on in their slanders

[4] These letters have not been preserved with the present one.

continuously because of the conviction on my mind that in reference to speaking against Ross I had been just as bad as themselves.

You will wonder that I grudge 6d. a day for my board. 3d. would more than pay all I ate, & my bed at Mabotsa was made just once in three weeks or once a month. Did you ever hear me complain of being ill nursed in my lion sickness? No. Mrs E. scarcely ever looked near me after the first few days, & to get my arm dressed even when crawling with maggots I had to send for Mr E. Occasionally he came of his own accord, but even when almost dead I would infinitely have preferred Bakhatla to dress it for me. It was evidently a grudge to him, & how could it be otherwise? He & she too were writing against me at the very time. Obligation on my part there is none, unless in addition to neglect I ought to feel grateful for Native corn & English corn boiled in milk. My stomach was well nigh ruined for ever. It is but very recently that I got over the bad effects of their eternal boiled corn. Corn boiled, boiled corn, like shovels full of the everlasting pills of the Antients might have ruined the stomachs of ostriches. O it is a blessing to be allowed to eat as one likes. I can never cease admiring the freedom. I was far too polite in most things. I would not do anything to give offence and, as I tell them, I believe my guilt in silent listening to their scandals is now justly punished in what they endeavour to fix on my character. If he troubles us more we shall send his epistles back unopened. If he has never been slandered, how very gratuitously wicked his & her slanders must have been.

We have put up the mill. It does well, but it is rather inferior to Hume's common mill; the latter grinds finer & makes much less bran. So we should be glad of the large one when you have an opportunity to send it. The trouble of sifting continually would be obviated. If we had the large mill for wheat we should try & make this the maize mill, if that can be done. Some small bits of wood came out of it when we tried it first, so I took [it] down to see from whence they proceeded. I was sorry afterwards, for Sechele was my assistant, and turning it generally the backward way he & I bothered with it the whole day and failed after all. But I got a thorough knowledge of it by the labour, & as soon as I came out of the room next morning succeeded.

A Family Scene in Private

We had a practical exposition of your Phantasmagoria scene lately. Mary has taken up the profession of Surgeon Dentist. I was the subject operated on. The twin of that you extracted became very bad one night, so up we got to it. I scarified & fixed on the tooth key, & then the new surgeon dentist gave a wrench, & I pulled her hand away in agony. It had come out a little way. I pulled & pulled with a pair of shoemaker's nippers, but every pull was like a haul at my entrails. On went the key again. Another wrench, & I roared out "murder". It came a little farther, but was still sticking doggedly. Another trial of the nippers, forceps, &c, and then another effort with the key, completed the first attempt at dentistry. We were a pretty sight in our ghostly dresses, I on the floor & Mary standing over me. It was dreadful. "Teeth drawn at Chonuane 1/- each." Mouth rinsed out afterwards with dirty water *gratis*.

31st July. The men whom I engaged to go out for their hiefers being at a distance were sent for, but a week or two having passed ere they arrived, as we were under the impression that Mr & Mrs A[shton] would [come] we delayed, thinking that the Bakua[i]ns would pass them on the road. I then went over to the Boers & tribes in that direction,[5] & returning yesterday found that Mr Jeffries[6] would pass by Kuruman. If three or four hiefers can be got they will be very acceptable indeed.

Will you remember to send some of my fine powder by some safe opportunity? It is, I believe, among some clothes. Will you lend me your box of stones from one opportunity

[5] This journey, made together with Paul, had two objects: (a) to persuade the Boers to abandon their threat of coming to disarm Sechele (31.7), to which they agreed; and (b) to explore the possibility of stationing Paul with Mokgatlê (17.iii.1847 Tidman).

[6] Gad Jeffries, a farmer living at Kalkfontein, Middleveld (Orange Free State), who often went on hunting and trading expeditions into the Interior (Leyland, *Adventures in the Far Interior*, p. 42; *S.A. Archival Records: Orange Free State No. 1*, pp. 279 ff.).

to another? I mean those you recieved from Dr Young.[7] I shall take great care of them.

[*No signature*]

34: To ROBERT MOFFAT
8 September 1846

[Bruce Collection.]

Chonuane
8 Sept. 1846

My dear Father,

As we are in daily expectation of the arrival of your better half,[1] we feel as if the worse did not deserve a letter. This is plain enough, is it not? It is perhaps rather a sort of nervousness, produced by stretching our necks frequently to see if the waggon is in sight, that quite indisposes us to write. We wish heartily she would come & relieve our suspense. Maybe after all she is snugly at supper, giving the meat two taps with her knife before she cuts it, by way of alaga-ing[2] it to make it more digestible.

A report furnished by Mr Lauga respecting the party of Mr Arkwright & Christie[3] made us think a little. We saw nothing improper in their conduct while proceeding Northward, and now that Mr A. returns we have neither seen nor heard anything which induces us to believe Mr L.'s report as having originated in him. Mr A. has been here three days & neither he nor his people have shewn any disposition

[7] Possibly George Young (1777–1848), of Whitby, "theologian, topographer, and geologist" (*D.N.B.*), though I have not found any record of Moffat's meeting him.

[1] Mrs Moffat, accompanied by her three younger children and escorted by "Boey [Boe, 24.8] and his friends", reached Chonwane on 10 September. Her journey, prompted by anxiety "about a daughter now enduring sickness and hardship in a new mission", is described briefly in J. S. Moffat, *Lives*, pp. 254–7.

[2] Tswana *alafa*, "to doctor, charm, heal".

[3] "A Mr Arkwright, descended from him who invented the spinning jenny, has passed us on his way Northward after game" (28.v.1846 Pyne). Robert Arkwright, 1st Dragoon Guards, and Lieut. James Christie, 91st Regiment, had left the Cape Colony in February "on a long expedition into the interior", and were back in Grahamstown in October (A. Gordon-Brown, ed., *The Narrative of Private Buck Adams . . . 1843–1848*, Cape Town, 1941, pp. 271–2).

towards illicit intercourse. He is the son of a clergyman, &
if there is truth in what Mr L. mentioned it must have been
perpetrated by Christie & not by Arkwright. The latter I
believe abstains from travelling on Sunday in accordance
with a request of Mr Ashton, and if he has so much respect
for a missionary as to accede in one particular he surely
would not be guilty [of] attempting to take a prostitute into
his company, a deed he knows would soon be published over
the whole country. We have found him agreable & kind, &
he has during his whole sojourn here behaved like a gentleman. I say thus much because I feel it would be unfair to
condemn any one unless the evidence is pretty strong &
decided. Both Mr A. & Ch. have English servants who have
been soldiers. They may have given occasion to the report
above referred to.

We go on much as usual. Walls of school six feet high.
Measurement 48 by 20. Has no wing. Hope to finish it this
month. We have much better soil for building where the
school is than we had in this house.

Apie came last week & passed on to the Bamangwato.
All is peace. But we are sorry to hear a report of Cumming
lying ill at the Bakaas. Hope it is not true.[4] Paul was in
jeopardy last week. Two buffaloes attacked a party cutting
reed, & after trying in vain to lift two Bakuenas from the
ground ran off. The men were hurt but will recover. The
guns were at a distance & they had no trees. A Hottentot is
left here with a broken thigh bone. For two things I can feel,
toothache & broken bones.

Mr A. presented me with an excellent gun in its case,[5]
&c. He has shewn great liberality, & is very thankful for
very small favours. Being here to do all the good we can, it
is pleasant to meet here & there with those who feel that we
are of some use. The land is full of Griquas seeking their

[4] While hunting in the North (July 1846), Cumming had a severe attack of
rheumatic fever, which kept him confined to bed for eight days (*A Hunter's Life*,
vol. ii, pp. 91 f.).
[5] In 1850 D. L. gave this gun to the Tawana chief Letsholathêbê, at L. Ngami,
in exchange for a promise of guides to Sebetwane (*Travels*, p. 75). Elsewhere he
described it as "a beautiful gun I recieved as a present from Lieut. Arkwright after
setting his collar bone and also the broken thigh of his servant. It must have cost
him £25" (24.viii.1850 Freeman).

new location, alias filling their bellies with eiland[6] fat. No new information respecting the Boers, except that they are anxious to know where Mosilikatse is in order to attack him. Ordered Sechele to send men to advise Sekhoma to find it out for them. This Sechele does not feel disposed to do.

I send you three full grown fruits of the Mōana kindly brought by Mr Arkwright. Will you when convenient send them & the thama to India?[7] The roots of the thama dry up & will not keep.

Am happy to hear you proceed with the translation. Will you put P.L. above Isaiah, as I.H. above Sehela 49?[8] I always laugh when I think of my hymns, spelled the new way too, sharing the fate of Pharaoh's fat kine.[9] They were devoured by the lean ones, & yet the ill-favoured are the worst in all the land of Egypt still. Something of the sort will happen if yours & his are brought into coaptation. How will the following motion in next Com[mittee] do? "That as certain friends of Mr L[emue], ignorant of the fact that he took no part in the translation of the New Testament, have produced the impression in the country that he has not recieved his full share of the honour belonging thereto, we now avoid the production of a similar impression by referring his translation of Isaiah to the judgement of our esteemed bretheren of the French Society."[10] Translate

[6] D. L. almost invariably uses this spelling for "eland" (*Taurotragus oryx*), the largest species of S. African antelope.

[7] Tswana *moana*, baobab; *thama*, a small shrub having edible beans and root, first described and identified by Burchell as *Bauhinia esculenta* (cf. *Apprenticeship at Kuruman*, ed. Schapera, p. 55). The specimens were sent to Dr Wallich at Calcutta (cf. 31.17).

[8] Tswana *sehela*, hymn. The initials are those of Prosper Lemue (16.2) and Isaac Hughes (1798–1870), one of the LMS missionaries at Griquatown. In 1843 Moffat published in London a booklet of 124 hymns in SeTswana, entitled *Lihela tsa Tihélo ea Morimo* ("Hymns of the service of God"), of which No. 49 (p. 43) has the translator's initials "I. H."

[9] Cf. 8.7. D. L.'s hymns were omitted from the second edition.

[10] Cf. 31.12. At its third meeting (March 1846), the District Committee had passed a resolution pledging itself "to promote . . . in as systematic a way as possible" the translation of the Scriptures, "and earnestly calls upon every member to assist in this work; and would respectfully invite Mr Lemue to cooperate with us in attaining this most desirable object." "That you may have an idea as to whether Mr Lemue's assistance deserves the name, I may mention that while still at Motito he took several portions of the New Testament to the French district committee

Isaiah by all means, & if we have nothing else we can at least compare. I cannot see that you should take any notice of his doings. If his own bretheren won't print it for him, why should we? Will bad translations please us more easily than them?

Is no protest to be entered against the keeping back of the Directors' letter? [11] Was it not concocted thus by E[dwards], R[oss], & I[nglis], the third triumvirate? I feel inclined to abandon the Com[mittee] as a root of rottenness.

We shall write by Vardon[12] & Oswel. They will soon be here. One date tree has come up, & we expect more.

[*No signature*]

35: To ROBERT MOFFAT

5 October 1846

Address: Revd. R. Moffat, Kuruman. Fav[oure]d by W. Oswel, Esqre. [Bruce Collection.]

which he had *re*translated, and when the bretheren referred the subject to Mr Cassilis, as best able to judge whether they ought to be printed, he decided that Mr Moffat's Testament was all that they required" (9.i.1850 Freeman).

[11] At the same meeting, which D. L. did not attend, a resolution was also passed (moved by Inglis and seconded by Helmore), "That a paper from Mr Livingstone having been read, it be rejected as informal and contrary to the Regulations". D. L.'s "paper", appended to the minutes, was as follows: "There are two things which if not improper to ask from the President of the Committee I feel anxious for. The first is, Mr Edwards having deliberately written to the Directors that 'He has reason to believe that I have accused him to the other brethren', let the question be put, whoever heard an accusation from me, and let the answer be put on the minutes. The second is in reference to Mr Edwards having propagated charges against me among the Brethren, and as he refuses to give me anything like these charges, in fairness the *Brethren* ought to furnish them for my use at the next Committee meeting." D. L., apparently on hearing from Moffat what had happened, soon afterwards (10.iv.1846) wrote to Tidman: "But when these requests were attempted to be read by the secretary, Mr Edwards & Inglis uproariously opposed their production. Mr Edwards vociferously declared that he had never written to the Directors the letter to which I have referred."

[12] Captain Frank Vardon, of the 25th Madras Light Infantry, who while hunting along the Marico River in 1846 had joined company with Oswell, then on his second trip into the Interior (*Oswell*, vol. i, pp. 134 ff.). Vardon, like Oswell, became one of D. L.'s close friends.

Chonuane
5 Octr. 1846

My dear Father,

The arrival of Capt[ai]n Vardon & Mr Oswel immediately after the departure of Mamary has prevented my writing by this opportunity. They are now preparing to start. Baba & his party also are making ready for departure.

Mrs M. may have mentioned our desires respecting a waggon of Mr Oswel. We find he is perfectly willing to oblige us in reference to the payment. Mentions ten years as soon enough for the liquidation of debt, and now desires me to write you a line & ask you to inspect the waggon for me. I have no skill in waggons whatever, and he is in the same condition with respect to that kind of knowledge. We wish the matter referred to your judgement. The length of time however given is a consideration which will outweigh any defect in the vehicle. Mr O. asked if it would be necessary to shorten the bands previous to sending it up. Will you give your opinion as to this step? I do not know what ought to be done. As to painting, I think it would be better to get the paint & oil, & we can do the needful here. Mr O. purposed leaving it at about a day & half from Colesberg. I have thought men might be sent down from Kuruman, and if you send a span of oxen, while the expenses of the men will be put to my account, all the goods you may send for or boxes waiting for you at Colesberg will or may be drawn along by your oxen. If you can make any arrangement of this sort, it will oblige us much. If not convenient at present, Mr O. will leave the waggon at the place appointed till some other time. The place appointed is Mr Nelson, Orlogpoort's river, 35 [miles] South of Colesberg.[1]

We have not been able to pay Baba because we have not money sufficient. There are forty-two dollars[2] for the carriage of goods, and some other work additional, about which as we have to count yet I set down as other ten. If you will kindly advance these two sums, it will still farther oblige us.

[1] The Oorlogspoort River, south and east of Colesberg, is a tributary of the Orange, which it joins close to Norvals Pont station. Nelson I have not identified.

[2] The rix-dollar, worth 1s. 6d., had been withdrawn from circulation in the Cape Colony in 1841, but continued for many years afterwards to be used as a form of currency in the Interior, especially among the Boers.

Edwards & I seem in the same predicament for money. Wish somebody would leave me a hundred or two. But nobody thinks enough of me for that. None of my forefathers were worth their breeches, else I might have had something. They wore kilts, poor fellows.

The gentlemen are on the point of inspanning, and as they are waiting here my thoughts have been confused. I shall send macaca[3] by Mr Cumming for enclosure in Mr Whish's box. His address, to be written on the lid (perhaps twined): Charles Whish Esqre, 144 New City Road, Glasgow. If sent Cape ways, care of Jamieson & Co., Cape Town.[4]

We hope to have time to write before Mr C. arrives. Excuse all the blunders in this. All are well. Robert IV[5] improving. Hope Mamary got out safely. Should like much to have a visit from yourself. You might scold me as you like. We could both speak plainly enough if together, & let the righteous smite me &c I should not grumble at any amount of faithful smiting.

Affectionately yours,
[*No signature*]

36: To ROBERT MOFFAT

27 October 1846

[Bruce Collection.]

27 Octr 1846

My dear Father,

As Mr Cumming leaves tomorrow morning I must write you a note. But I have but little inclination to writing at present. Robert has been very ill for three days past of bronchitis, or inflammation of the lining membrane of the air tubes of the lungs. How induced we don't know. A great many Bakuena suffer from colds & dysentery. Perhaps it arises from the intense heat & occasional disposition to

---

[3] *Mochacha*, the Tswana name for *Adenia glauca*, "a woody climber, with tendrils" (Miller, *The Woody Plants of the Bechuanaland Protectorate*, 1952, p. 60). On 9.x.1846 D. L. wrote to Whish that he was sending him a box containing curios, bulbs, and seeds, which had been taken to Kuruman "last month" by Mrs Moffat.

[4] A firm of merchants in Adderley Street, Cape Town.

[5] D. L.'s infant son.

183

showers. The damp air comes from the parts where rain has fallen, & that too often in the evenings. Very pleasant, but pernicious after the hot sunshine. He could scarcely breathe for one day. The mucus collected so abundantly in the air tubes, the sound was like the cooing of wood pigeons in his breast. That has been removed, but no medicine has any effect on the complaint. He has constant heat of skin, loses flesh, & is much troubled with his cough. Remedies which usually produce a speedy change do nothing in his case. The cough gradually sounds worse & worse. I am sorry I cannot speak of the favourable symptoms. I can only hope they will soon appear. His cheerfulness is quite gone.

Mr Cumming has kindly favoured us with an adze, so there is no need for that which went to Kuruman. We hope Mamary & party arrived safe. Mr C. will give all our news.

Have been shortening the bands of the waggon. Succeeded well with those of the naves, except making one rather too little. Three of the large bands fitted well, but one did not touch the wood at the weld, & when trying to send it in (when cold) I broke it although the weld was one of the best made. I take it slowly, welding one side, then the other. What is the proper distance to place the band from the hole of the bellows? Ought the centre of the band or the lower edge to be opposite the hole? I placed the band sometimes two, sometimes three, inches from the hole, but could not get a heat over the whole part to be welded. It either went over the upper or lower edge. My friends here say you put pieces of stone under the band to bring it into a proper position. What that is I can't ascertain. This sort of work has suffered a few days' interruption. School is finished. Only one small shower of rain yet. Olive grows briskly. Waggon tent suffered a severe fracture all along backbone, ribs all shivered. We shall patch it up & go Eastward as soon as Robert recovers. Corn crop lost this year.

Long ago you have heard of the departure of Baba to the land of the blessed.[1] He worked hard for us, ploughing &c. I could not reckon with him, being engaged with Vardon &

[1] "The rhinoceros is our frequent fare. Baba, a Kuruman convert, was killed by one last week. Unprovoked, it rushed on him and ripped him up" (9.x.1846 Whish). Cf. also *Travels*, p. 552; Methuen, *Life in the Wilderness*, p. 194.

Oswel, but said in parting, "I shall add ten dollars to the amount for carriage & reckon again with you." He said although I gave nothing for the work it did not matter, he wished to assist us. In their confusion after the accident they sent a man on horseback to Mabotsa & a man on foot here. The latter arrived late in the afternoon, & Mebaloe & I immediately set off, keeping up a gallop till it was dark. The moon rose about one o'clock, and a rhinoceros at the same time disputed our path, standing snorting at us. We went off at right angles with the path, & our minds being impressed with the accident concieved every big dark bush after that a real burile[2] moving & making towards us. Directing our course to a fire in the distance, we found it at a cattle post of Bakhatla, who gave the melancholy intelligence that the spirit of Baba had departed just about the time we left home. Had the man on horseback come here we might have witnessed his dying moments, & it would have been satisfactory to our feelings to have shewn respect to him though we could do little else. We returned in the morning with sorrowful hearts.

If an opportunity should occur, we shall feel obliged by your sending some Alphabets & first spelling books. We recieved by some Wanketze a parcel of (we supposed) letters addressed to Mrs M. After letting them lie some time, we concluded we might open it in order to take our share, & trusted you would take our word that we had not read any but our own. But after opening the envelope we felt what appeared only one letter, so we return it in nearly the same state it left you.

We send, if Mr C. will take it, a macaca root, hoping you will enclose it for Dr Buchanan in the box.[3] If you think it will do mischief it can be left out. Intend as soon as the present brush of work is over to collect some of the rarer bulbs for your botanic garden. I know one mocaca as big as a small water vatchy.[4] The upper portion (stems, leaves, &c) is used as a vegetable by Natives.

[*No signature*]

---

[2] Tswana *bodile*, the black rhinoceros (*Diceros bicornis*).

[3] The box consigned to Mr Whish contained a parcel of "roots &c" for Dr Andrew Buchanan, Professor of Medicine at Glasgow University, who had been one of D. L.'s teachers (9.x.1846 Whish).

[4] Afrikaans *vaatje*, a little barrel.

1847

15 March 1847

Address: (Care of Revd. Dr Philip, Cape Town) Mr Livingston, Almada St., Hamilton, Lanarkshire, N.B. [Wilson Collection.]

Kuruman
15 March 1847

My dear Parents,

It is now a very long time since I wrote you, and the reason has been a belief that . . .[1] you had "crossed the Atlantic". You seem to have adopted the silent system too, whether with as plausible a reason I cannot aver. But certain it is it seems quite an age since last I saw your handwriting. I need not ask you why you have not written. Were you ashamed that after uttering such a succession of ardent longings for emigration, when it came to the point you must confess you preferred oatmeal porridge for life rather than risk your precious bodies on the great roaring ocean? "Crossing the Atlantic", about which you spoke so often, is fine in poetry, & nearly equal to "transplanting old trees" as a figure of speech. But I hope you will be kind enough to mention neither the one nor the other to me so long as we live.

We feel very grievously disappointed in you. I could scarcely believe my eyes when, after all your protestations, hints, &c, you cooly tell me that all your hopes are centred on straw bonnet making.[2] There is surely a lack of energy somewhere. You surely do not believe that because two old men went into a marshy aguish spot & died that all America is aguish? Why, there are a hundred thousand places in America where a case of an old or young man dying of inter-

---

[1] Eight words heavily obliterated.
[2] D. L.'s sisters had decided to go into this business (cf. Letter 43).

mittent fever was never known. And as for Charles coming home to go to Kilmarnoch, I am glad to percieve by a letter just recieved that he is not so silly as to go to any such place for education. Well, you must please yourselves. . . .[3] At any rate I do not see the least probability of my ever being able to send any more.

We are at present out here for the purpose of attending a meeting of Committee.[4] Two years have elapsed since we went into the Interior. We shall soon return again, and hope to commence a new station by removing with the Bakwains to another & better part of the country. The want of corn & vegetables is felt very much where we are. We have but little water & cannot irrigate. Sowed at a distance last year,[5] and Sechele our chief sent a village of Bakalihari to watch it for us, but rhinoceros, buffalo & waterbucks got the better of them & eat up all our corn. Sechele our chief is very agreable. Has learned to read & takes much pleasure in it, but is not converted. We do not in the least regret leaving Mabotsa. We have far brighter prospects of usefulness where we are. Mr Inglis was lately expelled from Mabotsa by the Natives, and Mr Edwards had to give them a large present to allow him to stop[6]—this while we are treated with great affection by the Bakwains. We feel grateful to him who guides our steps.

Have been engaged in itineracy much of late among the tribes living Eastward of Chonuane.[7] The number of inhabitants is prodigious as we approach the coast. There the

[3] The passage omitted (portions of which are also obliterated in the MS.) consists of about 120 words, and relates to "missionaries making provision for their parents".

[4] The fourth meeting of the District Committee was held at Dikgatlhong on 8–9 March.

[5] "I am at present out at our garden, which, by the way, is no nearer than forty miles from our residence" (28.v.1846 Pyne, from Kolobeng).

[6] Inglis had come to Mabotsa in May 1846. "Mr Inglis having taken up his residence in my house at Mabotsa, where certainly there is no work for two missionaries, continued to talk of a station among the Bahurutse untill actually expelled by the Bakhatla. He then offered himself to the Wanketze & was rejected, proceeded to Colesberg for supplies, and now imagines that the Bahurutse will go with him to form a station at Mainaloe" (17.iii.1847 Tidman). Inglis returned to Mabotsa from Colesberg in April 1847. "From that time to the end of June, he was engaged in making preparations to occupy a new station among the Bahurutse" (LMS Report, 1848, p. 117).

[7] In November–December 1846 the Livingstones and Mebalwe had made a journey of more than six weeks' duration to the BagaLaka and other Transvaal tribes (xii.1846 Pyne, 17.i.1847 Watt, 17.iii.1847 Tidman).

population of the Bechuana country chiefly resides. Preached to many tribes who never heard a kinder message from a white man than a kick of the foot or shot of a gun. Sadly oppres[sed] are they, and they have no deliverer. Their oppressors are Dutch Boors, and as they sow the seeds of a future "Caffre war" now we need not be surprised that after they have guns they revenge themselves and think all white men alike. They manufacture cotton, tin, copper, & iron. The men work in the fields. Have been seeking a field for Paul, one of our Native teachers. The way is open. Mokhatla, a very friendly chief, would be delighted with him; but these Dutch Boors have taken possession of all the country where Mosilikatze reigned, and the Bechuanas live in the land of their fathers only by sufferance. These Dutchmen hate missionaries cordially. They believe we will tell the Government all about their nefarious deeds. They are our greatest obstacles.

If you see Mr Whish, tell him that a waistcoat made by Mokhatla (in the box)[8] was exchanged for another Mrs Livingston made. The latter Mokhatla was obliged to give to a Boor for permission to feed his cattle on his own father's land. We hope we shall yet succeed in our wish of settling Paul over there. Mebaloe is exceedingly useful with us. I shall write you a much longer letter soon. Did not send you anything in the box because I believed you would not be there to recieve it.

You need not feel hurt at my remarks on the first page, nor advert to them. I only feel grieved that you did not go to the States. You certainly would be much more comfortable there in almost any situation than you can be in Scotland. But you must please yourselves.

Kind love to Mother, Janet, Agnes, in which my dear partner joins. Mr & Mrs Moffat send affectionate greetings. Their son Robert is at Glasgow College, & may visit you.[9]

Ever affectionately yours,

[No signature]

[8] "A waistcoat, made by Mokhatla, a chief living East of Chonuane" is listed among the curios that D. L. had sent Whish (9.x.1846 Whish).

[9] Moffat's son "who was in Glasgow never came out this length" (D. L.'s father to Henry Drummond, 5.xi.1847).

Have heard from Charles, also from John. Will write both. Send John's to Canada direct, & Charles's in a letter to Janet by the same opportunity I send this. Hope to write Mr Naismith also.

D. L.

38: To CHARLES LIVINGSTON

16 March 1847

Address: (Care of Revd. Dr Philip, Cape Town) For Mr Charles Livingston, Almada St., Hamilton, Lanarkshire, N.B. [Livingstone Memorial, Blantyre. Published in part in Chamberlin, *Some Letters from Livingstone*, pp. 94–6.]

Kuruman
16 March 1847

My dear Brother,
Your favour of 25th July /46 lately reached this station. Another to my better half bore it company, and when we arrived a few days ago our hearts were gladdened by perusing them. We are right glad to hear from you. Our pleasure however had a little alloy of pain. You mention the failure of your health, and this although we know that you are in better keeping than that of your best earthly friends. We had fondly hoped that you should be allowed to devote yourself to that work in which we hope to live & in which we desire to die. Good however is the will of the Lord. This is not our home. We look for a better land where no obstacle will ever arise in our service through infirmity of body. Hope you will yet recover. Divine Providence will guide your steps. May the Almighty God lift upon you the light of His Countenance & bless you.

I have had no time for correspondence during the last eight months. Have travelled & builded much. But having come out to attend a meeting of Committee I have a little time to spare, & will make the most of it for my distant friends. Do not expect fine composition or fine anything. I am becoming more & more a barbarian. Can read but little, and yet must keep up some acquaintance with the medical

189

& other sciences. Could not now deliver a speech in English. My sentences are Sitchuanized[1] by constantly expressing my ideas in that language. Have lately been obliged to speak Dutch, of all languages the nastiest. It is good only for oxen.

You are aware I have left Mabotsa. It was my station. Edwards got there through my influence. But no sooner was he sure of being fairly away from Kuruman, where he had been an assistant missionary, than every means were put into operation to get the station to himself. He felt that he would be nothing beside me. This spirit dictated the letter which was published in the U.S. about the lion affair.[2] I was not aware of the spirit by which Mr and Mrs E. were actuated and was only anxious for the promotion of their honour and influence among the Natives. We have endured the scourge of tongues. All manner of accusations were made against me, and the poor unhappy couple believed that I had scandalized them. They thought I had been actuated by the same spirit as themselves. They had an intense desire to get quit of me, and actually came all the way out to Kuruman beseeching Mr Moffat to use all his influence with me to induce me to leave Mabotsa. Mr M. replied, "Why, Mr L. consulted us all as to the propriety of his going to another tribe in order that the gospel might have a wider range in the Interior." "O had I known that", said Edwards, "I should not have acted as I have done." Mr M. told him also, to his utter amazement, that no one had ever heard me say a word about him but of respect & kindness. Poor fellow, led astray by his own heart & desire to be great. I sincerely pity him. Inglis took up his abode in my house, but was lately driven away by the Bakhatla, & Edwards was obliged to bribe them by a large present to allow him to remain. They were loud in their denuntiations, "You have driven away our true friend", &c. I mention this that you may be prepared for trials of a similar kind as those we have experienced. But few pass through life without feeling sorrow, but few escape the scourge of the tongue. We ought to consecrate our whole being to the Divine glory, and do good

---

[1] "Sitchuanadized" (Chamberlin).
[2] I have not traced this letter.

whoever does ill. Pray for us that we may be faithful unto death, follow the Saviour through good & evil report.

We are very happy in our work at Chonuane. The chief Sechele is a sensible man, now reads pretty well, is fond of his Testament, and has an intense desire for everything connected with civilization. We are poor & cannot help much. But when he has no soap he washes his clothes with pipe clay. We hope his people will follow his example. He & his wives³ are our best scholars & afford us much satisfaction. None however are converted. This is the great desideratum. Our thoughts always light on it. The locality we now inhabit is not good, our water is scanty & bad, but we hope to remove to a better shortly. This will mean hard work for me, but it is all in the course of the service of a good master. So we cannot grumble.

This subject brings a remark of yours to my recollection. You worked a day or two on John's farm & got knocked up for several days after.⁴ Did you wonder at it? What a physiologist you are! Suppose you had worked two hours each day for the first week,⁵ three for the second, & four for the third, & so on, would you have been knocked up? Your system may not yet be fitted for work, but we cannot conclude that it never will be. You are not yet old. When I thought of writing to the Directors, it was with the persuasion that you would be qualified both physically & mentally for missionary labour, and a recommendation from any one in whom the Directors had confidence would have materially facilitated your acceptance. In China there is not much bodily or rather manual labour, & so in India. But here we have more manual exertion than mental. Commit thy way unto the Lord. Trust also in him.

We have recently returned from a long tour through the region lying Eastward of Chonuane. We visited very many tribes who have never seen a missionary before. The country is more populous than anywhere else in the Bechuana land. The near[er] we approach the coast the population becomes

³ Sechele then had five.
⁴ At the end of his first session at Oberlin, Charles "went to Canada in quest of a home in another brother's house in which to recruit his strength, but had to perform most of the journey on foot" (30.xii.1847 Tidman).
⁵ ". . . two hours for the first week" (Chamberlin).

the more dense; more civilized too, for they weave cotton, work in iron, tin, copper, and brass. The men too carry on the operations of husbandry. A large river called the Ourie[6] or Limpopo wends its way to the sea. It is more than 400 yds accross. But all the fountains have been seized by Dutch emigrants, commonly called Boors, and they treat the Natives very badly. Many of the Natives fled from our waggons when we were travelling, as if they had beheld an enemy. Poor people, they are destroyed for lack of know-ledge. They hate & kill each other, so the Boors find them an easy prey. The Bechuanas are admitted by all the Boors to be an honest quiet people, yet they treat them as slaves, make them work without wages, and beat them shamefully, lately attacked one tribe, killed a great number and took 400 captives. The booty amounted to 10,000 sheep and cattle beyond number.[7] Their Redeemer is mighty but they know him not.

Your question respecting the complete annihilation of the idea of a supreme being[8] in the Bechuana mind is rather difficult of solution. We come after missionaries have been in the country 30 years. Morimo[9] or God or Chief is at every man's mouth. Intelligent Natives say their forefathers spoke of God in the same way. A man escapes from an elephant or lion. He instantly exclaims,[10] "How good God is to me! What a heart God has to me!" A person is sick or dies. The exclamation then is, "God has no heart", i.e. He is not kind.

They have parables from which we who are better in-formed[11] can gather the idea of a future state. The know-

---

[6] Odi, the Tswana name for the Crocodile River (upper reaches of the Limpopo).

[7] In the winter of 1846 the Boers, led by Potgieter, had attacked the BaPedi, a Transvaal Sotho tribe, from whom they took booty officially estimated at 8,000 cattle and 6,000 goats (not sheep); cf. Theal, *History of South Africa*, vol. vi, p. 505.

[8] "Your questions respecting the idea of a supreme being . . ." (Chamberlin). The question may have been prompted by Moffat's statement (*Missionary Labours*, p. 243) that among the Tswana "No fragments remain of former days, as mementoes to the present generation, that their ancestors ever loved, served, or reverenced a being greater than man."

[9] *Modimo*, the Tswana name for God.

[10] ". . . escapes from an elephant. Now he instantly exclaims . . ." (Chamberlin).

[11] "They have parables from God. We who are better informed . . ." (Chamberlin). The story that follows is very widespread among the Tswana and other Southern Bantu.

ledge of some of these parables is universal, and if we can believe testimony it was so of old. Here is one. God sent a cameleon to say to men, "Though you die you do not vanish or become annihilated, you will return again." The cameleon being a slow walker was outstripped by the little black lizard sent by another, and the latter came first to man. The black lizard said to men, "One will come after me & tell you that when you die you will not perish but will return again. It is all a message of lies. When you die, you perish as an ox." When the cameleon came, men stopped his mouth by saying, "O we know your message. It is all lies."

There are cairns in the hills, and when a traveller comes to one he throws a stone or branch of a tree to it and says with a loud voice, "Hail, O king. Let it be well with me in the way I now go. Let me find game. Let it be pleasant for me among the people I may meet." [12]

From these & other facts we who are more enlightened can gather fragments which seem to point to a primitive faith & worship. But none of the Bechuanas in distant parts can connect these fragments together so as to form one rational idea on the subject of the Godhead or futurity.

They seem at one period to have worshipped animals. A little beetle is tied on the hair, and something like a prayer is sometimes made to it. If a Morolong (one of the tribes) kills a khoodoo,[13] he breaks out into a loud wail, "O I have killed my father, what shall I do, yo yo yo yo." If asked why they do so, "It is our custom, we saw our forefathers do so & we do the same." They laugh at it. Have not the smallest devotional feeling, unless spitting on the ground when they see the animal after which their tribe is named can be denominated such an emotion.

Am glad you decide not to go to Kilmarnock. It would be a false step. Father does not understand the matter. I

[12] "Small stone beacons, or kairns, were often noticed by us on our journey. To these the natives pay much respect, addressing them occasionally with, 'rumala khosee!' or, hail king! in passing; at the same time contributing a stick or a stone to the heap, and requesting success in whatever they may be engaged in. When questioned on this subject, they only say it is a custom handed down to them by their fathers, but that they believe chiefs have been buried there" (Methuen, *Life in the Wilderness*, p. 204).

[13] The kudu (*Tragelaphus strepsiceros*, Tswana *thôlô*) is the totem of the BaRolong (sing. MoRolong).

have examined the "new views", as they are called,[14] and find as you do many excellent things in connection with them. But still in relation to the fundamental points I believe they are quite erroneous. I came to that conclusion without any regard to "authority" of names or systems. They are favoured with success in Scotland just because the majority of the Scotch preaching has been outrageously wrong in the opposite direction. I question whether success would attend them where the "mercantile views", the "waiting systems", have not been prominent in the preaching of ministers.

Study thoroughly, my dear brother. If you become a missionary you will have little time then. I wish I had a thorough education. If your constitution is not ruined you would be better in connection with our Society than school keeping, because you would have both summer and winter for study. If you can afford it, go to some eminent physician and request his opinion on your health, also whether you may think of missionary labour. Our Society has been trying to get agents for China, & after trial of several have come to the resolution of educating sixteen expressly for that Mission. The funds are at present depressed, but will come round again. However, you will know best how to act.[15]

Let us hear from you soon & often. We answer all who write us, but find it beyond our temper's utmost stretch to write those who maintain a majestic silence. I thank you most heartily for the books you sent. Am sorry I cannot possibly send you any money. The reason, a most cogent one, is, I have none. We got letter after letter from home breathing the most ardent aspirations for emigration. We made a great effort, & sent £20 to enable them to emigrate. Think of the acknowledgement. It runs as follows: "John's views of emigration exactly correspond or coincide with ours. He says you may do something to a garden, but old trees seldom bear transplanting well." This after boring me for years with their wishes to emigrate. Probably there has

---

[14] See above, 30.17.

[15] ". . . but will come round again to success. You will know best how to act" (Chamberlin).

been a process of conviction, but of that I am ignorant. All I know was the intense longings side by side with "John's views of emigration exactly coinciding with ours."

I shall read D'Aubigne in our way homewards, and the work of Mahan also. Should have been delighted with his Mental Philosophy.[16] Admire Brown very much, a favourite work.[17] I read it in my travels. My wife will put in a line or two.

Yours affectionately,
D. Livingston

My dear Brother Charles,

Many thanks for your kind letters received about a fortnight ago. I feel sorry to hear your health has failed, but I trust you will soon recover. We hear you have grown very tall. We have hopes when you have done growing you will improve in health and become as strong as my dear husband. He has very good health, which is a great blessing in this country. He works very hard, building, gunmending, and all kind of work. We are now on a visit to Kuruman, where my parents reside, and hope to return to our own home in about two months. Hence I have not time to say much now, but hope some time or other to answer your kind letters. Accept the love of your affectionate sister.

Mary L.

39: To MRS N. LIVINGSTON

4 May 1847

Address: (Care of Revd. Dr Philip, Cape Town) Mrs Livingston, Almada St., Hamilton, Lanarkshire, N.B. *Postmark:* Hamilton, NO 25, 1847. [Wilson Collection.]

[16] J. H. Merle D'Aubigné, *A History of the Reformation in the Sixteenth Century* (1843 etc., translated from the French original); Asa Mahan, *Scriptural Doctrine of Christian Perfection* (New York, 1839, 7th ed. 1844), *A System of Intellectual Philosophy* (New York, 1845).

[17] "I am reading Brown's 'Mental Philosophy' carefully, & find it very useful in giving me more defined ideas with respect to what emotions are or are not sinful" (7.vii.1841 Watt). The book referred to is probably Thomas Brown, *Lectures on the Philosophy of the Human Mind* (13th ed., Edinburgh, 1841).

Kuruman
4 May 1847

My dear Mother,

Having come to this quarter some weeks ago in order to attend a meeting of Committee, we went, and on the second day were called back again by intelligence from Kuruman that a fine little boy of Mr Ashton was dangerously ill. His father and I rode 110 miles[1] in about 24 hours, but found that the child's body had been committed to the grave. We have remained here ever since waiting Mrs L.'s confinement, which we expect in a few days. We are all much the better of our visit. We were very thin when we arrived, but are now recovered. Robert is quite well, having finished teething, which plagued him much. I write you now because I shall not have many opportunities after leaving this. Have been learning some carpenter's work. Mr Hamilton has been teaching me to make windows. He is very old now,[2] yet sometimes dreams that he is walking about Glasgow seeking a job with his tools over his shoulder. I take a regular part in the services carried on here, and have assisted in erecting a school. But we both feel an intense longing to be back again in the sphere of our labours in the Interior.

I often remember you, how you used to keep us all cozie and clean. I remember you often assisted me, my dear Mother, to put on my clothes in dark cold winter mornings, and later in life made a good breakfast for me on Monday mornings before I went away down to College. A thousand things rise up in my memory when I think of you. May God bless you. Sometimes when I see a word in Scotch I remember it as it came from your mouth. But I shall never hear your voice more, nor shall ever on earth see your face again.[3] But I hope we shall meet in Heaven. May the gentle shepherd carry you in his arms through the dark valley & recieve you into his glorious kingdom according to the greatness of his mercy & love.

I have but little time in general to write. Am often so

---

[1] The Committee meeting was held at Dikgatlhong.

[2] Hamilton was born in 1776 (*Register*, p. 11).

[3] Hardly a cheerful prophecy, nor a true one, for D. L. met his mother again ten years later.

tired I cannot do it in the evenings. Yet this was not the cause of my long silence lately. I thought you must have sailed for America, and therefore considered it should be better to wait till I heard from you. Think John might have encouraged you to emigrate. He has plenty of food, & might have tried to make you comfortable in your old age. But he knows best. Is he not the firstborn, the excellency of dignity, the excellency of power? Poor Joseph, "separate from his bretheren",[4] has been farrier, builder, carpenter, glazier, doctor, minister, man midwife, blacksmith, boardsmith, tinsmith, shoemaker, waggon mender & painter, gunmender, hunter, fisher, and I don't know what else, but would not refuse his aged parents a place at his fireside. But perhaps it is better that you remain where you are. The corn laws being now abolished you will have but little difficulty in obtaining a livelihood. May you be blessed in your basket & store. If you try to make porridge of maize or Indian corn, let it be boiled for a long time, it then becomes better than oatmeal porridge. When supping them I often have thought how you designated them like sawings of wood.

I wrote you lately, viz. on our arrival here. We had recieved two letters from Charles & some publications sent by Mr Gurney or Sturge.[5] I wrote him at same time & sent it to your care. Father referred . . .[6]

I just now hear that I have not written to Janet so often as I ought to have done. She must excuse me. I shall remember her next.

There is war with the Caffres at present.[7] They are borderers, and have most of the vices of the Colonists with but few of their virtues. Their country is densely wooded and it will be difficult to subdue them. The Colonial Govt. has behaved with great kindness to them; salaried some of the chiefs, and gave large presents to others. But all the

[4] Genesis 49: 26.
[5] Possibly Samuel Gurney (1786–1856) and Joseph Sturge (1793–1859); the former was President, and the latter a life member, of the Aborigines' Protection Society.
[6] Eight lines heavily obliterated.
[7] The "Seventh Kaffir War" (also called "The War of the Axe"), between the Cape Colony and the Xhosa tribes on its eastern border, had started in March 1846. It lasted until the end of December 1847 (Theal, *History of South Africa*, vol. vii, pp. 1 ff., 57 ff.).

kindness has been lost upon them. They seem to have thought the concessions made by Govt. to them indicated fear or weakness, so as soon as they obtained guns, horses & ammunition the younger portion of them, those who know but little of the miseries of the former war, were determined to revenge the old feuds between black & white. The war has been a most unprovoked one on the part of our Govt., and since Pottinger[8] has come it will end in the complete subjugation of the nation. Whatever you may see in the newspapers or whatever can be said against former wars, the very warmest friends of the Caffre tribes declare that justice is [on] the side of our Govt. They came down on the Colony just like the Highlanders of old in their forays, burned nearly all the mission premises in the country, & carried off immense herds of cattle & sheep. Jan Tsatzoe,[9] who came to Hamilton with Mr Read,[10] joined what he thought the strongest party, viz. the Caffres. This is a great blow to our missionaries there, he has been a proffessor so long.

In this quarter the work of God is gradually progressing. There are occasional defections just as at home. The Native teachers Paul & Mebaloe are carrying on the work among the Bakwains during our absence. Remember us in your prayers. Mrs Ross is dead,[11] and Mr R. talks of going home.

[8] Sir Henry Pottinger (1789–1856) was installed as Governor of the Cape Colony on 27 January 1847 and retired 1 December on appointment as Governor of Madras (Theal, *op. cit.*, pp. 40 f., 54 ff.).

[9] Jan Tshatshu, chief of the AmaTinde (a minor Xhosa tribe) at King William's Town, had been educated at Bethelsdorp and converted to Christianity. In 1836 he accompanied Dr Philip and Read to England. After his return he became addicted to drink. In 1847 he and his people took part in the fighting against the Colonists. This led, *inter alia*, to his expulsion from the Church (J. Maclean, *Compendium of Kafir Laws and Customs*, 1858, pp. 135 f.; Theal, *op. cit.*, vol. vi, pp. 137 f., vol. vii, p. 14).

[10] James Read (1777–1852), founder of the mission at Kuruman and since 1820 stationed at Bethelsdorp and elsewhere in the Cape Colony, had been in England from June 1836 until November 1837 with Dr Philip, Tshatshu, and another Native convert, all of whom gave evidence before a Parliamentary Committee on Aborigines (Theal, *op. cit.*, vol. vi, p. 138; *Register*, pp. 4, 19).

[11] She had died at Motito on 5 December 1846 (*LMS Chronicle*, vol. 11, 1847, p. 132). "Mrs Ross is dead of dysentery. A loss to her husband & children, that's all. She may however have been useful sometimes" (17.i.1847 Watt); "Mrs Ross is gone. No loss certainly, not even to her own children. They were left to grow up in unrestrained heathenism" (9.viii.1847 Moore).

Inglis still talks of what he will do, but does nothing. It is lamentable to see a waste of public money to so little purpose. But he whom we profess to serve will yet set all to rights.

If Father is writing to Charles, he may inform him that Mr Moffat desires me to tell him that he has set him right in reference to the Yankees. When Charles calls them a "hypocritical nation" they must be bad indeed. One so intimately acquainted with them must know. Everything new we hear of them Mr M. remarks, "How confirmatory that is of Charles's opinions of these Americans". He & Mrs M. send you all greetings. I told him of Neil's[12] idea of respectable connections & he enjoyed the joke much.

Please tell Charles to write some account of the domestic manners of the Yankees, of individuals, &c. Also, dear father, write yourself more frequently. Open the letters if you like. Never mind what I say above. If you rewrite them and make additions it may be all the better. But perhaps I do not like it so well. Never feel uneasy about any expression you may recieve. I would not for the world pain one of you. Always remember that in writing we want the tone of voice, which might give another turn entirely to what may be penned.

Mrs L. unites with me in very kind salutations. She would be glad of a bonnet, I daresay. Janet's head would fit hers. Who cares for a fit here? She would like a pattern or two of gowns from Agnes. If you ever found an opportunity of sending such things, shall be glad of the seeds.

Have been favoured with a little girl, name Agnes; not a pretty name, but it is that of My dear Mother. All doing well. Thanks to God.[13]

[*No signature*]

[*Added by Mary Livingstone*]

My dear Mother, I have not much time to write to any one. I intended to have written Janet, but a bonnet of her

---

[12] In March 1856 D. L. sent a letter from Tete to "Niel L[ivingston] in Canada" (*Journal*); I do not know if he was the man mentioned above, nor how the two were related.

[13] This paragraph was added as a postscript at the head of the letter, in such a way that the words "not a pretty name, but it is that of" immediately precede the "My dear mother" of the opening.

own size will do for me. I am going to beg for David too, he is very much in want of wo[o]llen stockings for winter. Missionaries' wives have not much time to knit stockings in this country, as they have to act as domestic drudge.

40: To ROBERT MOFFAT

July 1847

[Bruce Collection.]

Banks of the Notoane[1]
July 1847

My dear Father,

Through mercy we are now near the end of our journey. Have met with no accidents. The health of all very good. For the mercies we enjoy we thank Him who has been our protector night and day. A lion came up to us at the Meritsane,[2] but was driven off by the shouting of the people. The lungs of Khalimele[3] you may be sure did their duty. We have heard the roar frequently since, but that is all, & we wish we may never experience more. We have been very unsuccessful in securing the game we wounded. Two spring- (Robert has just come over the back of the seat, head foremost & his heels whirled over on the table, but knowing the somerset is his own fault does not cry) -bucks, one sessebe,[4] & a pitse,[5] are all we have got. An ostrich nest twice, good eggs. The goats give a little milk morning & evening and are thus very useful. We have been very comfortable in this journey, for most of which we have to thank your handywork &c.

Mr Evans met us this evening. He has not succeeded with Sechele, but has with Sekomi. Cumming seems to have

[1] The Ngotwane River, flowing north and north-east, is a major tributary of the Crocodile. To get to Chonwane D. L. had to cross it somewhere beyond Mabotsa.

[2] The Mareetsane River, rising about 25 miles south of Mafeking, flows westward into the Setlagole, which in turn is a tributary of the Molopo. The crossing was about four days' journey from Kuruman.

[3] One of D. L.'s Native servants (cf. 30.7).

[4] Tswana *tshêsêbê*, the antelope *Damaliscus lunatus* ("sassaby").

[5] The Tswana name for zebra.

forestalled him. I feel sorry I was not there when Evans came through. I think Sechele has a prejudice against him ever since he was there in partnership with Greig. I might have removed part of it. I think it would be more for his advantage to deal with Mr Hume than with Cumming. The latter has always been very anxious that he should conclude a bargain to deal with him exclusively, & may have managed it so now.

We spent Sunday at Setlagole.[6] Had a meeting with Sehutsane's people there. Gasitsioe, son of Chose,[7] knows how to read. The chief too knows the letters, but cannot spell. He says he waits at Setlagole to see what the Griquas will do in his country before he returns to it. We could not come by a straighter course as we intended, the big waggon being too heavy for travelling through the long grass. We spent Sunday last near Raputse,[8] came along the Bakhatla hills yesterday, course nearly north, and today came down to the Ñotoane, course N.E. Even this is considerably shorter than the Mamoori[9] road. We could reach home tomorrow but prefer an easy stage, and make our entrance on Thursday.

Mosate, called Moshatta by the Bamapela,[10] means maloapa a khosi.[11] Bebenya, to gleam as lightening. The Barolongs call the sea Lopenole; pena refers to the fullness of the water or the absence of banks. Merisantse, a plaguy

[6] About 50 miles south-west of Mafeking, near Kraaipan railway station.

[7] Segotshane had been regent since about 1830 of one section of BaNgwaketse (cf. 7.5, the other being that under his half-brother Sebego); he was the younger full brother of Tshosa ("Chose"), whose son Gaseitsiwe became chief soon after the time when D. L. wrote.

[8] About a day's journey ("a good stage") south of Mabotsa (J. S. Moffat, Lives, p. 255).

[9] Mamuri, sometimes called Mimori by early writers, a small stream flowing eastward into the Mainelwe ("Little Marico") in the vicinity of Mosega; the road leading across it was thus to the east of that now taken by D. L.

[10] The BaMapela, so called after a former chief, are a tribe of BakaLanga, known to the Tswana as BagaLaka; they are a Transvaal Ndebele (Nguni) people living in the Potgietersrust District of the Transvaal. D. L. had visited them at the end of 1846, when he noted that there were several distinct "sections" of BagaLaka (20.v.1847 Dyke). "Their dialect," he says also (17.iii.1847 Tidman), "is somewhat different from that we use. But we were readily understood, and they easily accommodated their language to ours."

[11] Malwapa a kgosi, the chief's (domestic) compounds; mosate is the Transvaal Sotho word for the tribal capital, and more particularly for the chief's quarters.

fellow. Metsehula, the sea. Likahela, corn from every one, levied & given to the maroka or rain doctors. This is the word to which I referred as revenue levies. They say, Likahela tsa pula.[12] Mashoa is another word for makheto.[13] Lehañke as applied to a stone means hard, sehañke to a man perhaps bravery or hard heartedness. Boceleka, unmanageable? Tsikela. Konolola.[14] Tlatlarega, tlatlarietsa, sound an alarm. Shuma, breathe hard in sleep. Hema, not héma, means the same as hegeloa or homoga.[15] Serea, paltry. Heretlega, change the conduct. The thobane ea boguera is called khoroane ea khoti (or khuti, a hole).[16]

The above are what I have been picking up in the way. Will be happy indeed if any of them proves of use. Empekoani, something of cowardice. Am glad to have something as an inducement to pick up new words. I began to write an analysis of the language with . . .

[*Rest of letter missing*]

41: To ROBERT MOFFAT JUNIOR

13 August 1847

Address: [written by Rev. R. Moffat] (Care of T. J. Mathew, of Cape Town) Mr Robert Moffat, care of Miss Eisdell, 7 Walworth Place, Walworth, London. [Photostat copy, LMS Archives. Published in part by Chamberlin, *Some Letters from Livingstone*, pp. 110–14.]

> *Kolobeng, Bakwain Country*
> *13 August 1847*

My dear Brother,

We recieved your favour dated Augt /46 while at Kuruman, and returned at least in quantity an equivalent.

---

[12] *Dikgafêla tsa pula*, tribute of corn (paid to the chief) for (making) rain.

[13] *Makgêthô*, taxes.

[14] The word "unmanageable" is an interlineation immediately above *boceleka*. I cannot interpret either the latter or *tsikela*; *konolola* means "unfasten".

[15] Brown's *Secwana Dictionary* defines *hema* as "handle a weapon, avoid blows, parry", *héma* as "breathe, take a breath", *hegéla* as "sigh, pant, be out of breath", and *homoga* as "be rested from work, be refreshed".

[16] Literally, *thobane ya bogwêra* means "cane (or stick) of the boys' initiation ceremonies", and *kgorwana ya khuti* "small gateway or opening of the hole (or, to the hollow)". I cannot explain D. L.'s association of the two.

Let this large sheet be added to the former and leave quality out of the question, and you will never again be able to utter your complaint about "return letters". The circumstances in which I am at present placed, and the object I have in view in writing at present, are the following. The water of Chonuane being scanty and bad, and it being impossible for us to raise the staff of life in that locality, we felt it to be our duty to propose removal to a more salubrious situation. Many of the Bakwains were opposed to it, because Chonuane afforded good garden ground for Native corn, pumpkins &c. But Sechele declared he would cleave to us wherever we went, and having fixed on the Kolobeñ, a fine stream which drains that mass of hills which lies Eastward of Kuakoe,[1] we are now in process of removal thither.[2]

Our new station is at the point where the Kolobeñ emerges from the hills, and about 40 miles N.W. of Chonuane. I am engaged in erecting huts. Mebaloe alias David is thatcher, and I am architect. Paul remains with Mrs L. at Chonuane. The mass of the people are engaged in removing their corn & goods from stage to stage. Others are engaged in building. Mary feels her situation among the ruins a little dreary, & no wonder, for she writes me yesterday that the lions are resuming possession & walk round our house at night. Kolobeng means "the haunt of the wild boar",[3] but it seems to have been the haunt of everything wild. Hyæanas abound exceedingly, buffaloes in immense herds, and zebras quite tame in the thickly wooded country around. Elephants too have left their traces on what will, we hope, for the future only contain marks of the "pleasant haunts of men".

The evenings afford me a little time for writing &c, and as you express a wish to have a grammar of the language, I intend in the absence of any grammar of Sitchuana deserving the name to furnish you with a few remarks; and these I expect to be of more value to myself than to you, for I shall

---

[1] Kgwakgwê, a hill where the BaNgwaketse were living when Moffat visited them in 1824 (cf. *Missionary Labours*, pp. 394 ff.); it is about two miles west of Kanye, the present tribal capital (24° 59′ S., 25° 19′ E.).

[2] Since D. L. had returned to Chonwane in July (cf. Letter 40), the move to Kolobeng must have been decided upon very soon after his arrival.

[3] "wild bear" (Chamberlin).

send them to Father and entreat him to correct my observations, at the same time hoping he will add information on those points in which I am ignorant. I need scarcely remark that it is of the utmost importance to attain an idiomatic acquaintance with the channel through which we hope the streams of Divine mercy & consolation will flow to the benighted inhabitants of this region. I have heard it spoken by individuals who thought they had acquired a knowledge of it, yet using the English idiom they could only be understood by Natives who, being accustomed to Europeans, knew what was intended as well as the speakers themselves. Had they come to the Bakwains or to any of the Interior tribes they would not be understood by a single individual. The English idiom here would be unintelligible gibberish.

In the following remarks I shall not attempt to follow grammarians. The endeavours of some to reduce the Sicuana to the grammatical forms of Latin & Greek &c seem to me to have been complete failures. I shall attempt an analysis only, and should I stick fast in the middle it will be because I lack either time or ability or both. We will begin by what we can between ourselves dignify by the name of a

Phonetic Table of the Sicuana.

A is sounded as in Fāther, Māmmă, or Scotch way of pronouncing Latin. Example: bathu men, mālā bowels, mālă cold, gonă there, ñāpā (verb) pinch, lithāko walls, logoră a hedge.

E as in Pear, were, their. Ex. Sepha brittle, senya v. destroy, heta v. pass, leta v. wait (or watch).

É with accent as in Lemon, clerk, friend, dead. Séka v. judge, étă v. travel, réka v. buy, maséka leglets, séba v. backbite.

I as in Scotch, Latin or English dimìnish, belìeve, or as seek, peep, ream. Kika a corn mortar, thìpa a knife, bosìgo night, purĭ a goat, letsatsi the sun.[4]

O as in Hole, toad. Tlotla to honour, shotla v. mock, kopa v. beg.

Ō as in Broad, sought, broth. Tlōtla strain (a liquid), lōpa to ask.

[4] Chamberlin has *turi* for *puri*, and *letsalsi* for *letsatsi*.

U as in C*u*shion, cuck*oo*, soothe. Lekuka a milk sack, phupu a grave, ruta v. teach, pula rain.

Æ, dipthong, as English I in H*i*gh, l*i*e, al*i*ke. Tsam*ae*a v. go, r*ae*a say, tlatlal*ae*a v. load a gun, put one thing into or on another, as putting a kettle on the fire &c, baea v. place or put (as [Latin] pono).

Œ, dipthong, as in -que or *w*ig. UE is nearly the same in sound, but scarcely so full in sound as oe. Bakuena can be spelled so, or Bakoena, or Bakwaina or Baquena. Gague is pronounced as if spelled gagwe (his). Leshue filthy, sebegoe a thing found in the field.

Sh as in Di*sh*, fi*sh*, *sh*all. Ma*sh*i milk, sesheshe a blossom or flower, leshashe a coward, shoñkoe a plant (asclepias?)

C as in Italian vocce, or as ch in *ch*urch, lur*ch*, ç. *C*aka a battle axe, coga rise, cukūru a rhinoceros, all pronounced as if spelled with ch. The last in English orthography would be Chookooroo.

Ñ with the circumflex over it is the same as the Spanish ñ or English -ing in comi*ng*, writi*ng*, but in Sicuana it begins words as well as forms a frequent termination. Mo lehatsiñ in or on the earth, mo tseleñ in or on the way or path, mo thutoñ in teaching, mo nokeñ in the stream. All these are pronounced as if instead of ñ they were written ng. Ñoñola to mock or deride, ñoñorega grumble, are pronounced as if written ngongola, ngongorega, taking the initial from any word ending in -ing but allowing the i to be silent [in] the enuntiation.

G, gutteral as in Scotch lo*ch*, Dutch dag, χ the Scotch way. Gago thy, ñoñorega, riga throw down.

H is always an aspirate except in combination with s as sh. Phiri a hyæana, the p is pronounced distinctly & followed by the rough breathing. Ph is never f as in English.

Of the sounds which occur less frequently in Sitchuana, we have *e* like Dutch *u*, or Scotch way of pronouncing upsilon. Serum*e*ri a chrystal, motsek*e*ri a sling. The Bakalihari have the dipthong we possess in reb*u*ke. They pron[ounce] bathu as if spelled batheu.

Several letters interchange in different tribes, and these constitute the chief diversities of dialect. T interchanges with R: Rara, thatha, father. The Bamapela or Bagalaka say

Papa. H interchanges with v, & v is used too instead of sh: U tla shua, U tla vua, thou shalt die; lehatsi, levatsi. L & N interchange, & the l is ommitted in some words by certain tribes in which it is used by others: Ki tla tla, Ki tā tā, I shall come.

The letters used in printing Sitchuana, & which are quite sufficient for writing all the dialects, are A B C D E É F G H I K L M N O P R S T U V X Y Ñ sounded as above.

I shall now note a few words to shew you the importance of strict attention to the pronuntiation of Sicuana. They may serve as examples on which to test the above observations.

Mālā bowels	Libe sins
Mālă cold	Libi dried cow dung
Tlotla v. honour	Tsétla yellow
Tlōtla v. strain (a liquid)	Tsetla the bladder
Pholo health or soundness	Tséga laugh
Polo the penis	Tsega the covering of the
Lopa to ask	genitals (non descriptand)
Lŏpa an obscene word	Poiho fear
Kopa beg	Poio turning
Khopa stumble or trip	

The foregoing are what occur to me at this moment. Had I leizure it would be easy to shew you that the most egregious blunders may be committed by the ommission of the aspirate, or by substituting the long for the short o, the é for its neighbour e. In Mr Lemue's Proverbs[5] there are no lack of errors of the sort. Matlo, advents, is the word invariably used for maitlo, eyes. A Native will know what you mean if you make the a in mātlo very long, but never if pronounced matlo. Alaga, v. charm or heal, is printed halaha, which has no meaning whatever. I once heard in a pico (peetsho),[6] called for the purpose of proposing a missionary

---

[5] *Liperoverebia tsa Salomo, mora oa Davida, khosi ea Israele, tse hetolechoeng mo puong ea Sechuana, ki P. Lemue* ("The Proverbs of Solomon, son of David, king of Israel, translated into the SeTswana language, by P. Lemue"), published by the French Mission Press at Beerseba (Basutoland) in 1846.

[6] *Pitsô*, a mass meeting of tribesmen for the discussion of public affairs.

settlement in the tribe, the following statement, & it was reiterated on subsequent occasions, although I pointed it out to the individual by asking the meaning of the word of a Native in his presence: "Jesus *cleaved* to our sins." The word "cleaved" gives but an imperfect idea of the force of the word shualelela. It means adhere to & refuse to give up, as a man to his wife who, having left him, he follows and perseveres in attempting to bring back. He meant to say, "died for". I mention this for your own instruction. I often think of it as a spur to myself to attain a better knowledge of the language.

After the orthography, which I concieve to be nearly perfect as a means of reducing the language, it will be well to direct your attention to the system of *signs*, the frequent repetition of which forms a remarkable feature in all the dialects. Probably that and the changes effected by prefixes form its distinguishing characteristics as a tongue. Dr Adamson of Cape Town[7] thinks that the principle of repetition of signs explains the apparent complexity found in the tongues of barbarous nations, and that there is no necessity for the supposition that such complexity is an evidence that these tribes were formerly in a state of civilization. Nearly all the complexity of the Sicuana exists in the repetition of the signs of nouns, and though . . .[8] such an apparent prolixity seems to be, by carrying along the sign through the sentence or through several sentences to impart perspicuity & precision to the narrative, these signs cannot be translated into English except in some cases, and then it is by "That which" or "the" or "it". Any attempt to arrange them as pronouns would be a failure, for there are true pronouns besides. Indeed, I believe if a perfect grammar is ever made it will be by thinking as little as possible of the grammars of the Japetian[9] tongues. Before attempting to arrange them in classes I shall give you an example of common repetition. The sign of motse, a town, is o.

---

[7] Rev. Dr James Adamson, Professor of Mathematics at the South African College (now University of Cape Town) 1829–50; a man of wide learning.

[8] Word undecipherable in photostat copy.

[9] A name formerly sometimes applied to the Indo-European ("Aryan") family of languages.

Ga re na motse mo hatsiñ
Re batla moñue kua gorini
Kua Jesu o agañ gona
Ko ona o re o batlañ
Ki motse o o tlotlegañ
Ki motse oa rona.[10]

The sign of motse is in moñue in the second line, again three times over in the fourth, & in the fifth the word with its sign twice over.

Examples might easily be cited in which it is much more frequently used than in this, but in these it is quite untranslateable into the English (except by a multiplication of particles to an extent which would prevent most Englishmen from understanding their own tongue). Ga go e si go ko go utluale contains negatives and signs mixed together, which if we attempt to translate literally would convey no idea to an Englishman, but we know immediately as meaning, "it was never heard of". Such sentences must have puzzled Father amazingly at first. We who follow in his wake can form but a faint idea of the sweat of brain he must have endured in picking & dissecting these particles.

All nouns beginning with C, E, K, T, P, I, U, have e as their sign. Ex., Caka e, a battle axe; eñkho, a pitcher; kañkashi e, an oar; tolo, a khoodoo; pitse, a zebra; inta, a wingless insect of domestic habits yet not respected;[11] uñkoe, tiger. You may make the above into a rule to assist memory: initial Cektipu hath e; or any other cabalistic word you like to manufacture.

Before proceeding to another lot, you may remember that initial Cektipu forms the plural by the prefix "li". Licaka, liñkho, likañkashi, litolo, lipitse, linta, liñkoe (there is a slight u sound in the latter, & perhaps it ought to be spelled liuñkoe). The plural signs of this class are "li, tse, ri, tsa", according to their position in the sentence. These four signs have the same meaning, but are varied for euphony & in expressing tense & case.

[10] The first stanza of Hymn 168 in the Tswana Hymn Book, translated by Robert Moffat from "Pembroke" (No. 221 in the *Bristol Tune Book*).
[11] The Tswana word *nta* means "louse".

Initial mo has o. Molao o, a law; mosho o, morning; monyo, dew; mōko, chaff. But mila a street, mele the body, have also o. Probably in some of the dialects a street is called mola, & the body mo̩le. Setibele[12] has motsila, a street. Mo initial forms the plural by changing into e: Melao, mesho, mo'mbila pl. mila, mebila, mele pl. mebele.

Under this head may come proper nouns or nouns expressing individuality. Their signs are eo o, and the plural ba ba. Mothu an individual eo o, bathu individuals ba ba. It is remarkable that the Natives apply individuality to rhinoceros, sessebes, ostriches, swine, and to all foreign articles. Cukuru eo o, sessebe eo o, ince eo o, kolobe eo o,[13] kettle eo o, pan eo o, &c, & the plural bocukuru ba, bosessebe ba ba, boince ba, bokolobe ba, &c. In reference to foreign articles we object to follow the Natives & say, Kettle e, pan e, &c.

1. Any verb may be individualized by prefixing mo & ba, and using these as the signs of the singular & plural respectively; or 2. by the word mothu with the sign in the genitive preceding. Ex[ample], 1. molosi a fighter, balosi fighters, mothu oa tōo, a person of fighting; morisi a herd, barisi, mothu oa tisho, a person of herding; mopi (from bopa, to form or create), babopi, mothu oa popo; mohumi, bahumi (from huma, to be rich or become rich), mothu oa khumo, a man of richness (mahumo pl. riches); moloi a witch, baloi, mothu oa tōo; morōka a rain doctor, barōka; moroki a sewer, baroki sewers, &c. &c.

The sign of the plural "me" is e, but metse, water, has a. The Bakalahari say mādze a, & that probably was the original form of the word.

But I must now put a period to this, and whether I ever resume or not will depend on circumstances.

Sept. We have now got into our hut on the Kolobeng. The town has, as Dr Hamilton of Leeds[14] would say, an oppidal appearance, though still in process of building. Our

---

[12] SeTebele, the language of the MaTebele.
[13] "Cukuru", rhinoceros; "ince", ostrich; "kolobe", boar, pig.
[14] Richard Winter Hamilton (1794–1848), Congregationalist minister and author, "a man of ability and rather turgid eloquence" (*D.N.B.*).

corner, although we are attempting only temporary build-ings, has assumed a touch of the European style. Mebaloe, Paul, Isaac, & our man Friday (Morukanelo),[15] have for the first time in their lives got up square huts of poles & reed. The chief without any suggestion from me determined to erect the school. "I desire", said he, "that you be at no expense whatever. I wish to build a house for God, who is the defence of my town. I shall call upon all the people to cut wood &c. It will be my work." [16] He proposed likewise that after the school was built we should have an interchange of works, he doing some work for us which required a number of men, & we leaving that to him should put a square house together for his use. We were glad of the proposition, for the making of a water course must be our first effort & will require aid.

As the season is far advanced & we cannot well do without corn for two years, everything now is of a temporary nature. The school must be so too. But we hope both chief & people will be as favourably disposed when we do need permanent buildings, & this if they were converted I am sure they will be. We earnestly pray for this. Everything else goes on as well as we could wish, indeed better than we could have expected. But the immortal souls, these are still in dark-ness,[17] & need your prayers & those of every believer in Jesus to whom their state is known. A lady in the excess of her simplicity wrote to me requesting me to tell more of our success in order to stimulate her prayers.[18] Poor ignoramus that I was, I had told her of the degradation into which so many precious immortals had sunk, and that the gospel had little or no effect in the Interior even when preached again & again. I thought this stimulus enough to any one who longed that the glory of Jehovah should dispel the clouds of dark-ness & death which cover the earth. But the longer one lives the more one learns. All the success in Bechuanaland belongs through the Divine favour to those who preceded us[19] in

[15] Modukanêlê; he accompanied D. L. to Lake Ngami in 1850 (cf. Letter 65).
[16] See note 21.
[17] "But the immortal souls there are still in darkness" (Chamberlin).
[18] "Some Glasgow friends desired Mrs MacRobert to request me to 'tell them of success in order to stimulate them to prayer'" (7.xi.1847 Janet Livingston).
[19] "me" (Chamberlin).

the field. We are beyond their line of things, & have as yet seen none.[20] You must go still farther N. or N.E. & try for yourself. There is plenty of room. Itineracy is good if you have a permanent sphere, a focus.[21]

Septr. 30. We are all at present in pretty good health, thanks to Him who bestows this blessing. Our temporary huts finished. School nearly so. Will begin watercourse in a day or two. Mary salutes you & Helen kindly, & you may believe me as yours affectionately,

D. Livingston

If Sechele knew I was writing you he would send many salutations. I shall tell him I have sent them for him to-morrow. This goes early.

[*Endorsed by Rev. R. Moffat*] Kuruman 26th. My dear Robert, I forward this as rec[eive]d. I have not a moment for remarks. Very good so far as it goes. R. M.

42: To ROBERT MOFFAT

29 September 1847

Address: Revd. R. Moffat, Kuruman. [Bruce Collection.]

Kolobeng
29 Septr 1847

My dear Father,

By the arrival of Koulter[1] on his way Southwards we are put in possession of another opportunity to inform you how we proceed in this quarter. I need not say I do so with pleasure. I only wish you may enjoy as much in the perusal as I do in the writing. We are all at present in tolerable health, but the setting in of the hot season seems to try our stamina. Mary is troubled with shooting pains in the chest.

[20] "We are beyond their line & of things I have as yet seen none" (Chamberlin).
[21] The three sentences beginning "You must go . . ." are wrongly placed by Chamberlin immediately after "It will be my work" (see above, note 16), which makes it appear as if they were part of Sechele's words.
[1] Moffat endorsed the letter: "Recd. by Kauter, Octr. 24th". The man seems to have been leader of a party of Griqua hunters and traders who had been to the BaNgwato.

Had sore eyes but not severely, & is now recovered. She got them from the little one. Hope we may through the Divine mercy be favoured with health. We have so much to do it seems desirable we should, but we must be resigned to the will of Him who knows what is best for us & His cause. We feel it hot now. We have plenty of hills behind us, sufficient one would think to screen us from the influence of the Southern icebergs, and all burning Africa spread out before us to the North. But we are within the blessed sound of gurgling waters. They have nightingales in England, but of all the birds in the world commend me to the merry midnight frogs. You cannot concieve, yes you can, how delighted we were to hear the sound of waters at night, irrigateable water too.

In my last I informed you of our removal. Mebaloe & I built huts & removed into them. Paul followed, & is now roofing his. Your tent has done him good service. Ours is 24 by 12, & a pack house has since been added, 10 by 12 ft. Mebaloe's 16 by 12, Paul's the same size as ours. The town is still in process of building. Our corner has a touch of the European, for all are square, & Mebaloe is thatcher to all. Even our man Friday, alias Morukanelo, has got up one of the four-cornered sort, & declares he will never leave it, it is so beautiful. Our plan was to get up temporary houses & a temporary meeting house as soon as possible, in order that teaching might go on regularly during the time we should be occupied in making gardens. We have now got nearly to the point at which we can with good consciences begin to labour for the meat which perisheth.

The chief without any suggestion from me told me it was his desire to build a house for God, that I should be at no expense whatever with it. He even thought that we should do nothing in the work, but to this latter we objected, as it was for the work of the God of all. I think sometimes that he expects God will bless him for his good work, yet he expresses himself occasionally quite in the orthodox style. He wished to build a very fine house, but we cannot at present spend more time on it than making it a temporary affair of pole & reed. He employed all the males in cutting reed, & sent them a good distance to select the straightest wood they could find. We began it on Saturday morning & met in the walls on Sunday. Many hands make light work. Here it was not light work to keep them from doing too much. We made it 40 by 15. We found they had cut the beams too short for our plan, & rather than wait for longer put it up at 15 instead of 20. On Tuesday it was finished, except the closing in at the top, but the reed being deficient they have been off cutting it today. We shall probably begin to our watercourse on Monday next. Too late for corn, but we may yet have maize & vegetables. Another proposition of the chief is that we make an exchange of work. He takes the watercourse, & we build him a European house. We are glad enough to do this, for we are but few in number. I intend to give a door, an old one. I may make or sell him a window.

We have lost much time in removing, & we have yet to go & get the door frames & iron in the roof.[2] We shall burn both school & house in order that we may pick out the nails and prevent any Boor taking up his abode therein. When we returned we found many Boors on the place. Some were rather impudent, dogged Paul's wife untill she hid herself in Mebaloe's house. The latter has more firmness than the former. All of the Boors made off as soon as possible after we came. I did not shake hands with the fellows as I did when among them in our Eastern journey. I felt like the "cock on its ain midden head". One gave Sechele a bottle of brandy. Their children employed the time in digging licuse,[3] & ran among Paul's children as if equals. When we came I felt in doubt as to whether it was not duty to go immediately with Paul & settle him with Mokhatla, leaving the removal of the Bakwains to another year. Since hearing of the above-named conduct I fear it might be improper.

We were subsequently informed that, in our absence, deputies were sent by the Bakaa & Makalaka to ask our influence with Sechele to grant them liberty to live in his country as independant people. Sekhome is now using them in a very tyrannical manner, although living in their

[2] Of the old house at Chonwane.
[3] *Dichuse*, "wild crocuses, small [edible] bulbs" (Brown).

land. Since he has got guns he compells them to pay him tribute. (I shall return to him again.) Finding us absent they did not disclose their object in coming publicly, but informed the chief's brother in private. They passed on to the Bakhatla, & when there were told that I should never return, that I had fled from Sechele, &c &c. The messengers told what the Bakhatla said, & on leaving stated they would come again if the Lekoa[4] returned. One of the messengers is the son of Shue, the chief of the Bakaa. I know him very well. Shue's wife knows you.

The prospect of these two tribes coming nearer made me think of forming a sort of circuit with them & Mokhatla, & keeping one of our number always engaged among them, but present engagements prevent us from doing anything but at home. We cannot part with Mebaloe. He works so hard he is our right hand. Paul has never been accustomed to work, but is the best theologian by far. We sent a message to Mokhatla anent your present, but he has not yet made his appearance. It has been hurry scurry ever since we came, & will be for some time to come.

I forgot to mention above that Sechele is favourable to the approach of these tribes, because they are manufacturers in wood & iron. Sekhomi monopolizes all the trade in front of him. He will not allow any one to pass him Southwards. There is a good way to the Lake, but he keeps it shut, as you will hear by the Griquas. If any one went past him & opened up the way, he would be conferring a benefit on the tribes beyond. When will you go to the Lake? If you don't next season I may as a relaxation take a trip in that direction. I should like you to go, as you have become in a manner pledged to it.[5] I think it would be well if first visited by a missionary. The Griquas will certainly reach it next season.

Kañkashi is the name for the pole with which they shove off the canoe. I cannot get the word for the paddle which is used after they have got into deep water. To row is to hurua,

---

[4] *Lekgowa*, the Tswana term for a European.

[5] As early as 1841 D. L. had reported a rumour, put about by Ross, that "Mr Moffat has got £400 from some gent in England for the purpose of fitting out an expedition" to Lake Ngami (7.vii.1841 Watt).

go hurua mokhoro or mokoro. Go hurua ka likañkashi may perhaps do.[6] The i final is distinctly sounded. Bara means to swim. The people on the Lake are great swimmers. Lekaoe is the name given to a sort of skiff plaited together & made of reed. Licobobo & lituguana mean thicket, very dense, of both large & small trees. Mopakoana a curtain, a kaross hung up to act as such. A dreamer of dreams is called tlorolimpe, ki gore[7] torolimpe. Will that do for prognosticator? Island is in Sekwaina sekiri, Setlapized seori.[8] Setlaka sa gare has always reed in it,[9] but a piece of land with trees on it in a stream is always sekiri or seori. Seori can be applied to a promontory, & so can setlaka sa gare, but sekiri never. Koñkoñ an ignoramus (pelu pahu, I forget at present). Matlurra rough, so is maguata. Leposa, to drawl in singing or go lazily in walking.

But I must leave words. I am glad however of the opportunity to send out kañkashi, as likewise a riding ox which had I been at home I should have sent by Boe. I have had it three years & it has grown large in my possession. It is very tame & is easy in riding, so I think will just suit you. It has some objection in its own mind to the stick being put into its nose,[10] but that operation over it is as docile as possible. The boys here chirp to him & he comes out of the kraal very familiarly turning his tail to them in order to enjoy what learned folks call titillation. I hope you will be kind enough to accept it instead of your old one, and whatever you may say, think or do, with it, never think of returning it. A dear brother to whom I gave one returned it, after it had got its thigh bone broken, by telling his herd, "that ox belongs to Livingston". I have got a horse said to have been Mr Oswel's. Of this I have doubts, but it serves to get us eilands. If it dies I can get another ox, so you need not imagine I put myself about by begging you to accept this.

[6] *Go hudua mokôrô*, to row a boat or canoe; *go hudua ka dikankase*, to row with oars.

[7] *Ke go re*, that is to say.

[8] SeKwena, the language of the BaKwena; "Setlapized", SeTlhaping-ized, i.e. put into the dialect of the BaTlhaping.

[9] The word "setlaka" (*setlhake*, an island) has the same stem as *lotlhaka*, reed; "setlaka sa gare", the island in the middle.

[10] The stick or bit to which the reins of a riding-ox are attached passes through its nostrils.

We had horns &c for you, but all have been left at the Letlotleñ.[11] It is now too late for seeds. Your melons will be grown before Koulter comes.

We concieve Mr Hume is done for here. Mr Evans sold a dog trap, which I think I have seen in your garden, for 30 or 40 lbs of ivory. He called it a wolf trap. The first time a wolf got into it the animal shook it to pieces. I suspect Evans did not tell this when mentioning how Sechele tried to cheat him. We try to obviate the objections which rise up in the heathen mind by such deeds, by admitting that there are bad ones among us. At present they have a high opinion of the integrity of missionaries, & we hope we may be assisted to walk so as to maintain a consistency of character.

The pans you gave me have furnished us with sheep since we came. We have had eilands too, and being very fat tried to salt for you, but all went bad, so you must take the will instead of some good sehuba.[12] Buffaloes come occasionally into the town. Two came down our way one morning & we soon made them our own.

We took a claw hammer of yours by mistake, & in using it a few days ago knocked its head off. This is the only article I know of which should not have come. The reason I used it, after knowing it was yours, was it has a smoother face than mine & did not cause the nails to bend so as the others.

I find on application to Koulter that he has no loose oxen, and Apie's party have, so we shall send the ox with the latter. The party with whom Apie now is will probably be here next week. Sechele has been down to desire me to send you many tumerishos,[13] also to all his friends, among whom he considers Mr Ashton. He is anxious for some one to make gun stocks for him, many of the guns of his people being much damaged & split. Some one he calls Taote esiñ moreki[14] has sent messages to him to the effect

[11] *Letlotleng*, locative form of *letlôtla*, more commonly used in the plural (*matlôtla*) for the ruins of an abandoned village or dwelling; in the present context, the reference is to Chonwane.

[12] Brisket; by extension, tribute due to one's superior (who is entitled to that joint of meat from any animal killed by a dependant).

[13] Greetings.

[14] "Taute, not the trader". "Taute" is the Tswana rendering of the name "David", and the trader referred to here was David Hume, of Kuruman, who is still known in Kwena tradition simply as "Taute".

that he wishes employment in that line. He offers an ox &
kaross for each. Our people say it is one David Dickop at
Likatlong.[15] I promised to mention it to you, and that you
would mention it to the individual if at Kuruman.

In riding over here from Chonuane I had the misfortune
to lose the stopper of my powder horn. Could you lend me
an old one till I get one of my own? I am now without any.

When we came here, Sechele had all his powder (about
100 lbs) in his tent. The tent was smeared with fat to make
it impervious, the floor was covered with dried grass, and as
he always uses candles in the evening the candle stick usually
stood at the head of his bed. After drinking beer one evening
he & all his attendants got up & went into the kotla,[16]
leaving the candle burning. The wind blew it over into the
grass, & when the flame ran up the tent it was observed.
One of my guns being in the tent, S. ran in & snatched it
up. As he pushed back the flaming tent with one hand it
was severely burned. The tent was completely consumed,
but the powder remained untouched, it being covered over
by some paties.[17] All agreed it was a great deliverance.

We do not know when we shall obtain a supply of that
article. We do not look for Cumming, although he has left
some ivory with us. He has a Hottentot woman with him.
Got two Bakwains to accompany him. One of these having
gone out to hunt with him was threatened with being shot if
he did not find a buffalo's spoor. The man becoming afraid
pointed out the direction in which he believed the animal
went, but Cumming insisted it had gone another way. He
then shot one of his own dogs, told the man he should do so
to him. The latter again pointed out the direction in which
the buffalo went. Cumming seized him by the throat, beat
him with his fists, kicked him on the abdomen, & then
knocked him down with the but[t] end of his gun; this
made the blood spout out from his nose & mouth. The two
were alone in the field. A few days afterwards he ordered
the Bakwains to let his horses & cattle alone. He then
ordered one of his Hottentots to tend them. A horse very

[15] Dikgatlhong, an LMS station near the junction of the Vaal and Harts Rivers,
about 100 miles south-east of Kuruman.

[16] *Kgotla*, council-place.   [17] *Phaté*, skin mat.

soon fell into a lemena.[18] Cumming seized a Molala,[19] in the belief that he had digged the pit. One of his Hottentots held him by the feet and another by the head, & Cumming beat him till he expired. I asked the man particularly whether he saw the man was actually *gonogile*.[20] He said it was midday when the deed was done. The corps[e] lay there till the evening, and then some of the man's friends came & took it away to bury it. All the people fled when they saw the man actually dead. The Bakwains fled after nightfall.[21]

Cumming has gone on, telling the Natives he is going to his friend Mosilikatze. The Boors have lately attacked some of his outposts, and having found the Matibele of a different metal from the Bechuana fought and ran away, hoping no doubt to live & fight another day.[22] They say they are returning to ipakanya,[23] so say the Natives. Cumming does not know of this. If he comes near the Matibele, ten to one if he returns. If he should it will be a marvel to me. Donovan's party died at the Macapo or Bacapo.[24] Cumming was South-East of them where they (the Bakwains) left him. He seems driven away in his wickedness.

We have been to measure our watercourse today. Had we time we could irrigate a large tract of land, but we should require to go along a mass of boulders about 200 feet. We prefer to make an effort for a smaller piece because it can be accomplished soon, and if spared & find *that* too small we shall try the larger on a future occasion. Immense tracts may be irrigated down below easily. We hope the Bakwains

[18] "A pitfall with spikes at the bottom; a game trap" (Brown). Cf. *Travels*, p. 26, for a detailed description of one variety.

[19] "A person in the position of a serf; one belonging to an inferior tribe" (Brown), such as Bushmen or BaKgalagadi.

[20] Perfect tense of *gonoga*, "waste away, die" (Brown).

[21] Cumming's own version of this incident, which differs considerably from that reported on hearsay by D. L., is given in *A Hunter's Life*, vol. ii, pp. 167–9.

[22] In June 1847 a Boer commando headed by Potgieter had gone against Moselekatse, "who was found far north of the Limpopo. The Boers seized 1,600 cattle, but were unable to get them away, as the Matabele attacked them in such force that the commando was forced to retire. This expedition was therefore quite fruitless" (R. H. Massie, *The Native Tribes of the Transvaal*, 1905, p. 101).

[23] *Ipaakanya*, "to prepare oneself" (Brown).

[24] The "Macapo" are the MaTswapong Hills, in the general vicinity of Phalapye, Bechuanaland Protectorate; "Donovan's party" I have not identified.

may irrigate for themselves, and they profess willing enough
to try when they see how we succeed.

Completely disgusting the motloa, a small white ant,
very troublesome.[25] If the[y] climb up a wall or tree, a
little of the compound put on the path, they never think
of going that way again. We have not yet tried the white
ant masetlaoka with it. I shall enclose leaves of it & the
mehetolo.[26]

[*October*] *14.* Sechele sent his brother today with the
request that I should give him assistance to establish an
evening prayer meeting in his house. Thinking he meant a
private one with himself, I said he ought to pray himself in
secret. But going up this afternoon in order to encourage
him to do so, he took me aside and told me he wished to
have a social prayer meeting, in his own house, of his
children and all connected with them. He added he knew
he was living in sin,[27] but though he had not given up
those with whom he sinned he wished to pray in his family,
& hoped that some of his people would be brought to
believe. As he told me before that he always prays in secret,
he said "I do not give up that, I pray alone in secret, in the
field & in the town." Paul & I began, & we have arranged
that one of us go every evening. Always when affected his
eyes glisten. We wish it may be the beginning of conversion. His eyes glistened tonight. I suppose you remember
when you caught it such little things as these. It will be a
hard trial to part with his wives. Three of them are decidedly the best scholars, the most friendly, the best in
everything of all the women in the town. His love for reading is really striking. He has read all our books twice. He is
now in the Psalms, the second reading of the Testament.
No one ever goes up without being requested to give him a
lesson, & he never tires of either reading or explanation.

[25] *Motlhwa*, termites, "white ants". (This sentence is the first on sheet three of
the letter, but there is no sign of any hiatus between it and the end of sheet two.
It may be that D. L. in copying from his original draft accidentally omitted a
phrase or line.)
[26] *Masetlhaoka*, "large white ants, which eat grass" (Brown); *mhetolo*, the Tswana
name for shrubs of the *Indigofera* species (Miller, *Woody Plants*, p. 92).
[27] Because he was still a polygamist.

When Machuire or Macuire[28] was here, he & his party spoke in the most bitter manner against the gospel. "Why have you a house of instruction in your town?" "That is a dwelling house", said S. "But I have heard you built a school". "You heard truly." "Then your town is done for. We shall get all your people to be servants, & you will be left with your book in a leshupi,[29] motse o senyegile rure." [30] "Is the town gone?", said Rachose;[31] "ecoa o senyegilegale, o sencoe o phatlalaricoe ki mekhoa ea bagolugolu ba rona, yana ga gona motse." [32] Sechele told me that the words of Macuire were more bitter than anything he could have concieved, but he was only concerned lest some of his people should believe them, some (said he) who do not understand. He roundly denied the existence of God. We had been on our previous picture night on the magicians of Pharaoh throwing down their rods.[33] As it is rather a familiar meeting we were assailed by the question, "How could they do that?" I related a story you may remember as having happened at the time of the reformation at St Andrews, or perhaps Melrose Abbey, of a pretended cure of a blind man, & asked, How could they do that? It was of course a poser. The explanation of that & a few other tricks of jugglery awakened breatheless attention. On the succeeding Sabbath our attention was directed to the gospel character-istics of which Paul spoke so positively, "If we or an angel" &c,[34] and then in the evening the baruti of tsieco.[35] After

[28] Matswiri, son of Pampa; he belonged to the royal family of the BaTlharo living near Kuruman, but was relatively insignificant in status (cf. Letter 43, where he is called "a petty chief").

[29] *Leshope*, "a ruin, a deserted kraal with no part of it still standing" (Brown).

[30] "The town has truly become destroyed (or spoiled)".

[31] Ratshosa Motsomi, headman of some BaTaung (Southern Sotho) who had originally come from the south-east with Sebetwane, but remained behind when that chief left the country of the BaKwena in 1826 (Schapera, *Ethnic Composition of Tswana Tribes*, p. 57).

[32] "Whereas in fact it was spoiled formerly, it was destroyed and became scattered owing to the conduct of our ancestors, hence there is no town" (a reference to the split in the tribe caused by the assassination of Sechele's father in 1822, cf. 5.3).

[33] D. L. used a magic lantern in order to illustrate and explain scenes from the Bible (cf. *Travels*, pp. 230, 278, 298 f.); for the magicians of Pharaoh, cf. Exodus 7: 8–13.

[34] "But though we, or an angel from heaven, preach any other gospel unto you than that which we have preached unto you, let him be accursed" (Galatians 1: 8).

[35] Teachers of deceit, false teachers (2 Peter 2: 1).

Macuire came Sechele said to me, Here is a moperofeti oa tsieco;[36] and after telling some of his foolish sayings asked me, in the hearing of a great number of his people, "If Macuire had been alive when Jesus was in the world, would he not have been Juda Isekariota?"[37]

The party came in a very suspicious manner. We believed they came for plunder. They wished to remain on the opposite side of the stream, but Sechele insisted on their coming into the town. Their horses were becoming sick & dying, yet they lingered, always appointing a day for departure & yet remaining. Then came your packet, and as the report you sent agreed exactly with appearances I went up, though it was night, & put the Bakwains on gaurd. About 80 guns were washed in the morning.[38] The discharging of these frightened Macuire's people sadly. Sechele then sent for Macuire, & asked what harm he had done him that he had come waiting for an opportunity to steal his cattle, adding, "If you want to do it, begin now." Macuire of course denied any evil intention, except that of going on to some tribe beyond the Bamangwato & stealing what he could get. He was then asked, "& what evil have the tribes beyond the Bamangwato done you? You are still eating Sebegoe's cattle." He replied he wished to buy a waggon & live independant of game flesh entirely. Plunder was evidently his object, but fear operated to prevent him getting any. The Wanketse wished to surround him & his party at night & cut them off, but Kosiencu[39] prevented that. He who went out to plunder was within a little of leaving his bones among us. We thank Him who watched over us & shielded us from harm. Very probably the fear which prevented the accomplishment of their purposes was imparted by Him whose existence they denied.

Sorry to hear that Robert comes out without finishing his

[36] False prophet.   [37] Judas Iscariot.

[38] D. L. may be referring to the ceremony of *go fôka marumô*, "the cleansing (charming) of weapons", in time of war. In view of the common assertion, based on *Travels*, p. 35, that the BaKwena had only five guns when attacked by the Boers in 1852, the reference to 80 should be noted.

[39] Kgosientsho, often mentioned below as leader of a lawless party of Griqua hunters; the name, however, is of Tswana origin, though I have been unable to identify its bearer more closely.

course of study at College.[40] But we hope almost against hope that he may have been permitted to remain. Pity he listens to the foolish advice of Dr Anandale.[41] No degree is ever granted by University College of M.D., unless the candidate is a graduate in medicine or surgery of some other college (recognized by them), and has passed two years subsequently to the taking of that degree in an hospital or in public practice of his profession. If his head is affected by the racking of a winter session, the summer ought to be spent in preparation for the next. One or two medical classes might be attended for profitable exercise, but the main attention ought to be directed to lessening the labour of the coming session. The books to be read are well known, so there is no difficulty in preparation. However, it may all turn out for the best yet.

Sechele desires me to write for a Testament of the immitation Russia, a brownish colour. Perhaps a few of the finer Testaments may be sent by the next opportunity. We have none of any sort, & may need them before very long. We were quite in need of the Selections[42] before Boe came, and are glad of them. Sechele wished me to mention a Testament & Selection bound together, but I have the impression that you parted with all these. Also to ask if you have forgotten the umbrella of which you spoke by Siloishoe.[43] We left a tripod intended for him, also all the pictures we selected from your stock.

Isaiah is certainly an improvement on Proverbs.[44] I feel sorry in reading the prophet that you did not spend more time on the Proverbs. Jesia has many new words, at least new to me. I have not yet tried them, but will do so in my Eastern trip. Potlaka is so common here it seems preferable

---

[40] Moffat's son Robert had been studying at Glasgow, "preparatory to coming out as a missionary", but owing to ill health was obliged to return to S. Africa (J. S. Moffat, *Lives*, p. 261). He sailed from England in October 1847 (*LMS Chronicle*, vol. 11, 1847, p. 173).

[41] Not identified.

[42] *Likaélo tse ri tlaocoeñ mo likualoñ tsa Morimo*, 2nd ed., London 1841, Moffat's translation of *A Selection of Scripture Passages* (by William Brown).

[43] Not identified; Seloisho is a Tswana personal name.

[44] Moffat had recently published at Kuruman a Tswana translation of Proverbs, Ecclesiastes, and Isaiah, entitled *Mahuku a Morimo a a entsicoeñ kholaganoñ e kholugolu, eboñ Liperovereba tsa Solomon, le Moréri, le Liperofesho tsa Yesaia.*

to akotsa in "He that believeth shall not make haste." It means to hurry one, or be in a hurry. Perhaps my love for it arises from the meaning they attach to akoha. To Bakwains it means, "Come hither". Again & again have I called to a man working, Akoha, be quick (as I thought), but he would leave off immediately & run to me. I have not the smallest doubt but your Isaiah will bear comparison with any one in the country. The fewness of the typographical errors makes me think you do not regret parting with your old assistant, I mean he of captivity notoriety.[45]

Perhaps I too shall be honoured with "durance vile", but I feel in the path of duty when I devote a week or two of relaxation to the Eastern tribes. I hope Jesus is my shield, and with that hope & the path of duty before me I am not the metal to cower or turn tail to a Boerish storm. I should like Mary to come too, but she is sick of waggon life. It has been hurry scurry ever since we came. I feel very languid & think a trip will do me good. I have longed to visit the Eastern tribes for a long time, but have been bound hand & foot here. It is reported we shall have a visit from Potgeiter. Perhaps I may induce him to stay where he is.

Robert is rather a consequential sort of gentleman. He won't even bestow a look on the chief, and if any of the people presume to salute him by touching him, he either walks past scornfully or lifts up a stick to keep them at a distance. You might see him lifting up a stick to those he could not strike above the knee, yet he roars out Murder if a kid looks at him. Seems to like English better than Sichuana, and is very fond of his little sister. She is equally delighted with him. Both are favoured with good health. When we ask where Grandpapa is he points Southward, but I think he has but little recollection of Kuruman now.

My brother Charles will have finished at Oberlin by next

[45] Early in 1847 Edwards, while on a trip to the tribes south-east of Mabotsa, was arrested by a party of Boers and taken to the local landdrost (magistrate) to explain his presence in those parts. It appears from his own account (letter to Tidman, 4.v.1847) that he had been mistaken for "Sechele's missionary" (i.e., D. L.), and when the error was discovered the landdrost "was perfectly satisfied & then treated me with respect & hospitality". Edwards before starting work at Mabotsa had been responsible for most of the printing done at Kuruman since 1831.

year. Is desirous I should write the Directors & introduce him as a candidate for China. Is "engaged" to a young New Englander who is very anxious to go as a missionary.[46] Does not like the American Board[47] on account of its connection with slavery. Another Society has sprung up which does not recieve slaveholders' money; this he would join, but it will not be strong enough by the time he has completed his course. I never advised him to become a missionary, but when I recieved a letter which I sent you I proposed to him to think of China. If I had that letter I should send that as an introduction, but it has gone out of the way. All I can do now is give the Directors a little of his history,[48] and if they like they may proceed to examine him as to capability &c as in any other case. But, poor fellow, he is unmercifully poor, and how can he come to London as a candidate? He writes us from Lafayette, where he was keeping a school during the vacation & lodging in a baptist minister's house. It is to be hoped our good folks will send him our £30 since they do not emigrate themselves, but probably the dearth has eaten it up.

Did your Australian seeds vegetate? None of my English seeds have come up except canteloupe & prize melons & prickly cucumber. Some of Jeffries's have come to the surface. We have sandy soil on the surface, but a peculiar sort of clay forms a stratum which lies about a foot below and in some places is at the surface. The water from the canal runs through the sand along the clay & in several parts comes up to the surface. Where the sand is a foot in depth everything grows beautifully, but where the clay appears grass chokes other vegetation & water stands for

[46] In October 1846, Charles L. had written announcing his recent engagement to "Harriette C. Ingraham, a native of New England", whom he had met at Oberlin. "She is of a most excellent family, has a brother a graduate of Brown University, is sister-in-law to the Rev. S. Bristol. Miss Ingraham is a member of the senior college class, and by next August will have completed a regular college education. She has charge of a young ladies' academy at present (vacation). Is twenty one years of age . . . She has already acquired some knowledge of the four languages Hebrew, Latin, Greek and French. Knows how to do household work, a very indispensable item, you know. But above all I think she is imbued with a spirit of deep piety—has a strong desire to do good, wishes to go as a miss[ionary]."
[47] American Board of Commissioners for Foreign Missions, founded 1810.
[48] This D. L. did in a letter to Tidman 30.xii.1847.

some time after every shower. It needs but little irrigation. I intend to try what boring a hole through the clay to perhaps a lower stratum of sand will do. This lower stratum does exist in some parts. I do not know whether it is universal.

We gave a small room door to the town house. It gave so much satisfaction that a novel idea was originated. Rhinoceros not unfrequently come by mistake rushing through the town. Two came lately, & an attempt was made to skin one entire & stretch it out for a front door, but it would not do.

Manyetsa, "if I have taken anything by false accusation", as Zacheus said.[49] It seems a compound of mano & ya, eat bread of deciet. Have you got this word out your way? Ga ki rue khomu manyetsa is the way it is used, as if one should say, "I do not live by deciet". Ñaro[50] is just the thing.

But I am now very sleepy. If I have forgot anything you mentioned I shall advert to it again on reperusal of your letter. Kind love to Mamary when she comes,[51] also to Mr Hamilton & Ashtons. We remember them all kindly, though we do not write at present. All here are well.

I shall try to find a little strychnia for Andries tomorrow morning before Boe goes. We send nothing now because our own waggon will soon go.

16th. The strychnia, $\frac{1}{8}$ of a grain once or twice a day untill he feels the muscles of his back twitching. If this effect is not produced in a week, three times a day will be the dose. If Boe remains half an hour I shall make it up in pills $\frac{1}{8}$ in each. I know you have no time.

The leaves of the ant medicine are dry & crumble now. The enclosed is mehetolo. There is another plant which dyes the teeth black.

Affectionately yours,
D. Livingston

[49] "And Zacchaeus stood, and said unto the Lord; Behold, Lord, the half of my goods I give to the poor; and if I have taken any thing from any man by false accusation, I restore him fourfold" (Luke 19: 8).

[50] This word is not listed in Brown's *Secwana Dictionary*.

[51] Mrs Moffat had left for Cape Town in August with her younger children, who were to be sent to school in England (J. S. Moffat, *Lives*, pp. 260–2).

I enclose a letter to Robert with a few remarks in the way of attempt at analyzing the language.[52] After it is written I feel disinclined to send it, but it is tuntunyeritse, filled up to the brim, and I don't like to throw it away. Will you read it at a leizure hour & give me your remarks? I shall feel obliged if you point out in what I am in error. We shall not hear from you for a long time, but must be content. We imagine Mameri is at the Cape now. Remember us to Mr Hamilton & Ann. Mary will write her tomorrow morning.

I shall put down the contents so far as I remember. Kankashi, an oar. Lekaoe, a reed skiff. Lecobobo, a thicket. Lituguana, D[itt]o. Mapakoana, a curtain. Leposa, to iketla, drawl in singing. Metsehula seems well known as the sea. Lotoe too is known, but they say metse hula is on both sides of the country. Matlurra, rough. Tlorolimpe, a dreamer. Hurua, to row. Khoroane ea khute is the nearest to ensign; it is the thobane ea boguera I mentioned.[53] Sekiri, an island. Bara, to swim (Heb[rew], to create). Some Selections, first opportunity. Lobila, I was mistaken as to its use. It is a very small path, one trodden only once, or one which has been abandoned & is now nearly obliterated.

My time is up, so I must conclude,

Ever affectionately yours,
D. Livingston

43: To JANET LIVINGSTON

7 November 1847

Address: (Care of Revd. Dr Philip, Cape Town) Miss J. Livingston, Almada St., Hamilton, Lanarkshire, N.B. *Postmark:* Hamilton, MY 10, 1848. [Wilson Collection.]

Kolobeng
7 Novr. 1847

My dear Sister Janet,

We recieved your kind favour of 4 Jan /47 while at Kuruman. I have just finished a reperusal, and as I am not

---

[52] See Letter 41. [53] See above, 40.16.

quite sure whether I answered it or not I dedicate this sheet to you. We have been since our return to this quarter as busy as you were in the first week of your straw bonnet business. Every day has its multifarious duties, and very seldom can we find the day long enough for all we intended to do. Yet we work in good spirits. We are beginning a new station again, but this is a very different commencement to either that of Chonuane or Mabotsa. The people must have had some esteem for us to travel 40 miles and build a new town on our account. They seem to feel that we are their real friends, and manifest their kindness in a great variety of ways. They are in general more sedate in our meetings. Some join in our singing, and they erected the meeting house of their own accord. The chief undertook our watercourse in exchange for a square house we superintended for him. Last week a petty chief, a bitter opponent from the Southward, reproached Sechele for attending to the preaching of the word & building a meeting house. S. told me of it and said, "I am only sorry for my people, some of them may imbibe his sceptical ideas." He sent for his Testament and read it aloud for about two hours by the side of the scoffer.[1]

We have not yet any conversions to cheer us. All looks favourably, & that is all we can say. Some Glasgow friends desired Mrs McRobert to request me to "tell them of success in order to stimulate them to prayer". I wonder it never entered into the heads of the simple ones to enquire what stimulus we have to work on & pray on year after year, without seeing any fruit. At Mabotsa I never went to meeting without a sense of oppression on my spirits. I earnestly wished to communicate saving knowledge, but never felt sure whether I should find any one to whom I could deliver the message. I cannot tell how I felt when after speaking on the most important of all themes, and in the most earnest manner, I saw less indications of interest than if all had been idle tales. In asking individuals afterwards of what they heard I have recieved the answer, "If

[1] Since this is obviously the episode involving "Macuire", described more fully in Letter 42 in the portion dated 14 October, "last week" suggests either that the present letter was begun some time before the date given at the head, or that "November" should read "October". Letter 42, as already noted, was received by Moffat on 24 October.

you had told us of oxen or game we should have remembered, but this word of God vanishes out of the heart, it goes in at one ear & out at the other." It is different here. We have always a meeting, & the chief is never absent. The subject spoken on can be made the topic of conversation afterwards, & is so frequently without my presence. We hope for good results from what we see, but this is still the day of hope, no fruit yet crowns our labours.

I do not know whether you new view folks pray for the outpouring of the Holy Spirit. Nothing but a special influence on their hearts will ever change these people. But this will perhaps stir you up to a vindication of your orthodoxy, so I forbear. I should have preferred to have heard that Mr McRobert was still preaching new views to being worried & laid aside by you "bodies". Really, Janet, I do not know what is come over you. How sweetly you Independants used to sing of recieving all into your communion of whom you could hope Jesus should say, "Well done &c, Enter &c." But the deed of the Glasgow churches shews another way of dealing.[2] Then one of the excluded churches turns round to its pastor & says, "Come now, you do not think as we do, off with you"; & Father seems pleased with it. You have got too strait laced for us since we left. If I ever come back again you will look queer when I invite you to the English chapel, won't you?

You find fault with me for my remarks on Mr Philip. I should not have said anything about him deceased, but I wrote about him alive & in the public newspapers sending forth challenges to all & sundry to take up the gauntlet with him on the subject of—what? Missions, Holy Spirit's influences, church polity, corn laws? No, on none of these, but on Homoeopathy,[3] or the doctrine which teaches that about a trillionth of a grain of common salt will have a

[2] "The unhappy result of the controversy" (about the "new views", cf. 30.17) "was that the 'Four Churches in Glasgow' felt compelled to withdraw from fellowship with the churches with which they had corresponded" (Ross, *Congregational Independency in Scotland*, p. 131). The church in Cambuslang, of which Mr M'Robert was pastor, was (like that in Hamilton) among those differing from the Congregational churches in Glasgow on the point at issue.

[3] The mention of homoeopathy suggests that this refers to William Philip (1.14), cf. Letter 45, but I have not traced the "challenges" of which D. L. writes, nor his own "remarks".

powerful medicinal effect on a person who is in the habit, as every one is, of taking several grains every day.

Missionaries are dispised in the Colony, & why? It is no longer a mission field. Every one knows it but missionaries. And what does the world think of us squabbling in the newspapers? A gentleman from India said to me, in allusion to these affairs, "Is it not disgraceful?" Since my residence in this country I have noted some providential events, & find no difficulty in explaining them, although at home you all speak of them as dark and mysterious. I tremble for myself, for I see that, in many cases, as soon as there is a departure from usefulness there is a period put to life. I do not say this in reference to Mr Philip in particular. I do not suppose his usefulness was impaired, but the Colonial system of missions having in him a warm supporter Providence seems to be rooting it up, in order that the benevolence of the churches at home may be turned into other channels. I do not enter into the subject of the Colonial mission farther than to say that the Colony is better supplied with the gospel and means of education than any part I know in Britain. You think the Tahitian affairs mysterious. It is no wonder to me that the missionaries were expelled & the Natives oppressed. God works in different ways [in] different parts of the earth. I cannot now enter on the subject in such a way as you could understand. A train of thought is suggested every time I think of the departures of certain good men, & I pray I may be kept humble & useful, & content to be guided by the Divine will alone even unto death.

Am glad to hear you succeed in your business. You must always try and improve. One fashion or shape will not last long, however much you may excel at it. If convenient it would be well to make an annual visit to Glasgow at the time the fashions change. Try & excel in all parts of your occupation.

Am sorry to hear by a letter we recieved since this was begun that Agnes's arm is affected. To me it seems rheumatism. Let her try quinine in doses as large as she can bear, say 6 grains three times a day. To a common bottleful of water add an ounce of Epsom salts, about a teaspoonful of Vitriol, & two drachms of Quinnae. Dose a wineglassful, three times a day. Keep the bowels open. Attend to them particularly in using the quinine. If it causes unpleasant feelings in the head she must decrease the dose. A burgundy plaster or common strengthening plaster, spread on soft leather & while hot before the fire sprinkled over with quinine or muriate of morphia, may be applied to the part or near it. The latter medicine is dear, a very small portion is got for a shilling. If Quinia does not do, request from Dr Thomson a trial of Colchicum in combination. If her appetite is bad the iodide of iron may improve it. A blister of the size of a crown piece, applied about 4 inches from the joint, above it & on the inner part of the arm (or the portion next the body), & when the blister is well risen the cuticle stripped off with a pair of sharp scizzors, & then [the] exposed surface sprinkled over with morphia, might do good.

During the period of "doctory", as the Yankees have it, she might keep her bowels open by making an effervescing draught of carbonate of potash (which you know as pearlash) & vinegar. A teaspoonful of the ash, & as much vinegar as takes away the unpleasant taste of the ashes when mixed in the waters. About a table-spoonful if strong enough in half a tumbler of water, the ash having been dissolved in a like quantity, then mixed & drank while fizzing. Pearl ash is the impure carbonate of potash. Very often the latter is not very much purer.

We have been requested to establish a prayer meeting in the chief's house, a good sign. We have it every evening, about 8 o'clock.

Child squalling. That is the music in which I conclude this letter.

Yours affectionately,
D. Livingston

3 Jan[uar]y 48. This letter now goes of[f] to Colesberg. Am thankful to say we are all well. Have heard from Charles, and a letter for him accompanies this to Scotland. Are you letter-openers? Remember the fate of Sir James Grahm.[4]

---

[4] Sir James Robert George Graham (1792–1861), statesman, "became highly unpopular, especially after his admissions of tampering with foreign refugees' letters, 1844" (*D.N.B.*).

44: To ROBERT MOFFAT
November (?) 1847[1]

[Bruce Collection.]

[First leaf missing]

". . . him cattle he would make rain." Sechele imme-diately ordered him to be beaten & expelled the town. A lot of fellows with sambucs & switches of moretloa[2] soon convinced his godship that he was made of clay. Being ex-pelled he went to Moseelele, with whom perhaps he has found quieter quarters.

Our rain maker is the chief of the Babiriri[3] here. The sly rogue said the rain was in the chief's mouth, that he had only to give them leave to dig up a child which had died at Chonuane last year. He opposed this for some time, but the people became very clamourous and he allowed them, but still no rain. They then had a meeting on the top of the hill, & Sechele made a noble confession of his determination to depend on God alone. The people gave a shout of hu or hoo, in derision I believe, which might be heard a mile off. They wished him to order a stone to be rolled down the hill as a sort of augury. Very well, said he, down with your stone. But no rain came, so he ordered the Babiriri chief to give up, but that worthy with a brother of the chief refused. They know they have the majority of the people on their side.

Sechele makes no scruple of ridiculing the rain making. The most annoying thing about it, he says, is they make the conditions of success to depend so much on his doing certain parts of the operations. He feels his position very uncomfor-table. He would like to take a long journey to the Cape or

---

[1] The year in which this letter was written is fixed by the contents, and the month (approximately) by Moffat's endorsement: "Copied for Mr Parker, Birmingham, Decemr. 25th". (J. F. Parker was a friend to whom Moffat often sent extracts from D. L.'s letters, cf. Moffat to Tidman, 24.i.1849).

[2] Sjambok (Afrikaans *sambok*), rhinoceros-hide whip; *moretlwa*, the Tswana name for *Grewia flava*, canes of which are commonly used for whipping people.

[3] BaBididi, an Eastern Tswana people. The section among the BaKwena came there as refugees during the period of MaTebele rule in the Western Transvaal, *c.* 1825–37 (Schapera, *Ethnic Composition of Tswana Tribes*, p. 56).

England to obtain quiet to study the Bible without the distractions attendant on his position. Poor man, as he is only partially enlightened he needs our sympathies & prayers. We have some of the influential men on our side, I believe from a conviction that we are right, but the old gentlemen, although all are friendly, stick most pertinaciously to use & wont. You will remember us & them before the throne of our great high Priest.

The prayer meeting in Sechele's house is usually well attended. I make a few remarks on the portion read. He rings a small bell for all within hearing to come. Have you heard anything of a bell for us? We need it, for the hand bell being so much used is becoming loose. Mr Edwards might give us his for any use he makes of it. We do not make any enquiries, but hear that things are in a sorry state over the way. The chief lives out at a post, & nobody comes to meeting except to annoy. The only individuals in the school are a few Kurumanites. The people who live near Mr Inglis[4] are those which composed two villages East of Mabotsa which Mebaloe & I visited regularly for a considerable time. They were all very friendly in their conduct to us, but we do not know how it goes on with them now.

Sechele sent a pair of khoodoo horns for you this evening. He salutes you with them, & Mrs M. & Mr Hamilton. I burned a lot of horns at Chonuane in the belief that I should soon be able to collect more for you, but have only got two rhinoceros horns as yet. I send a few bulbs. Will get more soon. They will cost nothing worth thinking about. There are no waterbucks nearer than the Ñotoane a day off. I have spoken to some hunters about the skin, but have not yet secured one. We send out three pieces of rosewood. We went about half a day from this to a large plantation of them, & picked out what externally would have made excellent planks more than a foot in diameter, but after trying five we found all had a large cavity inside. We got quite tired of cutting, and came away believing we should have better success on a hilly situation. We levelled four small ones, & send the three best. Two are hollow, but believing that Mr Ashton might find some of the wood

4 Inglis was then stationed at "Matebe" (Pôwê, 25.5).

useful in chair making we put it in & leave the division of it to your discretion. I say nothing of it to him, so you can take what pleases you best. It cracks immediately wherever the bark is taken off, so I send it unbarked.

[*No signature*]

1848

45: To ROBERT MOFFAT

March (?) 1848

[Bruce Collection.]

[Top third of leaf torn away]
... be some mistake in the newspapers, some bottomless slough of dispond between this and Kuruman. My reason for thinking so is, some months after our return[1] we recieved a packet of letters by two Griquas. You mentioned then that newspapers had been forwarded, I supposed to Motito. Several months elapsed and then, although our expectations had been raised, we recieved only two Advertizers, & one Grahm's Town Journal.[2] The present parcel contains six or seven Advertizers, making 8 or 9 since we left Kuruman. I think it right to mention this, because more may have been sent, & if lost by having come by way of Mabotsa the risk may be avoided in future. A portion of the Patriots[3] sent this time we read in Kuruman in March or April last year. It is probable those intended to be sent may still be with you. You need not however put yourself to much trouble about them.

Very glad to hear of Mamary's safe arrival at the Cape.[4] The other communications awaken very many thoughts, forebodings, regrets. We feel especially sorry that Robert's prospects have taken the turn they have done.[5] But poor

[1] From Kuruman, where the Livingstones had been in the early part of 1847.
[2] *The South African Commercial Advertiser,* published in Cape Town three times weekly since 1824; the *Grahamstown Journal,* published weekly since 1831.
[3] *The Patriot,* a journal "of Nonconformist sentiment and intelligence", published bi-weekly in London since 1832.
[4] Mrs Moffat and her children had reached Cape Town in October 1847 (R. U. Moffat, *John Smith Moffat,* 1921, p. 21).
[5] Robert Moffat, junior, on his return from England became a surveyor in Government employ. "He always remained a firm and true friend of the natives,

234

short-sighted mortals as we ought not to presume to prognosticate. He seems determined to try what can be done by means of scientific knowledge. Theology is not to be named in the same day with science. The very decided preference he mentions for the latter has made me conclude that a visit to this country is necessary to teach him that it is only the mere handmaid of the former. The $\frac{1}{100}$ part of a century will convince him that the gospel is the only power competent to effect much among heathen. Most sincerely do I sympathize with him in his aspirations for the benefit of Africa. It is cheering to read his effusions. Love for poor humanity has not left this world, although when in a state of dispondency we are tempted to think it has & growl out, "All seek their own, not the things of Jesus Christ". If he tries the experiment in some part where Natives are well inclined to or have believed the gospel, he will not be disgusted by their apathy. They will shew him due respect. His health will be improved. . . .[6]

. . . What a mercy to be guided by the overuling hand of Him who is omniscient. We are often delivered from dangers & know nothing of them. How much gratitude we owe for the deliverances of which we are aware. When returning from the Eastward[7] it was necessary to cross a dry river, the banks of which were very steep. Paul & I jumped down to look for a ford, the waggon continuing its course along the bank abreast of us. We came into a part with grass longer than ourselves & full of game paths. I was thinking, "this is a very lionlike place", when Paul proposed mounting the waggon, his thoughts being in

and was subsequently of great service to the Bechwana Mission in a commercial capacity; but anything short of his entire consecration to direct missionary work failed to satisfy his parents, with their intense devotedness to a cause to which it was their desire to feel that they had given not only themselves, but their children as well" J. S. Moffat, Lives, p. 262).

[6] Top third of page torn away.

[7] Early in February D. L. had gone on a journey among the Eastern tribes, "one object of which is to recruit & remove the languor of body & mind which affected me before I begin the erection of a permanent dwelling" (13.ii.1848 Watt). In D. L.'s Journal, the encounter with the rhinoceros described below is entered under the date 17 December 1848 (cf. Blaikie, p. 92). That portion of the journal, however, was compiled in 1853, from notes recovered after the destruction of Kolobeng, and D. L. apparently confused the present journey with one he made at the end of the year.

the same train as mine. I turned my face waggonwards, and when within 20 paces of it found a female black rhinoceros, having just calved, between us & the waggon. The beast, enclosed by us & the waggon, had its attention providentially directed towards the latter, & Paul & I ran into a rut. The animal made a furious attack on the waggon. Its horn glanced on a spoke & split it up as if it had been a boiled carrot. The felloe[8] split too with the shock. It knocked the other parts of the waggon, but broke nothing. Isaac was in the waggon & thinks he shot the beast, but it went away with its little red calf. We heard its snorting as we stood in the rut, & our guns being in the waggon expected every moment to be visited, but we were down the wind.

When at Mokhatla's we were within one half day of Pretorious[9] & went to see him. He had gone to cut wood, but his wife was very kind. Pressed us to remain, & we should have complied, but we saw 4 Bamapela children in the house, stolen slaves. My heart grew sick & I left. My people by my advice tried to steal them by telling them where we should spend Sunday. They said they had often ran away, but Mokhatla caught them & returned them to their owners. Mokhatla told me that he invariably assisted them to escape, untill a lad having come to him requesting to be shewn his way to Sechele's, he sent men to take him forward but his feet became . . .[10]

. . . We expected Morukanelo tonight, but suppose you may have been absent when he arrived. I may as well tell you some more of our wants: A trowel; large & small beads; a ladle, & bullet mould; hiefers if you can get them, at any price (Boers charge 20 dollars for those two years old); she goats; a musket if you have one to spare; trees; vine cuttings; fruit stones for seed; pictures;[11] the large vice mentioned.

We should have been at the house now had the waggon been here. We do not like to spoil the new one. We have all

---

[8] MS. has "felon".

[9] Johannes Lodevicus Pretorius, who had settled near the present town of Rustenburg in 1839; he is referred to again below (Letter 50) as "our friend Pretorius".

[10] Leaf of MS. missing.

[11] The words "Fruit . . . Pictures" deleted in MS.

the window & door frames ready, beams too, & will bring the roof home next week. Some are making bricks for the partitions. Had an excellent crop of potatoes. Maize not quite so bad as we expected, but will manure for crop of English corn. Some worthy sent us a large assortment of plates for shoe heels, and a lot of nails which I imagine are meant for nailing lead on the roofs, thick cast-metal things of about ½ inch in length. I think I must sow them in the garden, & if they do not grow longer my vexation will go with them into oblivion. The pictures I selected were left with you, I do not know where.

23 March. I had written the above in expectation of the return of the Griquas, but Sekhomi seems to have delayed the fulfilment of their desires longer than they expected. Right glad we were to see the old waggon again. We each thank you most sincerely for the apples & other fruits. They are a great treat to us, both young & old enjoy them (the apples) much. It was well you did not send potatoes. We have a large supply, and nearly all are of good size & quality. Whether the size is owing to my having selected good seed, by making the cook cut off the small end of all the large potatoes for seed, I do not know, but it is comfortable to think & believe that one has had some agency in effecting a good result. I thank you for the seeds, & will certainly try what can be done in the way of raizing trees &c. The ginger is about a foot high, but no appearance of flower. The olive does well.

The chest was sold immediately to Sechele for an ox. The guns went off & both seem well pleased, but that is all. Mebaloe told me he has about 40 dollars of the price. Sechele will give his in ivory. Hope this will be convenient. I must not omit to thank you for the powder horn. It will now be of use. I do not like to keep two things when one is enough for my wants, so I gave it [to] Sechele to be put in the place of that he gave me. He was disappointed in not recieving a supply of soap as well as we. We can only sell two of the bars sent, and as these will soon be consumed it may be well if you remember to procure a good supply for us. We can always dispose of it for sheep &c. We are very thankful for the tea. You could not of course know that we were in need of it.

Please send the vice by all means. That which we have at present has shewn symptoms we do not like. The thread inside came wriggling out. I took or broke off the part which protruded, & now it cannot be opened very wide without getting dislocated. The thread seems to have been made of a bit of wire soldered on to the inside of the box.

You will observe I mention the non-appearance of the Advertizers. Mr Frideaux[12] sends 18 or 19 by this opportunity. Had these come before I penned the above I should not have said anything. I suppose I have now recieved a fair share of what have come to hand. I believe everything came safe. A small phial of Cayenne pep[p]er came on a former occasion. Mary reminds me we have never thanked you for it. If we forget anything please put the neglect to anything but ingratitude. A tomahawk puzzles me. Mary says it is for meat, but what is the use of the hook if not for pruning trees? What wild Indians we are, not to know the use of our own weapons! I think I have seen butchers use the hook in splitting open the backbone. The Native melons here & at Mokhatla's are excellent. We shall send some seed, also of one, very large red flesh, we had this year. The Native melon with bands of dark green along the rind grows so large, Mary Robert Agnes & I cannot manage one at a sitting. The people have given us a good supply. The green flesh was excellent. Canteloupe not so good.

We have fairly began our new house. Beams were sawn by two Boers. We have nine workmen of the Bakwains. Khalimela of stentorian lung celebrity[13] is a factotum; knows everything, for "he has been to Kuruman & was taught by Moshett".[14] He tells this so often, we cannot avoid a smile now when we hear it. He makes a good effort at waggon driving & is one of our under sawyers.

By the way, as I am on the subject of workmen I must beg

[12] Jean Frédoux (1823–66), of the Paris Evangelical Missionary Society, had joined Lemue at Motito in 1845.
[13] See above, 30.7, and Letter 40.
[14] Moshêtê, the Tswana pronunciation of Moffat's name.

if it is possible for you to get heifers for us to make an effort on our behalf. There is nothing we need more than these. The men will work most cheerfully untill the house is finished if only promised a two year old hiefer. Although you should pay 16 dollars for them they will be a cheaper mode of payment than any other. When I told them of the difficulty I experienced in procuring them, they said, "Never mind, although you only get $\frac{1}{2}$ of them next year & the other half two years hence we shall be perfectly content." We bought ten cows when married. These may be said to constitute our stock still. We have not been able to add to their number. But I need not enter into a long disquisition on cow tails. You will understand that anything in the namagari[15] line will be extremely acceptable & useful if you can procure them without inconvenience.

Mebaloe gave me 24 dollars when we went out to Kuruman last to endeavour to purchase two hiefers. I intended to try & induce Moyahe[16] to sell them when at Likatlong. Mentioned it to him, but was called away suddenly.[17] After reaching Kuruman I sent, I forget by whom, the money to Mr Helmore, & a note requesting him to use his influence in the matter. I never afterwards heard a word about it. As he will soon be over to eat fruit again with you, perhaps you will be kind enough to give him a hint.

Have you any iron rod fit for making ramrods? Have made some out of band iron, but the process of hammering out is very tedious and they break after all if trod upon. Had the hammer been large it would have been very useful. We have the loan of a stone hammer from Mr Ashton, but felt the want of a large one. Will you purchase for me one of Mr Hume's adzes with the opening for the insertion of the handle wide? I bought one from him, but it admits a very small handle & hurts the hands. There were several, such as that you bought for Paul. Not a thin oblong one thus ▯.

In regard to sending to Colesberg for supplies for us

[15] *Namagadi*, a female (used of animals); in the present context, a heifer or cow (*kgomo e namagadi*).
[16] Not identified; Mojahe is a common Tswana personal name.
[17] Cf. Letter 39.

when an opportunity occurs, it will be better for you to make a guess at our wants than wait till we mention them. If we get too much we can with pleasure say stop. If we are in want we may in impatience be disposed to growl out, "Why didn't you think of us?" Sorry the bell has not come. If the wind is against us we cannot make ourselves heard through $\frac{1}{6}$ part of the town. We can procure buffalo heads. Great numbers are killed daily. They leave the horns in the field. We have gone through with our pictures & are now at a loss for subjects in our Tuesday evening meetings. We speak on the wonders of creation, but have nothing to illustrate them. You will remember the pictures mentioned next time a waggon comes this way.

Have had no time to examine translations or anything else for a long time. Am very glad you have finished Isaiah, &c. Go on with whatever may seem best for the great cause, whether prophets or priests, & never mind though "every fool will be meddling". I do not understand you[r] misgivings as to purity of motive. You had desired, resolved, intended, to translate as much as you could of the Divine word before you ever heard of any other translation. You would have proceeded to the work although we who may snap if we can had been all dead & rotten. Your motives were in operation antecedent to all that carping which some of us may indulge in. Never mind. The scriptures in Sicuana will live, but no more will be known of the petty jealousies which may now peer out than we now know of the bickerings brawlings backbitings & flytings which took place between Solomon's 300 wives & 600 concubines. Pity but we remembered more vividly that we are immortal & might live so as to be always doing eternal good to our perishing fellow men. I wish I had a constant desire to do all for the Divine glory. In building, ploughing, &c I often feel as if these operations were not those in which I ought to be so continuously engaged. Think I should not feel so in translating, printing, &c. But one always feels the evils of his own situation most.

In your medical practice you seem to have been pretty successful. I observe in a memoir of Mr W. Philip of Hankey in the Scotch Congregational Mag. a boast of his successful homoeopathic treatment of small pox. Only one sixth of his patients died, while in other parts the fearful mortality of $\frac{1}{3}$ obtained.[18] Suppose his patients to have been 100, $\frac{1}{6}$ is sixteen per cent. In Calcutta the mortality among the Natives is 5 per cent. There vaccination does not prevail. In London previous to the introduction of vaccination the mortality of those who caught the disease was 8 per cent, or $\frac{1}{2}$ that at Hankey, and now when vaccination is very general in the metropolis the mortality is 2 per cent. *Compare two with sixteen.* $\frac{1}{3}$ & $\frac{1}{6}$ are both very high rates of mortality, & certainly there is not a bit of room for boasting. The mortality in small pox depends occasionally on the virulence of the case which communicated the disease to a village. Innoculate a number from a bad case, & all have it very badly, & if from a mild case all have it mildly. This is the rule, & to it there are of course exceptions. The small pox medicine is vaccine virus, and all one can do if the disease is severe in a vaccinated village is to ascertain the cause of unusual severity & endeavour to prevent others coming within the range of that cause. If I saw some exposed to the infection from a severe case, I should propose innoculation from a milder case, that they might have the disease in its mildest form. If all were mild cases, what room would there be for me to boast, especially if all were as I suppose the Hankeyites are generally vaccinated? This subject starting up in my mind leads me to enquire if you have got vaccine virus for us yet. The question (as many others) is I believe superfluous. It will not remain long at Kuruman, wherever else it may lodge.

You may give a child jalap, scammony, magnesia. A very little of the two former does if a little calomel is added.

---

[18] Philip (1.14) had been drowned in the Gamtoos River on 1 July 1845. While a divinity student at Glasgow he had also taken "a regular course of medical training" and qualified as a doctor (*LMS Chronicle*, vol. 9, 1845, p. 172; *Evangelical Magazine*, vol. 24, 1846, p. 3). The "memoir", published in the *Scottish Congregational Mag.*, vol. 6, 1846, pp. 4–8, 49–54, states (p. 6) that he had become interested in homoeopathy, "embraced the system with enthusiastic ardour, and determined to practise it", and (p. 49) that immediately after his arrival at his mission station "the small-pox broke out among the people, and he had above twenty patients continually on his hands. He treated them all *homoeopathically*, and was so successful, that he only lost a *sixth* of his patients, whereas, in other places, there was the fearful mortality of a *third*."

Three or 4 grains of calomel pass off by stool without causing salivation in children. In severe cases I give this amount immediately, & the bowels are moved freely in a few hours. Sweet oil does in young children instead of castor oil, also a plaster of jalap or rhubarb in cases where nothing is retained on the stomach; but I have not tried this on black skins. In your skin case you cured the woman of the effects of the pills. The pills I have not doubt cured the skin disease. I have not yet met with a case in which the arsenic failed to cure. I have had bloody stools from it & all the symptoms you mention, but these were invariably the signal for the disappearance of the disease. Your case may however be an exception. The medicine ought to have been continued, but in diminishing doses.

The Griquas have come, so I must make haste & conclude all I have to say. I intend writing a report to the Committee tonight & will enclose it. If you do not go you will be kind enough to forward it. If they do not recommend my expense to be paid, I shall send a bill to Cape Town, & no matter who grumbles.[19]

Some Bakwains go out with the Griquas on their own business. They will bring letters back, I daresay. Will endeavour to procure bulbs, seeds &c, according to your desire, but am afraid to promise much, for am so hurried I can't do half I would. We have done but little for some time back. It seems so. Doors & window frames, beams, litlomesho,[20] & on Tuesday we begin to cart stones. This is all. Some bricks too. When we begin to the walls we shall soon get them up, & then we shall begin to believe we have done something. Thanks for the loan of the sail. I have not felt the want of wire. A nail filed round does in putting on steel on a pan.

If an infant bleeds at the nose even pretty freely, I

[19] The fifth meeting of the Committee, at which Moffat was in fact present, was held at Griquatown on 15–16 May 1848. One of its resolutions, carried unanimously, was "That this meeting transmit to Mr Livingstone an extract from the Directors' letter of 3rd Septr 1847 containing a resolution subject to his station and a vote of £30 to defray the expenses of erecting a dwelling house at Chonuane—at the same time expressing its dissatisfaction at the *irregular* way in which that money had been voted by the Directors, inasmuch as no application was made *to the Committee* by Mr Livingstone for any sum of money to defray his expenses."

[20] Rafters.

should do nothing except apply cold to the head & back. If severely . . .[21]

. . . We have made a beginning for the phalalo,[22] £7. 7. o. Morukanelo gives a pound nearly, & Sechele another. Mebaloe has come in to request tumerishos[23] to all. They are not so heavy, so I enclose them. I cannot lay my hands on the Directors' letter. Have sought for it but cannot find it. I enclose the report & return. If you do not go you will please send it. If you go perhaps you will hand it to the Secretary. Let Mr Ashton see it.

Mary desires me to write for shoes from you, No. 6, & put them in the account. By the way, I may say we had better not let our accounts run on so long as the last. When it runs up to hundreds it makes me nervous, & I begin to think of the workhouse, poor law union, or whatever they call it. When you have time you may let me know how we go on in the debtor & creditor line.

We send back the letters with many thanks for the perusal. Love to all in the house, Ann &[c]. Mr Hamilton must excuse me again. Am sorry I cannot write him. Mary sends tobacco for him. One portion comes from the Bamapela, another (the largest) from Mokhatla. Far-fetched things are usually valuable, far-fetched ideas but little worth.

Believe me yours affectionately,

D. Livingston

The reason of the 8 shillings is Edward's charge of £3. 8. o additional in an account for which we had previously settled. It was £5, & subsequently changed to £8. 8. o.

46: To MR AND MRS N. LIVINGSTON

5 July 1848

Address: (Care of Revd. Dr Philip, Cape Town) Mr Livingston, Almada St., Hamilton, Lanarkshire, N.B. *Postmark:* Hamilton DE [*rest undecipherable*]. [Wilson Collection; brief extracts published in Blaikie, *Personal Life*, p. 86, Seaver, *David Livingstone*, pp. 109 f.]

[21] Leaf of MS. missing.
[22] "Church contributions for Mission work" (Brown).   [23] Greetings.

Kolobeng
5th July 1848

My dear Parents,

An opportunity having recently occurred of transmitting letters Southwards by one of our Native teachers proceeding in that direction in order to arrange the affairs of a son recently deceased, I felt extremely sorry that I had not a letter ready for you, & the more especially as I dispatched one for Charles to your care. I begin now in hopes that this may have the good fortune to overtake his ere it reaches you. If it does not, perhaps undeterred by the pillory & universal execration which befel Sir James Grahm you may be induced to commit a similar deed to that which has given his name an unenviable notoriety.[1] We recieved a letter from Janet subsequently to that of Agnes, and lately we were delighted by the arrival of a short one from you enclosing one from Charles. All have been gladly welcomed. Janet's was answered, & although I have the impression that I had done equal honour to Agnes my rib informs me I am mistaken, and if Agie will forgive me I shall promise her the next effusion I can produce.

I have written twice to Charles within the present year, and am very glad to hear from him that he has at last recieved some of my epistles. I should much prefer his being connected with our Society to being united to any other (except perhaps the Church of England Do.). Time would be given him to acquire some medical knowledge, & this would be of very great advantage to him in his future course. People who have but a small amount of knowledge of the healing art, no more perhaps than mother, possess the means by which much perplexity & long continued regret are avoided in the event of residing at a distance from medical aid. I always feel thankful for the knowledge I obtained, and besides escaping from doubt & unavailing sorrow, which frequently succeed a fatal issue in one's own family when ignorant of the most approved modes of treating disease, it is something to follow in the wake, in our own feeble & imperfect manner, [of] the great Physician, the great missionary to our fallen world. It is a great

---

[1] See above, 43.4.

privelege to be a missionary of the cross, & greatly we need the prayers of all who feel an interest in the great cause, that we may be faithful unto death.

We are highly favoured in our people, thanks to our gracious Lord & master. All are respectful, & some shew great kindness. Our meetings are attended by attentive audiences. We have much cause to hope that the gracious spirit of God is working his own work in their hearts & enlightening their darkened understandings, for when spoken to in private several acknowledge that they pray in secret. We do not like the idea of any making hasty professions, and it takes a long time to clear away the rubbish which obscures their perceptions. All our hopes for final success are centred in the operation of the Holy Spirit. For a long time I felt much depressed after preaching the unsearchable riches of Christ to apparently insensible hearts, but now I like to dwell on the love of the great mediator, for it always warms my own heart, and I know the gospel is the power of God, the great agent[2] which he employs for the regeneration of our ruined world.

The chief is our steadfast friend. This is a time of scarcity, in consequence of the crops having again failed, but he remembers us as often as he can. He killed a zebra for us lately, & last night sent over the breast of a gnu (or as the Dutch call it a wildebeeste), & although it is one of the most fantastic looking wild beasts you can imagine it tastes like an ox. If Janet or Aggie saw a troop of them rushing along, whisking their tails round in every direction, having manes like the lion & unicorn in the Royal arms, only instead of a crown horns bent forwards thus, she would immediately conclude she saw a squad of the king of the forest coming to devour. The , zebra tastes like what you may imagine a horse does, but though it has all the flavour you experience when near the latter animal, custom makes our teeth water over the yellow bilious-looking fat under its beautifully striped skin.

Two days ago we entered our new house. What a mercy to be in one[3] again. A year in a little hut through which the wind blew our candles into glorious iciclles (as a poet would say) by night, and in which crowds of flies continually settled on the eyes of our poor little brats by day, makes us value our present castle. O Janet, know thou, if thou art given to building castles in the air, that is easy work to erecting cottages on the ground. I am still making doors for it. A big wolf came the night before last & took away a buffalo's skin from the door. Mary wanted me to go & see whether the room door were fastened, but in reference to a celebrated deed of brother John I advised her to take a fork in her hand & go herself, as I was too comfortably situated to do anything of the sort.

The children have been much troubled with ophthalmia, but we hope the change of situation will prove beneficial. One of my letters must have miscarried, for the impression on my mind is very strong that I informed you the name of our first born is Robert Moffat Livingston. His sister is called Agnes after our dear mother, & as the Natives have no hard g in their language she is usually named Nannee, which is as near Nannuck as possible. Robert is somewhat like your humble servant, but more like Charles was when younger; speaks a little in both languages, & is as great a carter as Charles was when he bought Will Forest's[4] horse with a shilling. He transforms everything into waggons & oxen. Even at dinner the potatoes are ranged into oxen to the meat as the waggon. Nannee is a frolicsome little lady with black eyes & hair, always merry, generally wakening in the morning with a loud laugh before her eyes are open. They are both of course too young to know anything of their far distant relatives. May He who feeds the young ravens remember them & carry them in his bosom to the abodes of everlasting peace. We commend them to your prayers.

As for ourselves, we wish to spend our lives in the great work of our Lord Jesus. Let the whole earth be filled with his glory, amen & amen. I never yet had a wish to return home. I have no hope of seeing you on earth, & though I should not it matters but little, for we all I trust have hopes of meeting again before the great white throne. I think if

[4] Not identified.

compelled to return from any cause, my desires to see & converse with you once more would become stronger the nearer I came to your residence, but it would turn out somewhat like our old newyearsdays, the anticipation would be finer than the reality. But the glorious prospects we have through our gracious Redeemer will in the realization far exceed all we can concieve. Let us all be faithful unto death. I should like to see Charles & understand the effects education have had on his mind & grace on his heart. He would think me a "stom mensch",[5] an unlearned & ignorant man, for all my plans of mental culture have been broken in upon by continual manual labour. We shall meet however where there are no incumbrances to the study of the works & ways of our Great Parent.

Do you know rose wood? It is a dear article at home. I am making doors & shelves of it. When cutting it, for we have to begin at the beginning of every thing here, the milk in the bark splashes into the eyes of the Natives & produces as much pain as so much Highland snuff would do, but we escape entirely, although we take a turn at cutting with them. The great difficulty we experience in raising European vegetables consists in the abundance of insects of the grass-hopper tribe. They devour every green thing. But I have hit on the plan of sowing turnip, cabbages, &c at the beginning of winter, and they do famously. If you send any more seeds, let them be thoroughly dried in the sun previous to being packed. I have just recieved a packet from India, entirely spoiled by the gentleman putting in some leaves of the banian in a green state for comparison with a variety of that tree here.

We have good hopes of several of our people. Some con-fess, when asked, that they pray in secret. All of them respect us. They see we wish their welfare. This is a great point gained, and we ascribe success thus far entirely to the grace & power of the Holy Spirit. We would say now, as we hope to do at all future periods of our course, Not unto us, Not unto us, &c. We have really attentive audiences on Sabbath. Talkers are occasionally seen, but these are sure to be strangers or very irregular hearers, & our more attentive

5 Afrikaans '*n stomme mens,* a dumb or foolish person.

attendants always reprove any irregularity observed. We commend them to your prayers that they may be saved.

Am sorry to hear of Agnes's continued affliction. It is difficult for me to form an opinion on it at such a distance but I should not dispair of motion being to some extent acquired. She ought to move it as much as possible even though the exercise should be attended with pain. Motion induced by muscles of the arm affected has a better effect than if performed by those of the other limb. A certain beneficial nervous influence is sent to the member by the mere effort. I should be inclined to try quinine in considerable doses still, or iodide of iron as a tonic acting on the general system.

Janet was rather in too great a hurry with her tooth. It is a wonder she did not think of having the aperture in the tooth stopped up by some experienced dentist. She ought to use a tooth brush morning & evening, with warm water in the winter, give up sugar in both tea & coffee (we do so always), & avoid acids. You must not blame Dr Thomson, for some teeth are so form[ed] that the thin portions of bone which came out must break off before the[y] come out. The roots are in general inclined towards the middle line of

the body , & the instruments are constructed for

operation in that way. But some teeth vary from the natural mode, the roots being inclined to the outside, & the pressure of the instrument hooks them more firmly in untill either tooth or alveolae as the thin portions of bone which you saw breaks. The instrument ought in these cases to be removed & placed between the teeth & cheek. But one cannot remember everything. I thought Dr T. a very cautious intelligent man. Will you present my kind remembrance. There is usually a cause for the decay of teeth, & drawing one does not remove the cause. That one would not have affected the others, but the cause whatever it was may still do so. Artificial teeth decay in the same way natural teeth do if the stomach is out of order. One night last year, after returning from a distance where I had been living on sun-dried meat (rhinoceros), very hard, & which seemed to

have broken a tooth, I got up at the middle of the night &
putting on the tooth key I made my rib give the wrench.
I roared out murder, & she of course stopped in the middle.
Another tug & another yell, & then a third brought it
out.[6] Janet may reflect on my wisdom as a set-off to her
folly as animadverted on above.

1st August. An opportunity occurs, so I send this as it
is. The chief has applied for baptism. Put away his superfluous wives. They being daughters of influential persons,
much excitement & opposition, more than he or we expected. But all will be overuled for good by the grace of God.
Love to all,
D.L.

[*Added by Robert Moffat*] 4th Sep[tembe]r. The box of
/46 from Glasgow for Mr Livingston has just arrived
here (Kuruman) all safe, and goes tomorrow. R.M.
Kindest Xtian love to all. R.M.

47: To ROBERT MOFFAT
11 August 1848

Address: Revd. R. Moffat, Kuruman. [Bruce Collection.]

[*First sheet missing*][1]
. . . fat grenadier. Our afflicted brother Ross will look
daggers at Mrs M. after reading her letter in the Chronicle.
Fancy an "epidemic" "chronic" complaint, & Epsom salts
producing very considerable effect in dysentery. Mrs M.
calls it acute, of course.[2]

[6] See Letter 33. The incident occurred in 1846, not "last year".
[1] The date is fixed by Moffat's endorsement: "Livingston, 11 Augt. 1848.
Acct. of Sechele's decision copied for Parker."
[2] An extract from a letter to Tidman by Ross, announcing the death of his wife,
was published in the *LMS Chronicle*, vol. 11, 1847, p. 132; immediately following
it (p. 133) was an extract, on the same subject, from a letter by Mrs Moffat to her
son Robert, then in England. Ross wrote that "In the latter part of September
[1846], my beloved partner began to be afflicted with an epidemic, at that time
raging in our District in the form of chronic dysentery"; Mrs Moffat does not
refer to an epidemic, but says "she caught cold; and this was followed by an attack
of acute dysentery". Neither mentions Epsom salts.

We are out of window glass. Size same as the church, but we are not in immediate want. Do not purchase any planks from Hume for us. Willow is devoured by insects here, even when painted as the doors we made at Kuruman were. A few of your superior locks are needed. A corn mill if good, & you recommend them, so they must be so. That we have of Mr Hume is a very poor thing, & the other will not grind maize. I thank you for the offer of the shower bath, but neither of us need it, & we don't like to have it merely to look at it. We may feel the want of it yet, but we may die too before the feeling arises. Some good tea if you please. The last was bad & very dear, two very absurd qualities met. Will you lend me the third volume of Prichard, & Leibig's Agricultural Chemistry,[3] by some careful conveyance? I have "What to Observe"[4] still. I do not mean to keep it altogether, but the long confusion has prevented me from making the use of it I wished.

Robert has had a very bad cold for a long time. Has been much reduced in flesh by it, but we hope the fine weather which now begins will have a favourable influence. The epidemic constitution of this year has manifested itself here in ophthalmia & thoracic affections. Disease has been prevalent in Mabotsa & in the regions beyond us. With you, if I am not misinformed, it has been chiefly seen in disease of stomach & bowels. It is interesting to note the epidemic constitution of seasons, for the diseases which appear seem to come in cycles of certain numbers of years. Agnes is very well. Mary enjoys good health, but much troubled with pains &c, & these are not to be wondered at, for she has much work on her hands. I do not wonder at her not writing her mother before she arrived.[5] She carried on both infant & sewing school herself in addition to her numerous domestic duties, & then she could not know whether the good lady would ever come back at all.

Apoplexy sometimes occurs as the effect of plethora. A

[3] J. C. Prichard, *Researches into the Physical History of Mankind*, vol. III (1841): *Researches into the Ethnography of Europe*; J. von Liebig, *Organic Chemistry in its Application to Agriculture and Physiology*, ed. L. Playfair (1840, 4th ed. 1847).
[4] Not identified.
[5] Mrs Moffat had left Cape Town early in March, and was back at Kuruman in the middle of May (J. S. Moffat, *Lives*, pp. 267, 269).

clot of blood is found on the brain if the death has been sudden, but sometimes the clot is absorbed, the patient having lived long enough for the purpose, and people finding nothing in the brain have said it had simply lost vitality. But it is now well known that apoplexy results from the very opposite state to plethora, & two modes of treatment are required. I do not apprehend apoplexy in Mrs M.'s case.[6] She might do better than read medical books & think on her sensations. A certain influence is always sent to an organ affected by the mind, & generally an injurious influence. Think as little as possible on her head. The means which rouse her into activity in the morning repeated at midday. A shower bath perhaps with the feet in warm water. Never to think about dying, but about living to purpose, believing that He who has our times in His hand will manage our exit for us & make it just what it ought to be. This is the sort of advice I should give if I had time to write it out, and I might add if she intends to leave us anything to send it by Paul,[7] for we shall assuredly be more grateful for it now than we shall ever be at any future time. The only thing we shall care about recieving will be her blessing after she is gone.

The valves of the heart are affected in Mr Evans's case in all probability, but what the peculiar affection is can only be ascertained by the stethoscope. He is liable to sudden death, yet may live long.

With kind regards to Mr Hamilton, Mrs M., & Ann,

Believe us, yours affectionately,

D. Livingston

Salutations to Paul.

48: To ROBERT MOFFAT

2 September 1848

Address: Revd. R. Moffat, Kuruman. [Bruce Collection; brief extract in Gelfand, *Livingstone the Doctor*, p. 43 (where the date is wrongly given as 1846).]

[6] She had been "much reduced" by her journey (cf. Letter 48).

[7] As indicated in Letter 46, Paul had gone to Kuruman "in order to arrange the affairs of a son recently deceased".

Kolobeng
2 Septr. 1848

My dear Father,

By the recent arrival of Monye Mabole[1] we were favoured with communications from the South, and now by the arrival of Motseabona[2] & party from the Bamangwato we have an opportunity of returning you thanks for your favours. We wrote lately by Aron[3] and have now but little to communicate. Monye Mabole brought 15 out of the 17 hiefers. One he said had been killed by a wolf near to this, & of the other he could give no account whatever. The Bakwains were of opinion that he had made away with both. I sent him for the horns of that said to be killed by a wolf. He brought a bone of some animal or other, but not being a comparative anatomist I could only look at it as a Motchuana does at the stars. I felt a little angry at first, but changed in feeling when I reflected that I might have lost ten, as Mr Ross did,[4] and any harshness on my part might have had a bad effect on his & other minds, & perhaps be the means of preventing their salvation. He brought one of his own & two of the principal men of the tribe here to intercede for him by means of it. I declined recieving it, but deferred rewarding him till some future time. He was apparently pleased to get off, and I am sure I am pleased with your promptitude in procuring the animals for us. We are out of debt in so far as animals are concerned, & have placed four of the number to our original stock of ten. We have never been in want of milk, but our old stock is in need of an infusion of new hands, or rather teats. This country is favourable for us in respect to cattle. If you recieve

[1] Not identified; the name suggests that he was a Tswana tribesman.

[2] Motsewabona, "one of the Kuruman people", who made frequent hunting and trading expeditions into the Interior (Moffat, *Matabele Journals*, vol. ii, p. 151).

[3] Arend Jonge, generally called by his baptismal name Aaron Joseph; a runaway slave from the Cape Colony, who after leading a nomadic life among the tribes of the Interior had become relatively wealthy through trade and ultimately bought his own freedom from his former master. He was the first convert to be baptized at Kuruman (1829), and subsequently made many hunting and trading expeditions to the north. Cf. *Apprenticeship at Kuruman*, ed. Schapera, p. 106, for references to some of the contemporary publications in which he is mentioned.

[4] I have not found any other reference to this event.

any from Mr Solomon[5] for us, please send them under Paul's charge or some one else whom you have confidence in.

The trees you sent were extremely acceptable. If you could have spared a few more they would have been equally prized. We have only two peach trees now & no apricots, but we hope some may come up. We have about 10 orange trees two feet high, two olives, and a lot of this country['s] trees which we thought of grafting, but they have not yet budded. Am sorry some of those you budded have had the new branches knocked off. Some of the country trees we put in the ground without roots, & it is said they will grow. We cannot bud or graft till next year. Do you steep your tape in gum, or what? The superb Claremont carrots came up splendidly, but a swarm of locusts left their place a blank, & we had sown all the seed sent. Our river has dwindled down to a dribbling rill, & we fear if rain does not come soon we shall have but a poor account to give of corn. Some is withered & will be useless. When we came in August or July last year it was a large stream, so we think its present insignificance may be attributed to the great drought of last year. We comfort ourselves by reflecting that at Chonuane our state would have been worse, for it is dried up, & Kolobeng according to the testimony of the antients is the only stream in the Bakwain country which never dries up entirely.

We went last week to Lōe for recreation & health to the children. Spent four days in the field, & returned invigorated. The much talked of Lōe[6] is a circular pit in a sandstone rock, and at present dry. Around the margin are a number of rude footsteps carved thus 🐾, apparently the

[5] Edward Solomon (1820–86), LMS missionary at Griquatown 1842–51 and Philippolis 1851–55; then left the LMS and became a pastor at Bedford, Cape Colony (*Register*, p. 52).

[6] Lôwê, about 12 miles north of Mochudi (Bechuanaland Protectorate), is said by the Tswana to be the place from which the first human beings and animals emerged on earth. It is "a hole *c.* 9–12 ft. deep, in a rock in a dry river bed. On the rock surrounding the hole there are engravings of footprints of men and wild animals. The Tswana believe that these are the footprints of the first creatures, and that one of them, pointing towards the hole, is the footprint of the one-legged Creator, who retired into the hole when he was disappointed with his creatures" (Breutz, *Tribes of Marico District*, p. 67).

work of children. The "spoor" with one exception goes into the pit. The exception is that of Matsién, the former of the Bechuanas.[7] As the story goes, he returned into it while men left it, but the spoor if intended to represent anything shews the opposite. They (the people) shew the old towns of the Bangwaketse, Bamangwato & Bakwains, Mashona &c &c, & all the Eastern tribes. The tradition seems to refer to the splitting up of the people into different tribes from Loe as the central population. The remains of old towns shew them to have been very large.

Mokhatla's men have just been to recieve their gun &c. The lock has been admirably done. I sometimes fail entirely in producing fire from steel. Do it over again, & it does well. Cannot understand the cause of failure in the first instance. Can you tell me?

I have some horns for you. I missed the opportunity for collecting seeds. The house engaged too much of my attention, & the man who usually does that sort of work for me & understands what we want being absent I held on expecting him till the season was past. Our beads too were at a low ebb before the last supply arrived. I am at present collecting some of the heads of the game for you, leaving the skin & under jaw entire. I think they will be interesting at home. Cumming intends to make an exhibition of his trophies in the Egyptian Hall, London, & make his fortune by them.[8] Will the heads be acceptable as above? I intend to put up a few in our lobby if Mary will give me leave to ornament it for her.

Am sorry to hear Mrs M. has been so much reduced by her journey. Thought her made of a piece of clay that would not wear out in a hurry. We do not like to hear her speaking about dying. Better if she were saying, "Now all our children are away, let us begin a new mission or something

[7] Matsieng, the one-legged Creator god (D. L.'s "former") associated with Lôwê; the place is nowadays still often called by his name. According to some traditions, he was the servant of the god Lôwê and the first chief of the Tswana.

[8] On returning to England, Cumming displayed his trophies both at the Egyptian Hall, Piccadilly (a building that could be hired for public shows), and subsequently at the Great Exhibition in Hyde Park (1851); he then "went about the country for some years, lecturing and exhibiting his lion skins . . . He was very popular and made a good deal of money" (A. Gordon-Brown, ed., *Narrative of Private Buck Adams*, pp. 281–2).

of that sort, let us go forward." But you will perhaps say, "Poor fellow, that's all he knows about it, wait till he feels the infirmities which creep on our frail bodies." The complaint with which she is troubled will invariably if severe require depletion. No matter where the pain manifests itself, when more than usually severe immediate recourse to bloodletting & other depletory measures are required. There is a tendency to congestion & an irregular distribution of blood, & she ought to think as little about her head as possible. When the stomach is stimulated by food of an exciting quality, a considerable quantity of blood is attracted to it & the spleen. The quantity is diminished in the brain & other organs. Purgatives have the same effect in drawing blood to the bowels. The mind does not act well after a full meal, as both blood & nervous energy are sent to the stomach. If one thinks much about stomach or any other organ, too much nervous influence is transmitted to it, & sometimes too much blood too. You need not be afraid to bleed if you observe fullness of system in connection with unusual pains in either head or any other part. Habitual medication is not good in any case.

Monday Evening. Sechele sends you a khoodoo's head which was killed in the town this morning. It has too much grass in it, but that can easily be remedied by wetting the skin again. I shall see what Motseabona can take tomorrow. He seems very willing to oblige, but he may not have much room. Have been to cut some pieces of tough wood today for ribs to the new waggon. After cutting up these we hope to build a smithy as our next engagement. After Paul comes we hope to itinerate somewhere, probably Eastward. Give him our love if still with you.

We are living in the hope & belief that progress is being made. Opposition exists, but not towards us. It manifests itself in hatred to the gospel. Some woman or other wished the lion which bit me were here to finish me. But all are civil. We cannot detect a particle of difference in the conduct of the mass of the people towards us, which is a cause for gratitude. They curse Sechele very bitterly. He says their curses are such, formerly he would not have said a word to them, he would have shot them instantly. The children are returning to the schools, & the meetings are improving. We have appointed two to converse with the chief in order to [have] a report at next church meeting. We should have been glad had Paul been here for the sake of his experience in such matters. I feel my heart trembling when I think of the danger of recieving one who may not be a true believer, or refusing one who is. We need Divine protection, & hope it may be granted to us. He mentioned his intention of calling his youngest child Setefano,[9] in allusion to himself as wishing to be (like him) the first follower of Jesus in this country. Mosielele tried to get one of the wives while she passed through his place on her way to her own people.[10] When she refused he issued a new edict against going to chapel. Sechele intends to send over an entreaty to him to allow his people to attend if they wish it.

We feel surprised to hear of so many people leaving the Kuruman. We could not credit reports which came to us about so & so leaving, but we now hear that these persons have actually left, and they predict that many others will follow. What can be the reason? If in your place I should feel inclined to look upon it as an indication that I ought to leave too. How hard you work for them, & everything is supplied for them that they need in the clothing department &c. Are they not too well off? Here when I do a little gun work (& between you & me I sometimes do more harm than good to a lock) I am both thanked & paid for it. We are both looked on as benefactors. A general interest is felt in our prosperity. Now you, having both the means & ability to do a great deal more than we, seem to be left as if your value were unfelt. Do come in here & let us have a tour among the Eastern tribes; and if, after you have seen their numbers, friendliness & need, and contrast them with your present sphere, you can say you ought to remain where you are, I shall be content to bear any epithet you choose to put upon me. I am quite aware of the extent of the field you now occupy, & that the Kuruman has always since I knew

[9] Stephen, after the first Christian martyr.
[10] Before being baptized, Sechele had divorced all but one of his wives and sent them back to their parental homes.

it given a poor idea of its greatness, but the people leaving so
may render it needful for you to go through the building
operations of a new station somewhere else in your district.
Now would it not be well to look at other spheres before
you think of anything else? You may think all this premature,
prejudged or something else as bad as either, but I think
you will not refuse me credit for a sincere desire for your
honour & usefulness. A tour will do your health good.
You will get new words for translation, &c &c. I hope you
may be guided by Him who cannot err.

I felt glad to hear that you or rather Mrs M. had put a
stop to the Patriot. It has of late become excessively nausea-
ous to me. The filthy quack advertisements stuck at the
bottom of some of the pages create an unpleasant feeling in
my mind every time I reach them. Holloway, a Jew I believe,
draws thousands of pounds annually from the public purse
by falsehood,[11] & the editors of the Patriot for the sake of
a rather higher rate of payment admit his lies into the news
part of the paper, & thereby become the vehicles by which
a portion of the religious world too is drawn into the vortex
of deception. Life is in innumerable cases sacrificed every
year by advertizing quacks. I have thought many times of
late of proposing another paper instead of the Patriot.

We should have been glad to hear how Robert has got
on &c, but you are in the same state of ignorance as ourselves as to his movements.[12] You will of course let us know
when you can how he succeeds, & what the benefits he is
likely to confer in his new sphere. Also of Betsy & Jane,[13]
how they fare in England. I have no doubt but they will be
provided for, when or if it becomes known they need to be
provided for.

Our soap, you may remember when looking over the

[11] Thomas Holloway (1800–83), "patent medicine vendor; son of Penzance inn-
keeper; . . . advertised extensively in all languages, . . . made large fortune" (D.N.B.).

[12] R. Woffat, jr., had arrived in S. Africa from England in January 1848 (LMS
Chronicle, vol. 12 (1848), p. 62), and in May was appointed "surveyor and member
of the Land Commission in the territories between the Vaal and the Orange River".
On 30.i.1849 he wrote to Rev. J. J. Freeman that he had not yet seen his parents
since his return.

[13] Elizabeth Lees (1839–1919) and Jean Gardiner (1840–1927), the youngest
children of the Moffats, who had been sent to England for schooling at the end of
the previous year.

account, being sixpence per lb ought to be £1 instead of £2. Sechele was glad of his, but having given the last box for an ox we could only ask a better one this time, as it was dearer soap. The animal is not worth 30/–, but we prefer to bear the loss of the difference to appearing to take a profit from him. I need the glue both for joining & the house. The latter is unfinished inside. I am tired of it, & leave the finishing to some other time. It is simply white-washed. I have not good locks. Did you ever get the brace & bits from Birmingham which I requested you to order for me? Mine went this way & is now held by a reim.[14]

All this country news will be communicated by Motseabona. The Griquas are standing to the West of this high & dry on their way to the Lake. They can, it is reported, neither go backwards nor forwards, & wait for rains.[15]

With love to Mrs M. & Ann,

Believe me, affectionately yours,

D. Livingston

Tuesday morning. As Motseabona cannot take either of the boxes we let them remain. He takes some horns for you. Three rhinoceros or four.[16] One is 3 ft 1½ in length, the longest mohohu[17] I ever saw. The khoodo is [from] Sechele for you. The pallahs[18] need the bony part to be steeped in water & scraped in order to be pretty. You must tell me if I send too many of these things. I think they will be interesting to friends at home. The chief's brother brought a waterbuck's skin &c carefully prepared, but it was an old animal & only one horn, so I declined it.

[14] Afrikaans *riem*, thong.
[15] "A large party of Griquas in about thirty waggons made many & persevering efforts at two different points last year, but though inured to the climate & stimulated by the prospect of much gain from the ivory they expected to procure, want of water compelled them to retreat" (3.ix.1849 Tidman). Blaikie, who quotes (p. 103) the version of this passage that appeared in the *Journal of the Royal Geographical Society* (vol. 20, 1850, p. 138), has "engineers" for "Griquas"!
[16] "or four" deleted in MS.
[17] Tswana *mogohu*, the white rhinoceros (*Diceros simus*).
[18] Tswana *phala*, the impala or rooibok (*Aepyceros melampus*).

49: To ROBERT MOFFAT
November 1848

Address: Revd. R. Moffat, Kuruman. [Bruce Collection.]

Kolobeng
Nov. 1848

My dear Father,

We gladly welcomed our friend Paul back again after his visit to the Kuruman, and the etceteras he brought were as welcome as he. We had recieved a most gloomy view of the state of Kuruman from Motseabona & felt quite sad over it —everybody talking of leaving & many actually left, you too among the talkers of leaving. We really did not know what to make of it. I was on the point of offering you this house in order that you might go on undisturbed in your translations. Anxiety to see some little fruit from our labours among the Bakwains was the only thing in my mind that prevented. And, after all, the mountain in labour brought forth a ridiculous mouse. Paul gave such a glowing account of the numbers & state of your young people we felt quite cheered. Above all, to see Sebube come forward & choose a station for himself is quite exhilarating.[1] I felt inclined at once to go over & help him with his house, but thought afterwards it would be better not. Let all the praise of the commencement be given to whom it is due, & all the disgrace of attempting to hinder his settlement rest on the head which could tell you with tears & groans that he *always* assisted Native teachers. Sebube will tell you of his message to the Wa[n]ketse not to recieve him. Fortunately his influence is there, as almost everywhere else, somewhere about the degree Zero.[2]

We delayed the baptism of Sechele for two months after

---

[1] Sebubi, a Tlharo tribesman, for several years previously an evangelist at an outstation near Kuruman, had recently gone to work in the same capacity among the BaNgwaketse under Senthufe at Kgwakgwê near Kanye. He subsequently moved to Ranaka (also called Tlhorong), a few miles away, where his descendants are still living (cf. Schapera, "Short History of the BaNgwaketse", p. 11).

[2] The reference is to Edwards, who had vainly tried to get Sebubi to assist him at Mabotsa (Moffat to Tidman, 24.xi.1848).

his formal application.[3] As he had for a long time previous professed firm belief in the truth of Christianity & his general conduct seemed to be influenced by the belief, we did not feel so much hesitancy as we should have done had there been no previous indications of change. He was tested in the interval by his own people in several ways, & by the renowned chief Moshesh[4] in a way that might have influenced one who was insincere at heart. He had sent some men with karosses about four or five months previously in order to purchase a horse. Moshesh recieved the messengers very kindly, and as I gave them a note to the missionaries[5] requsting any members, who might feel disposed, to act kindly towards them & for their spiritual good, the poor fellows were well taken care of. Moshesh gave them about ten head of cattle & two horses, a great deal for poor people in this country, & sent a private message to the chief that whatever he wished, whether guns gunpowder horses or cattle, he must apply to him & he would supply them; & tell him to allow his people to believe if they like, but he (Sechele) must never believe. "I am a king", said Moshesh, "& I won't put myself under the authority of another (viz. God); I have my kingdom as well as He, & people would laugh at me if I believed & put myself under the power of another. Tell Sechele that." Sechele told me, although it was a private message, & added, "Ki le ka nyatsa, gone ga a itse se o se buañ, ka a re Morimo ki khosi ka ena." [6] I should not like this private message to get wind. The answer seemed satisfactory to us.

We were happy to have Paul with us in recieving him. Many of the people were shedding tears of sorrow. For what, do you think? That he was so far left to himself as to drink the brains of men. "It seemed water", said one to me,

---

[3] Sechele was baptized on 1 October 1848.

[4] Originally chief of the BaMokotedi, a small and unimportant Southern Sotho tribe, Moshesh (c. 1785–1870) by shrewd diplomacy and conquest welded together many different tribes and remnants of tribes into what is now the "Basuto nation" of Basutoland. He was by general consent the outstanding South African chief of his time, widely famed for his intelligence and statesmanship.

[5] Letter to H. M. Dyke, 7.iv.1848.

[6] "I treated [his message] with disdain, because he did not know what he was saying, for he said that God is a chief like himself."

"I expected to see something tala[7] in it." "Ka ua ba nosa yalo", said another, "ua reñ?" [8] They in general believe the satanic suggestions of wicked persons who tell them that baptism is being caused to drink men's brains, & the Lord's supper a scene of impurity. They love darkness rather than light. The youngest child he desired to be called Setefano, in allusion to his hope of being the first among the Interior chiefs who will embrace the gospel.

He endures a good deal of trial from his people at present. We have no rain, one good shower alone this year, while all around us the rains have been abundant. The Kolobeñ gets smaller & smaller. It has not run into the watercourse for the last three weeks. The people say to him, "There is Mosielele, he has plenty of rain & he hates the Word; our chief loves it, & we have none." This is the fourth year of scarcity. They had always abundance of corn untill the Word came. Last year at this time we could not make our watercourse contain its water, but two dry seasons following each other seems too much for it. If the prince of the power of the air has no hand in it we feel unkindly towards the old rogue.

We are cutting corn, seem to have a pretty fair crop. The friends who sent the chairs would be pleased if they knew they came just two days before his baptism,[9] & their first use was on that occasion, & one of them by the wife he has retained.

The gun gave great satisfaction, but two months nearly have elapsed before he could bring himself to fire with it. He told me he did not know what to do with it, it was too fine to shoot out of it hela.[10] He intended to keep it till he got a waggon, & then he would shoot with it occasionally & then put it into its bed. But a big buffalo made a mistake yesterday and came blundering through the town. He fired the first shot into it. It is now loaded in both barrels. He wonders who made the different parts, & as there are three names for conjecture, viz. Tipping, Lawden &

[7] Green.   [8] "When you make them drink like this, what are you doing?"
[9] "The ladies connected with Carr's Lane chapel, Birmingham, sent two chairs to Sechele. They came safely and arrived just two days before that on which we had resolved to baptize him" (1.xi.1848 Tidman).
[10] Merely, simply, i.e. without special reason.

Parker,[11] it is supposed one made the stock, another the lock, & a third the barrel.

The gun acoutrements are welcome. Have you no finished common musket cocks? The percussion are not at present so useful as these would be. I have completely failed in all attempts to make a screw thread in the inside of the part of the tumbler which projects. The taps have a portion tapering at the point which only scrapes, & before the real screw comes into operation it is either down to the bottom or broken. Can you give me any hint or instruction on the point? Any finished pans? Time is everything here. And any new ideas you may have acquired on putting fire into a pan?

Can you provide us with $\frac{1}{2}$ muid of good seed corn for next sowing? That we have is mixed with Bengal &c. The seeds are very welcome indeed. None of my beans did [well], yours come on splendidly. The Scotch kale was excellent at Mabotsa, but the two plants preserved for seed were planted close to each other & a curious interchange was the result. The kale gave its breadth of leaf to the turnips, & contented itself with becoming a "thistle" with a short stalk. The turnips are now things with leaves like bananas & enormous branching inedible roots. A few seem to have escaped the contagion, but I doubt whether they will be worth propagation. Of Mr Oswel's seeds the custard apple did best. We have six growing vigourously. Many more came up but were devoured by insects. Several beat roots & a plant called Pringall[12] have come on, but these are all.

If you can procure sheep as cheap as the last, but at some future time, you will oblige us by them. But *no more* goats. They are very useful in payment, but a skin disease unusually fatal these two last years renders it unprofitable for us to keep them any time on our hands. The sheep do extremely well & we can pay with them. Heifers will always be welcome, preferred indeed to every thing else.

[11] Tipping & Lawden were "gun and pistol makers" at 40 Constitution Hill, Birmingham, and Moffat's friend Joseph Parker was a "gun barrel maker" at 13 Newton Street in the same city (*Slater's Directory*, 1852, Birmingham section, pp. 38, 39).

[12] Possibly *Pringlea antiscorbutica*, the Kerguelen cabbage.

We can get 9 or 10 sheep in exchange for one. It will be well to avoid spending any money on our behalf for some months, or till next year's salary comes due, except for hiefers & tea. We shall want but little besides. If you can procure good tea for us we shall remember you every time we drink it. If you cannot get what we like best, the next best although inferior must do. Although it should be like rotten hay & we say so, we do not dream of attaching blame to you, because you are not the tea dealer. As for the ham, we never doubted your kind intentions in sending it, & our remarks had a reference to the future rather than the past. We never dreamed of sending back anything bought for us, never having once looked on you as the dealers. We are not Mahometans either. We are glad you admire the cap. We shall send that perhaps.

What in the world has become of Robert III?[13] We are exceedingly anxious to learn. Mary is afraid he has been in the commando against the Boers. I imagine he would be employed in some way at the time, perhaps as aide camp or what not, for what will not conjecture conjure up.[14] The worst of conjecture is its indefiniteness to those who have but little of the imaginative & excitable in their composition.

I am very glad of the musket. Have you never recieved the powder ordered? You must not forget that one of the bellows ought to come this way. I intend giving that we now have to Paul when settled with Mokhatla, which use will I feel sure meet your approbation. As soon as we plough we shall make the attempt to fix him there. Paul is preparing. I felt favourable to the proposition that Sebube & Paul join at the Bañuaketse at first, but on reflection came to the conclusion that we ought to attempt introducing the gospel into both places, & if both are as favourably recieved as Sebube has been, each may in time be furnished with an

[13] Robert Moffat, jr. He was at that time "inspecting farms, delimiting boundaries, and granting temporary title deeds", in the Vaal River (Harrismith) district of the Orange River Sovereignty (letter to Freeman, 30.i.1849).

[14] In July 1848, following upon the proclamation (February) of the Orange River Sovereignty as a British colony, some of the local Boer inhabitants rose in armed opposition with the aid of reinforcements from the Transvaal. They were defeated at the battle of Boomplaats (29 August), which put an end to the rebellion. The younger Moffat, then on his way to take up his official duties, apparently waited at Colesberg until the fighting was over (letter to Freeman, 30.i.1849).

associate. Sebube does not seem to need any energy from Paul, & I do not expect soon to find one better adapted for commencing a station than Paul. If Paul is not allowed to remain in the prosecution of his work, we shall then think the way open for him to go over to the Bañuaketse. The attempt would have been made sooner had we not been engaged in removing hither &c. This has caused more than 12 months delay. A long time to some this may appear, but no portion of my life passed quicker, & though I have not done all I wished, verily I have not been idle.

It occurs to me at this moment that as on earth, when employed in what we enjoy, the time passes so quickly we do not percieve its course, so the employments of heaven will completely saturate the periods of adoration, & in the opposite state existence will drag on heavily, there will be no employment to disturb the everlasting ennui of prolonged eternal despair. What a wearisome time Judas has spent since he went to his own place, & what a mercy to be allowed to spend our lives in labour for him whom we shall yet see in glory. A great mercy indeed that he makes that labour pleasant.

Many thanks for the gun aparatus. Have you none of more or greater finish? We want time very much to drill holes especially. The two loading rods have been bought by Sechele. I have got wherewithal to pay for them. He is anxious to pay for the double barrel[e]d gun & will do so soon, for he has sent to the Bamangwato in expectation of ivory. It has been promised. If successful, the little rifle will be bought about same time. S. does not know what to say about his gun, he is so pleased with it. Among the multitudes of words, expressions of gratitude to Tipping, Lawden, Parker, you & myself are not wanting, and the Overuling Providence which protected in the way is duly acknowledged. I think you would be pleased by his expressions in prayer. He has a great deal of opposition to bear with, & you need to remember him that he may be established in the truth.

We teach a little English to him, Paul & Mebaloe, & a few others, but have only one English Primer. Can you furnish us with some, & a few English Testaments if you have them? We were glad of the books you sent lately. I had the impression that you had handed over the book department to Mr Ashton. Our schools have diminished since we recieved the chief, or rather since the wives were dismissed, & so has the attendance on the services.

Mokhatla's lock was done extremely well. I seldom hit, giving the pans so much fire.

The weather is excessively warm, from 93° to 95 in the coolest part we can find in the shady parts of our house. I worked under some mimosas as long as I could, but the heat gave me headache, a complaint I never knew till lately, so we built a smithy. Mary is more troubled than formerly by the pains peculiar to her condition.[15] I never looked to the clouds so much in my life as I have done these few months past.

Mary desires me to say that she did not send sugar by Motseabona, because she did not possess full confidence in his honesty. If the trouble of drying quinces is not greater than that of preserving them, we should prefer them so. She will send sugar by next opportunity. Sebube is here on horseback.

I have read with great pleasure the Broadmead lectures by Foster. Have you his works selected from the Eclectic?[16] I shall send the former out some day. Leebig gives an outline of the present state of organic chemistry, as an appendix to Agricultural Chemistry, which is excellent. You must remember it in some of your journeys.

Any word of vaccine virus?

Affectionately yours,
D. Livingston

Love & kind salutations to Mrs M., Ann & Mr Hamilton. Mary desires me to transmit thanks for Cheevers recieved[17] &c. The Christian Treasury[18] is excellent. We

[15] She was expecting the birth of another child.

[16] John Foster, *Lectures delivered at Broadmead Chapel, Bristol*, ed. J. E. Ryland, 2 vols., 1844–47; *Contributions, Biographical, Literary, and Philosophical, to the Eclectic Review*, 2 vols., 1844.

[17] Presumably one (or more) of the works of George Barrell Cheever, author of *Lectures on the Pilgrim's Progress* (London, 1846), etc.

[18] A journal, "containing contributions from ministers and members of various evangelical denominations", published weekly in Edinburgh and London since 1845.

thank you for perusal. Be sure & read them before you send them. I was much ashamed when I knew or was put in mind that you never read the Echo,[19] & the shame returned the other day when a number of that ill-fated work stared me in the face.

[19] Possibly *The Evangelical Echo*, "containing accounts of the Lord's word in various parts, and articles on subjects of general interest to Christians"; produced in phonetic script, only two volumes were published (1847–8).